GMIT LEABHARLANN / LIBRARY
091 742785
http://library.gmit.ie

Is Féidir leabhair a athnuachan sa leabharlann, le fón nó ar líne
Books may be renewed in the library, by phone or online

Gearrfar fineáil ar mhireanna atá dlite thar téarma
Fines are charged on overdue items

Uimh. Seilf: Barrachód:
Shelf No: Barcode:

Dáta Dlite Due Date	Dáta Dlite Due Date	Dáta Dlite Due Date

Is Christianity True?

Is Christianity True?

by
Michael Arnheim

Published 1984 by
Prometheus Books
700 East Amherst Street
Buffalo, New York 14215

Published by arrangement with
Gerald Duckworth & Co. Ltd.
The Old Piano Factory
43 Gloucester Crescent, London NW1, England

Library of Congress Catalog Card No. 84-42861
ISBN 9-87975-262-9

To the memory of

my grandfather

Wolf Shames

Contents

Preface

On a train speeding between Euston and Manchester I fell into conversation with a plasterer, whose cheerful disposition and frankness, coupled with the unmistakable intonation of his speech, marked him as a Mancunian born and bred. Our conversation began on a safe enough topic, the declining value of money, which my fellow traveler attributed to the introduction of decimal coinage. I was intrigued. It was, after all, over a decade since the coinage had been changed. But my northern friend was adamant. Decimalization, he declared, was one of the three biggest "cons" in history. "What were the other two?" I immediately inquired and, quick as a flash, came the reply: the graduated pension fund and "JC." I was stunned. "JC?" I repeated quizzically. "Yes, Jesus Christ of course." And in what order should these three biggest confidence tricks be placed? On this point my fellow traveler was equally forthcoming: "JC—number one."

I wonder how my new-found friend would have reacted to the knowledge that in the briefcase lying on the table before me was a nearly complete manuscript on that very subject. Perhaps he will come upon a copy of this book in the Euston bookstall, or—who knows?—even in the one at Manchester Piccadilly.

For this is a book intended for anyone who has ever given even a fleeting thought to the question of the validity of the claims of Christianity. It is a book for the inquiring mind, for the seeker after truth about one of the most engrossing subjects many people can imagine.

Some of the ideas in this book were first unleashed upon an unsuspecting audience in a paper I read to Professor Henry Chadwick's Patristics Seminar in the Cambridge Divinity School, and I am grateful to the Regius Professor himself for reading the manuscript of the book and for his useful comments on it. Others who have been kind enough to read the manuscript in whole or part and from whose comments I have benefited are Professor John Emerton of St. John's College, Rabbi Louis Jacobs, Frederic Raphael, and my dear friends Dodie and Greg Brooks, to all of whom I owe a great debt of gratitude but none of whom is responsible for any of the views expressed in the book.

Most of all, this book owes its origin to the inspiration of my grandfather, the late Wolf Shames, a scholar of towering erudition coupled with tolerance, wit, and wisdom, and it is to his memory therefore that I dedicate it.

St. John's College   M. T. W. Arnheim
Cambridge, 1984

Author's Note

Except where otherwise mentioned, biblical passages are quoted from the Revised Standard Version.

All other translations from the Greek and all Latin translations are my own.

Where the views, attitudes, or beliefs of "Matthew," "Mark," "Luke," or "John" are mentioned or discussed, no theory as to the authorship of the Gospel in question is to be implied. Authorship of the Gospels is not my concern in this work.

Introduction

More than any other religion, Christianity stands four-square on the acceptance of an historical improbability: namely, that one particular man was no mere mortal but "the Christ," whose death changed the course of human history forever and who continues to exist as "God the Son," part of an indivisible threefold Godhead.

Islam certainly reveres Muhammad, but at no time has any claim been advanced for him beyond that of prophet, a title which, however defined, stops well short of imbuing its holder with divine status.

As for Judaism, it rests on no one figure—not even Moses, who can lay claim to no more elevated a title than that of prophet, an appellation he shares with a score of other Jewish leaders and teachers. What is more, neither Moses nor any of the other Jewish figures—including the patriarchs Abraham, Isaac, and Jacob—is ever portrayed as anything but fallible, frail, and imperfect.

Even Zarathustra, founder of the Zoroastrian faith (still practiced in Iran and by the Parsees in India), imbued though he is with miraculous powers, never ceases to be a mere mortal.

Of all the religious leaders of history and legend, the one who comes closest to Jesus in the honors accorded him is probably Buddha (or, to be more precise, Siddhartha Gautama the Buddha, *Buddha* being a Sanskrit title meaning "the Enlightened One"). Yet, unlike the Christian Gospels, none of the voluminous writings on the life of Buddha is included in the Buddhist canon, and, though divine honors are indeed paid to him by many of his devotees (especially in the so-called Mahayana form of the religion prevalent in the Far East), where Buddha *is* worshipped as a divinity, he has generally ceased to have any real connection with the historical founder of the religion.

In Christianity there have been a number of deliberate attempts to separate the spiritual nature of the central figure from his physical or historical self, or, to put it another way, to sever "Christ the Savior" from "Jesus the Jew."

3

During the first millennium and a half of Christianity Christians of every rank and persuasion automatically accepted the details of Jesus' life found in the Christian scriptures as "the gospel truth." (The continued use of this phrase in English idiomatic speech, incidentally, shows just how recently it was that the Gospels were taken for granted as the touchstone of truth.)

Even the Protestant Reformation, which caused such upheavals in Christian thinking, addressed itself to the excrescences upon Christian belief and practice that had grown up during the Middle Ages rather than to testing the authenticity of the claims put forward by the Christian scriptures. Indeed, if anything, the Reformation resulted in a more rather than less literal and fundamentalist approach to the Gospels. To replace the authority of the Roman Catholic Church and its priesthood, Martin Luther offered what he called the "priesthood of all believers," a doctrine which placed scriptural authority at the center of the religion.

It was only in the wake of the rationalism and skepticism of the Enlightenment that the historical accuracy of the Christian scriptures eventually came to be questioned. With the application to the Gospel of the methods of historical criticism applied to secular sources, the Gospel accounts were declared by scholar after scholar to be unreliable. By the early twentieth century the so-called "quest for the historical Jesus" was bogged down in negativism. The Gospels, according to an influential school of Protestant theologians, were to be taken as theological rather than as historical documents, and they could yield no authentic information about the life and deeds, or even the sayings and teachings, of Jesus.

Such a conclusion might have been expected to have a cataclysmic effect upon Christianity. For, after all, there could surely be no Christianity without Christ, and could there be a Christ without Jesus? But if Jesus were so shadowy a figure as to belong more to the realm of myth and legend than to that of history and fact, the whole edifice of Christianity must surely crumble.

Not so, said the radical theologians. The truth of Christianity was independent of historical proof, and historical evidence was therefore quite irrelevant to the validity of Christianity.

How then *is* one to decide on the truth or falsehood of Christianity? For Rudolf Bultmann, one of the most influential Christian theologians of the twentieth century, the key element was what he called an "existential encounter with Christ," which did not depend upon any intellectual critical process but rather on a leap into the dark—or, to put it more crudely, upon an acceptance of faith on trust.

J. Knox and D. E. Nineham, two leading British theologians, similarly reject the possibility of basing Christian faith upon historical evidence but resort instead to the church as the basis of faith, thus becoming caught in a circular argument. As Donald Guthrie remarks: "Neither Nineham nor Knox has recognized the inconsistency of appealing to the testimony of the Church when they have already denied the historical accounts, which they regard as the products of the Church." [1]

With this we are back to square one: By what criterion may the truth or falsehood of Christianity be judged? To base one's acceptance of a religion upon blind faith or unsupported trust gives one no right to claim the superiority of that religion over any other religion, nor does it entitle one to assert the truth of that religion. And yet no religion in the world is more insistent than Christianity upon its claim to truth or more confident of its superiority to all other faiths.

More than any other religion Christianity revolves around a single historical figure, and in the absence of any viable alternative method of testing the validity of Christianity we have no option but to begin at the beginning, focus unblinkingly on Jesus and test the truth of the Christian claims made for him.

Did Jesus Exist?

Before we can proceed any further we must ask the most basic question of all: Did Jesus exist? This is no longer as contentious an area as it once was, and there can now be little doubt that Jesus *did* exist as an historical person.

For one thing, we have a certain amount of non-Christian evidence of his existence, though some of it has clearly been doctored by Christian copyists in order to give Jesus a more favorable non-Christian press, so to speak. The well-known reference to Jesus in the pages of the pro-Roman Jewish historian Josephus is an example of this:

> At about this time there lived Jesus, a wise man, if it is right to call him a man at all, for he was a performer of miracles and a teacher of men inclined to accept the truth with joy. He attracted to himself many Jews and many Greeks. He was the Christ; and when, on the instigation of the leading men amongst us, Pilate condemned him to crucifixion, those who had initially revered him continued to do so. For on the third day he appeared to them

alive again, just as the divine prophets had foretold this and countless other marvels about him. (*Antiquities of the Jews* 18:63-64)

As it stands this passage could never have been written by Josephus. The categorical statement, "he was the Christ," could only have been written by someone who accepted Jesus as the Jewish Messiah, which Josephus did not. That the passage as we have it has been tampered with is now generally accepted, but unfortunately it is impossible to be sure how the original might have read. We have a clue, however, in Josephus' description of James as the brother of "Jesus, the so-called Christ" (*Antiquities* 20:197 ff.), a form of words more in keeping with what we know of Josephus' religious outlook.

Interestingly enough, it was only this fleeting and negative reference to Jesus by Josephus that was known to the Christian Church father Origen, writing in the mid-third century. Origen cites this brief reference on several occasions, but never mentions the longer passage quoted above, which presumably was either not yet in Josephus' text or else was passed over by Origen as not being authentic.

The only other non-Christian reference to Jesus worthy of mention in this connection is another well-known passage, this time by the Roman historian Tacitus, who wrote about three-quarters of a century after the death of Jesus:

Christus, the founder of this sect, had been put to death by the procurator Pontius Pilate in the reign of Tiberius. Checked for the time being, the dangerous superstition broke out once more, not only in Judaea, where the evil had started, but even in Rome, where everything dark and disgusting from all over the world gathers and grows. (*Annals* 15:44)

This passage not only confirms Jesus' existence but also corroborates the manner of his death, though even without Tacitus' testimony we would probably have been quite safe in accepting the fact of his crucifixion from the Gospel accounts. For, as we shall have occasion to see, Jesus' execution was clearly the cause of acute embarrassment to his followers, so much so that it is impossible to believe that it could have been invented by any of them. The *fact* of the crucifixion—though not its details or the circumstances surrounding it—also happens to be one of the few points of agreement amongst all four Gospel accounts.

So, we can confidently assert that Jesus *did* exist and that he met his death by execution.

Christmas

We are now nearly ready to embark upon the task of testing the validity of the Gospel accounts of Jesus' birth and deeds, his sayings and teachings, and his trial(s) and crucifixion. But before launching into these central questions, it is worth disposing of some of the non-scriptural traditions surrounding Jesus' date of birth.

It was not until more than three centuries after Jesus' death that Christmas first entered the church calendar. The reason for its late appearance is essentially twofold. For one thing, no one knew Jesus' date of birth, and, secondly, it was felt not to be quite appropriate to celebrate his birthday as a religious holiday "as if he were a king Pharoah," in Origen's phrase.

Why should the church have abandoned this eminently sensible view and elevated Christmas to the position it has since held in most Christian denominations, namely that of the second holiest day in the calendar? It is undoubtedly a reflection of a change about which we shall have a good deal more to say in due course: a shift in the portrayal of Jesus from "Son of God," an essentially Jewish and totally human figure, to "God the Son," an image drawn from pagan polytheism.

As for the *date* of Christmas, the chances are no better than 1 in 365 that Jesus' birthday fell on December 25. A number of different dates have contended for the honor, including May 20, April 19, November 17, March 28, March 25 and January 6, and it took nearly five hundred years before December 25 came to be generally accepted. The reason for the choice of this date owes nothing to historical evidence but a great deal to the influence of other religions.

It was no accident that December 25 happened to be the birthday of the Unconquered Sun (*Sol Invictus*), the chief festival of the Mithraic cult, a popular mystery religion of the later Roman Empire, which shared quite a number of elements with Christianity, notably its emphasis on rebirth and salvation.

The association of Christmas with lights and fire may well be a carryover from the more general celebration of the winter solstice of December 21, especially in northern Europe. The yule log, the brightly lit tree, and the candles still so much in evidence at Christmas time are all clearly pagan traditions of this kind, which, in keeping with the usual church policy of the Middle Ages, were adapted to Christian use rather than condemned out of hand.

It is also probably no coincidence that Christmas tends to fall close to the week-long Jewish festival of lights, Chanukah, whose date, determined by the lunar calendar, generally falls within a week or two of December 25. But Chanukah is not only the festival of lights; its principal purpose is to celebrate the deliverance of the Jewish people from the hands of a deadly enemy bent upon their total destruction, the Seleucid King Antiochus "Epiphanes" of Syria. In other words, Chanukah has something of a Messianic context, an ethos never very far from the surface in all the Christian nativity tales.

The commercialism and general merriment that characterize the modern celebration of Christmas derive from a pagan festival, the Roman Saturnalia, a week-long celebration of which December 25 was the last day. It may come as a surprise to many a twentieth-century Christian preacher fulminating against the commercialism of Christmas and calling upon his flock to "put the 'Christ' back in 'Christmas'" to learn that the exuberant spirit he condemns was the *original* Christmas spirit—or, at least, the original spirit of December 25.

Renumbering the Years

A bugbear of many a young schoolboy's life is the requirement to count years backwards if they happen to fall before the Christian era. This concept of "minus dates" is not only cumbersome to use but, more seriously, gives the *totally false* impression of a sudden cataclysmic break in world history between the year 1 "B.C." and the year 1 "A.D."

Even for the devout Christian the year 1 "A.D." has no significance, as it was *not* the year of Jesus' birth, though the sixth-century Roman monk, Dionysius Exiguus, who first introduced the present system of numeration, had assumed that it was. The modern consensus is that Jesus was born four years earlier; this ties in with the Gospel view (Matt. 2:4) that he was born in the reign of Herod the Great, who died four years before the date chosen by Dionysius Exiguus for the commencement of the Christian era.

NOTE

1. Donald Guthrie, *New Testament Introduction*, 3rd ed., 1970, 195n. See R. Bultmann, *Theology of the New Testament*, 2 vols., 1952 and 1955; *Primitive Christianity in Its Contemporary Setting*, 1956; D. E. Nineham, *Saint Mark* (Pelican Commentary), 1963; J. Knox, *The Church and the Reality of Christ*, 1964.

I

The Birth of a Myth

Jesus' Birthplace

Jesus was born in Bethlehem. Or was he? It is one of the best known "facts" of Christianity, on the strength of which the town of Bethlehem has developed a thriving tourist trade.

But is it true? Was Jesus really born in Bethlehem? Unfortunatly, even the writers of the Christian scriptures disagree among themselves. Matthew and Luke both say yes, while John (7:41-42) and Mark (1:9, 6:1) give the impression of never having heard of Jesus' supposed Bethlehem birth. They assume that his birthplace was Nazareth, a small town in the northern region of Galilee, at the opposite end of the country from Bethlehem.

But even the accounts of Matthew and Luke do not really agree. Luke is well aware that Jesus was associated in the minds of his contemporaries with Nazareth, not Bethlehem, so he feels obligated to explain to his readers how it was that this Galilean happened to be born so far from home.

We today are much more accustomed to the idea of babies being born far from home than was the case then. Nowadays we even hear of births taking place in taxis or on board airplanes in midair between continents. But the period we are concerned with was one when travel was slow, troublesome, and dangerous and when most people spent their whole lives in one little village without venturing more than a few miles in any direction from birth to death.

That is why Luke clearly finds it so necessary to offer us an explanation of Jesus' birth in Bethlehem. And what *is* his explanation? It is the familiar story about the Roman census. An imperial decree was issued, says Luke, which required that everyone return "each to his own city" (2:3). In the case of Joseph and Mary, this meant that they had to travel all the way from Nazareth to Bethlehem, which was Joseph's "own city."

On the face of it this sounds convincing enough. There is nothing like a little detail to win the confidence of an audience! Further investigation, however, reveals that the whole story is bogus.

What, after all, *is* a census? Today, of course, we live in a much more numerate age than has ever existed before, and we are forever counting, measuring, calculating, and checking every conceivable thing, sometimes (or so it would appear) for no reason other than to exercise our numerate skills. In most modern states a census is taken every few years, and all it is is a head count, to see how big the population is. But, despite the seeming meaninglessness of it, it has an eminently practical purpose. The object is not only to see whether the population as a whole has grown or declined but also, among many other things, whether there has been a shift of population from some regions to others. In other words, a census is a very practical exercise. What interests the census-taker is where people *are,* not where they once *were* or where their ancestors may happen to have come from.

The Roman government, being essentially made up of down-to-earth, practical administrators, was even less interested in figures for their own sake than most modern governments. The Roman census in fact had a specific practical purpose: taxation. The government wanted to know how many people there were in each locality so as to be able to calculate the tax due from each. And where would Joseph have paid his taxes? Not in Bethlehem, even if his family *had* originally come from there, but in Nazareth, where, as even Luke is quite happy to admit, he was actually a resident. Seen in the light of history, therefore, nothing could be *less* in keeping with the true nature and purpose of a Roman census than a move from a person's actual place of residence to some remote supposed birthplace or ancestral hometown.

One little snag, though, is that the Roman census would not have affected Nazareth in any case, as Galilee was not under Roman rule but had its own ruler, the "tetrarch" Herod Antipas, son of King Herod.

But that is not the only problem connected with the census. Luke is obviously very anxious for us to accept his story about Jesus being born in Bethlehem, so he gives us a lot of detail in explaining it. He actually goes so far as to specify the name of the Roman governor under whom the census was held: Cyrenius. There certainly *was* a governor of that name (or Quirinius, to put it in its proper Latin form) and, what is more, he is known from Roman sources to have held a census. But the mention of him by Luke in connection with the birth of Jesus creates more problems than it solves. Above all, there is a problem of date. Quirinius certainly conducted a census—but at a time when Jesus would have been ten years old. As it happens, Quirinius' census can be precisely dated by means of the very detailed account given by the historian Josephus (*Antiquities of the Jews* 18:1). According to him, Quirinius was sent to conduct his census shortly after Judea had been annexed by Rome, which occurred in the year 6 or 7 of the current era. This census was obviously intended to be an initial "stock-taking" now that Judea was to be governed directly by Roman officials.

Some Christian commentators have cheerfully admitted that Luke's dating of the census is a decade off and have simply left it at that. But most Christian writers on the subject have recognized that *if* they make this apparently trivial admission of error on Luke's part, the whole story of Jesus' Bethlehem birth falls apart. This has led to some desperate attempts to justify Luke's account of the census.

Aided by an inscription describing an unnamed Roman military official, apologists have rushed to suggest that perhaps Quirinius had had an *earlier*—and totally unrecorded—tour of duty in the area and that the anonymous official was none other than himself in this role, conveniently dated to the time of Jesus' birth. Besides the total lack of evidence for jumping to so improbable a conclusion, there is another little snag: *the generally accepted date of Jesus' birth was at a time when Rome had no jurisdiction either in Bethlehem or in Nazareth,* so there could have been no census to coincide with Jesus' birth.

This is because Jesus was born during the lifetime of King Herod "the Great." How do we know that? We have it on the authority of Luke (1:5), together with that of Matthew (2:1). The problem is that Herod died in 4 BC, fully ten years before Quirinius' census, and during Herod's reign no Roman census could have been held in his territory, which included both Judea and Galilee, that is, the locations of both Bethlehem and Nazareth.

It is clear from this that Luke has really tied himself into a knot. On the one hand, he dates Jesus' birth to 4 BC *at the latest.* On the other hand, he associates Jesus' birth with an event that happened a decade later. Which story do we believe, and does it matter?

Yes, it does matter. It matters because acceptance of Jesus' birth-date as falling in the reign of King Herod will finally put an end to the story of the Bethlehem birth, which, as we have already seen, is to be rejected on other grounds in any case.

One of the best-known details of the Bethlehem story is the incident about the inn and the manger. The charming and pathetic scene painted for us by Luke (and, incidentally, by him *alone* of the Christian scripture writers) has so captivated generations of children and adults alike that no one has stopped to ask some basic questions. Such as: What were Joseph and Mary doing looking for accommodation at the inn in the first place? Hotels, inns, hostelries, and the like were few and far between in the ancient world as a whole. Travelers normally stayed with friends or relations. Why did Joseph and Mary not do so? After all, was this not Joseph's hometown? That, according to Luke, was the whole reason for his journey to Bethlehem. Or are we to believe that there was not a single member of his family left there?

The more closely we examine the Bethlehem story, the more it disintegrates before our very eyes. To take another point: Why did Mary accompany Joseph to Bethlehem? Not only is it foolhardy for a woman in the last stages of pregnancy to undertake a long and perilous journey, but no one has ever claimed that Mary's family came from Bethlehem, only Joseph's. If Joseph and Mary had been husband and wife at the time, that would explain her accompanying him, but they were *not* married. (There is more on this interesting fact.)

So far we have confined our discussion to Luke's account of the birth of Jesus. But what about Matthew, who also places the birth in Bethlehem (2:1)? Unlike Luke, Matthew says not a word about any census, nor is there any mention of an inn or a manger. On the contrary, Matthew's account gives us the impression that Bethlehem was the permanent home of Joseph and Mary, and Jesus is said to have been born in a "house" (2:11). When Nazareth is first mentioned, Matthew finds it necessary to give a special explanation of Joseph and Mary's decision to settle in Galilee rather than in Judea (2:22), thus perpetuating the initial impression of Bethlehem rather than Nazareth as Joseph and Mary's normal place of residence.

But, if this had really been the case, then why does Luke tie himself in knots in order to *explain* the couple's presence in Bethlehem? Presumably because Luke knew that Bethlehem was *not* where they came from but felt impelled to get them there by hook or by crook in order to establish Bethlehem as Jesus' birthplace. Matthew is equally concerned to set the birth in Bethlehem, but he adopts a different technique. Instead of inventing a story in order to transfer Joseph and Mary from Nazareth to Bethlehem, he slyly gives us the impression that they had been living in Bethlehem all the time! But his concern about a Bethlehem birth for Jesus comes out nevertheless. It comes out particularly in his (slightly distorted) quotation of the well-known passage from the prophet Micah (5:2) predicting that it would be from

Bethlehem that the Jewish Messiah would arise (Matt: 2:6).

Here we have the key to the whole problem of Jesus' birth. Both Matthew and Luke want to prove to their readers that Jesus was the Messiah predicted in the Jewish prophetic writings. One of the essential prerequisites of the Messiah was that he be born in Bethlehem. Therefore, in order to "qualify," Jesus *had* to be equipped with a Bethlehem birth. If we had only Matthew's account of the birth and not Luke's, we might well have believed that Jesus had indeed been born in Bethlehem. But Luke gives the game away by concocting an elaborate and demonstrably false story in order to "prove" the Bethlehem birth, thus unwittingly tarring the whole episode with the brush of fiction.

By contrast with both Matthew and Luke, John, the author of the fourth Gospel, is not much interested in establishing Jesus' credentials as the Jewish Messiah *in the traditional Jewish sense*. John's Gospel, it is generally agreed, was written for a non-Jewish readership, which explains why the claim that Jesus was the Jewish Messiah as prophesied in the Jewish Scriptures is played down in this book.

In other words, John had no axe to grind as regards Jesus' birthplace, so it is all the more intriguing to see what he has to say about it. Interestingly enough, he relates an incident which bears directly on this issue. He tells us (7:40 ff.) that the Jews of Jesus' time were debating the question of whether or not to accept Jesus' claim to be the Messiah, the chief objection to acceptance being Jesus' Galilean origin (7:41). Those rejecting Jesus' messianic claim confront him with the prophetic prerequisite: "Has not the scripture said that the Christ is descended from David, and comes from Bethlehem, the village where David was?" (7:42) Does John make Jesus or one of his disciples object and explain that Jesus *was* indeed a descendant of David and that he *had* been born in Bethlehem? No. On the contrary, John takes it for granted that Jesus did *not* meet these prerequisites of Jewish messianic prophecy. For John this did not matter; therefore there is all the more reason to believe him on this point.

Jesus' Genealogy

The verse I have just quoted from John also introduces another very important question: Jesus' genealogy. Jewish prophetic writings made it clear that the Messiah had not only to be born in Bethlehem but also had to be a descendant of King David. That is the really important requirement and is the reason for the insistence on a Bethlehem birth. In fact, the only reason for requiring that the Messiah be born in

Bethlehem was precisely that Bethlehem was the city of David.

But, even if, for argument's sake, we were to accept Luke's improbable Bethlehem birth story, that story itself reveals that probably neither Joseph nor Mary had relations living in Bethlehem. So what about the requirement that the Messiah be of Davidic descent?

As we have just seen, John does not even try to persuade his readers on this score. As usual, however, both Matthew and Luke are more concerned to fit Jesus into the Jewish messianic scriptural mould. Both writers accordingly give us a detailed family tree tracing Jesus back to King David. Matthew's family tree (1:1-17) actually starts with Abraham, the first of the Jewish patriarchs, while Luke (3:23-38) outdoes him by going all the way back to Adam! At first glance, this all looks very impressive. After all, how many modern families are able to trace their ancestors back for a thousand years, which is the difference in time between David and Jesus?

Closer scrutiny raises a number of questions. First, there is a huge difference between the two genealogies, even in the number of generations separating Jesus from King David. Matthew specifically tells us that there were twenty-eight generations, fourteen from David to the Babylonian Exile and another fourteen from the Exile to the birth of Jesus (1:17). Luke gives no figures, but a count of the number of names he mentions as Jesus' ancestors yields a total of no fewer than forty-one generations for the same period that is represented by Matthew's twenty-eight. For the thousand-odd-year period Luke's forty-one generations average out at just over twenty-four years apiece. Matthew's fourteen generations from David to the Exile average out to about twenty-eight and a half years each, but his last fourteen generations have a mean span of a whopping forty-one and a half years.

So what? These discrepancies are so big that they cannot be ignored. What they reveal is an attempt on the part of both writers to juggle the figures. The two genealogies are very different from each other, but one thing they have in common is the number seven. We have already noted Matthew's tally of twenty-eight generations from David to Jesus. But, what is perhaps even more significant is the fact that there were traditionally supposed to be fourteen generations from Abraham, the founding father of Judaism, to King David. This is specifically mentioned by Matthew as well (1:17), but he took it straight from ancient Jewish tradition (for example, 1 Chron. 2:1-15). It seems that Matthew was determined to find the same numerical pattern in tracing the line from David to Jesus as was already accepted in the descent of David from Abraham. But why fourteen generations each time? Because seven was considered a sacred, mystical, or even a magical number in ancient times, and fourteen is simply twice seven. There were *seven* days in a week; the *seventh* day was a day of rest; Jacob worked for the hand of Rachel for *seven* years, and then, when cheated by his father-in-law, for another *seven* years; there were *seven* years of plenty in Joseph's Egypt, followed by *seven* years of famine—to mention just a few of the many hundreds of examples of the significance of seven and its multiples in ancient Jewish tradition.

Luke's family tree uses the number seven as well, but in a different way from Matthew. There is a total of seventy-seven generations in his line of descent from Adam to Jesus (3:23-38).

In other words, both Matthew and Luke are determined to bring Jesus' genealogy into line with traditional Jewish genealogies, using the mystical number seven in order to invest Jesus' birth with an aura of divine destiny.

But this fiddling with the figures, together with the numerical discrepancies between the two genealogies, can hardly inspire us with much confidence in either.

This numerical question is, however, a minor problem by comparison with the ones we run up against when we start looking at the actual names in the two supposed lineages. Between David and Jesus, a period of a thousand years, only two names (three, if you include Jesus' father, Joseph) occur in both lists. These are the names of Zerubbabel and his father Shealtiel (Matt. 1:12; Luke 3:27). Now Zerubbabel was a leading figure in Jewish history at the time of the return from the Babylonian Exile, about five hundred years before the birth of Jesus. Zerubbabel was recognized at the time as the leader of the Jewish people and it seems quite likely that he was indeed a descendant of King David. From the point of view of Matthew and Luke, however, a more important question was whether Jesus could possibly trace his lineage from Zerubbabel. Both Matthew and Luke attempt to do so, but with totally conflicting results. Not a single name is common to their two genealogies between Zerubbabel and Joseph. Even the name of Joseph's own father, Jesus' grandfather, is different in the two lists. Matthew calls him Jacob, while Luke tells us it was Heli, two quite irreconcilable names. (Joseph's grandfather, called Matthat by Luke and Matthan by Matthew, is the one person between Zerubbabel and Joseph to have even the *possibility* of being common to both genealogies.)

Only one conclusion can be drawn from this discrepancy between the two supposed genealogies: both Matthew and Luke are determined to trace Jesus' descent from King David. Indeed, they *have* to do so in order to maintain that he was the Messiah predicted by the Jewish prophets. But, it is quite clear that they had no *evidence* of his actual descent, so each simply invented a lineage to link him with Zerubbabel and thus with King David.

Needless to say, this problem of the irreconcilability of the two lineages has not gone unnoticed. So desperate did some Christian commentators become that they resorted to the claim that the two genealogies were not meant to be the same. Matthew's family tree, they maintained, is that of Joseph, while Luke's is that of Mary. In this way it was presumably hoped not only to solve the problem of the irreconcilable differences between the two genealogies but also to invest Mary as well as Joseph with Davidic ancestry. Unfortunately for them, however, the texts themselves are only too clear. Luke's genealogy does not mention Mary's name at any point but makes it quite plain that this is Joseph's lineage (3:23).

It certainly would have been more convenient for Christianity if Luke *had* attributed the descent from David to Mary rather than to Joseph. For, according to the theory of the virgin birth Joseph was not Jesus' father in any case.

In other words, Jesus' descent from King David *through Joseph,* which Matthew and Luke are so anxious for us to accept, negates another of their most cherished beliefs, namely, the idea that Jesus was the "Son of God" and his mother Mary a virgin. Belief in a virgin birth is even more difficult to accept than Jesus' descent from David, and it does not make things any easier for Christianity when it is realized that these two unlikely beliefs are by their very nature mutually exclusive.

The Virgin Birth

What is the evidence for so remarkable and miraculous an event? As usual, the Christian Gospels themselves do not agree. Once again, Matthew and Luke alone claim a virgin birth for Jesus, while Mark and John make no mention of it. In general, the absence of some supposed fact from a source is not very good evidence against the truth of that fact. After all, every writer must select his facts from a large pool, and he will do so in accordance with what *he* considers significant, the point being that no two writers can be guaranteed to have exactly the same set of priorities. But a virgin birth is so remarkable and so miraculous an event that it is hard to understand how any author could omit a mention of it—and least of all an author as concerned as both Mark and John were to show that Jesus *was* a remarkable man of miracles! We can only conclude that these two writers either did not know the story of Jesus' virgin birth or else did not believe it. In either case, it is a telling blow against our acceptance of it.

Both Matthew and Luke link the story of the virgin birth directly with their claim that Jesus was the Jewish Messiah. Luke has the angel Gabriel appear to Mary and announce the impending birth of a son to her (1:26-36). In Luke's graphic depiction of the scene, Mary is somewhat agitated at the news, making the specific statement that she has never had sexual intercourse (1:34). In addition to this emphasis placed on Mary's virginity, Luke makes several other points here:

1. Mary, though unmarried and a virgin, is betrothed to Joseph (1:27).
2. The conception is to be seen as a sign of divine favor to Mary (1:28, 30).
3. The unborn child is to be "the son of God" (1:35).
4. King David is described as the child's "father" (1:32).
5. The unborn child is to "reign over the house of Jacob for ever" (1:33).
6. The child is to be named Jesus (1:31).

The description of David as the child's "father" is obviously meant simply as "ancestor," and this statement serves as a shorthand for claiming that the unborn infant is to be the Messiah. But, how can the unborn child be at one and the same time the "son of God" and the son of Joseph? The answer is that he cannot, for, as we have already seen, his claim to Davidic descent depends on Joseph's paternity, the very attribute which is here being denied him.

The statement about reigning over "the house of Jacob" shows just how traditionally Jewish an image of the Messiah is presented here. "The house of Jacob" is just another way of saying "the children of Israel," Jacob or Israel being one of three Jewish patriarchs. In other words, the Messiah is seen not only as a savior but also as a ruler over an earthly kingdom, something about which we shall have more to say in the next chapter.

Matthew's briefer account of the annunciation (1:18-25) is similar to that of Luke, except that he has the angel appear to Joseph instead of to Mary. In addition, as usual, Matthew uses a Jewish scriptural quotation to "prove" the truth of his claims—on this occasion, one of the very best-known of all messianic prophecies, derived from the prophet Isaiah: "Behold, a virgin shall conceive and bear a son, and his name shall be called Emmanuel." (Matt. 1:23)

I say *derived* from the prophet Isaiah advisedly, because there is one very significant difference between Matthew's version of the prophecy and the original (Isa. 7:14). Isaiah's prophecy is not about a virgin at all but simply about a young girl or young woman. The Hebrew language, in which of course the prophecy is written, has two quite distinct words. There is the word *betulah,* a word frequently found in the Jewish scriptures with the specific meaning of "virgin." In Chapter 22 of Deuteronomy, for example, *betulah* and the abstract noun formed from it, *betulim,* "virginity," occur no fewer than six times in a sexual context. Isaiah himself uses the word *betulah* on five occasions, even where there would merely be an assumption that the girl in question was a virgin. But in the prophecy we are concerned with, Isaiah uses a different word altogether, *almah,* a much more general word referring simply to a young girl of marriageable age.

Is there some reason for the prophet's choice of vocabulary here? The word *betulah* is used only of girls without any sexual experience. But in the passage in question Isaiah is dealing with a married woman, who either is already pregnant or else is shortly to become so; someone, in other words, who could most certainly *not* be a virgin. It is clear from the context that Isaiah is not talking here of some messianic figure of the far-distant future but of a *specific* unborn child, namely the son of King Ahaz, the later Hezekiah, one of the "good" kings of Judah, who lived some seven hundred years before the time of Jesus! It would have been quite wrong for Isaiah to refer to Ahaz's queen as a virgin, which is why he does not use the word *betulah* but the more general word *almah.*

In fact, not only does the prophet use a different word but he also prefixes it with the definite article, *the.* Correctly translated, what Isaiah is saying here is *"the* young woman shall conceive and bear a son," which confirms our initial impression that Isaiah is talking about a particular young woman whose identity is known to him.

There might never have been any doctrine of virgin birth in Christianity had it not been for the way in which the Isaiah passage is translated in the Septuagint, the authorized translation of the Jewish scriptures into Greek, which was the form of the Bible most familiar to the Jews of Jesus' day. Greek was the lingua franca of the whole of the Eastern Mediterranean seaboard, and it was used by Jews as well as by their non-Jewish neighbors.

Greek does have a word, *neanis,* corresponding to the more generalized meaning of the Hebrew *almah,* but it is comparatively rare. This may be the reason why the Septuagint translators used the much commoner word *parthenos,* ("virgin"), properly the equivalent of the Hebrew *betulah,* to represent the word *almah* in Isaiah's prophecy.

Luke was probably not even of Jewish origin, so it is unlikely that he would have been able to read the Bible in Hebrew even if he had wanted to. Though he does not quote Isaiah, he does relate the virgin birth directly to his claim that Jesus was the Jewish Messiah. So, if he did get his idea of the virgin birth from Isaiah, then it could only have been from the Greek version, in which Isaiah is made to prophesy the birth of a son to a *virgin,* something he had no intention of doing.

But what about Matthew? He was a Jew and, what is more, his biblical citations are sometimes drawn from the Hebrew Masoretic Text (that is, the authorized Jewish scriptures). He is also said (by a certain Bishop Papias, who wrote in about the year 130) to have "composed the *logia* in the Hebrew language." There has been a good deal of discussion of this statement, as the meaning of the term *logia* is not quite clear. It is a Greek word literally translated as "oracles," and so probably refers to the biblical "proof" texts which Matthew is so fond of quoting; he uses no fewer than sixty of them altogether. But, of course, even if Matthew really did go to the Hebrew Bible to find these passages, he may nevertheless have been influenced by the Septuagint in translating Isaiah's "young woman" as "virgin."

But there may also have been other reasons for this. For one thing, it is quite clear that there had always been a big question mark hanging over Mary's sexual morality. Unlike the story of the virgin birth, however, these doubts about Mary are reflected in all four of the Christian Gospels, and, in addition, in non-Christian sources. It was clearly a subject that caused the early Christians acute embarrassment.

Both Matthew and Luke specifically describe Mary as *betrothed* to Joseph at the time of Jesus' conception but not yet married to him (Matt. 1:18; Luke 1:27; 2:5).

In fact, from Luke's account it does not appear that they ever got married. They are still only betrothed at the time of the supposed journey to Bethlehem (2:5) and Luke never broaches the topic again. In other words, as far as Luke's narrative is concerned, Mary appears to be an "unmarried mother." Even today, when unmarried mothers in certain countries actually receive a special financial allowance from the state, there is still quite a stigma attached to being an unmarried mother. How much greater that stigma was in ancient times, and especially amongst the Jews, can be seen from the penalties for adultery detailed in the book of Deuteronomy. The extreme penalty, stoning to death, is reserved for the betrothed girl who voluntarily commits adultery before her marriage (Deut. 22:23-24) or the bride who turns out not to be a virgin on her wedding night (Deut. 22:20-21).

In Matthew's version of the story, Joseph and Mary do get married, but not until after Mary's pregnancy is discovered and after Joseph is prevailed upon by an angel to have second thoughts on the subject (Matt. 1:18-25). His first thoughts, once he knew Mary was pregnant, were to send her away secretly, though he would have been entitled, as Matthew specifically tells us, to "put her to shame" (1:19), that is by announcing her adultery publicly and having her punished for it.

In both Matthew and Luke, therefore, all that stands between Mary and a charge of adultery is the claim that her pregnancy was caused by divine rather than human agency. This same claim is also the only shield Jesus has against a charge of illegitimacy.

Resorting to such a far-fetched explanation of the birth as a way out of the impasse may be a measure of the desperation felt by these two Christian writers. Significantly enough, nowhere else in the Christian scriptures is there any mention of a virgin birth for Jesus. This includes all Paul's epistles, as well as the Gospels of Mark and John. Moreover, while omitting any mention of any claim for Jesus to divine paternity, these two authors do reveal something of the doubt surrounding his legitimacy.

In the middle of a heated argument as reported by John, "the Jews" are made to taunt Jesus by remarking: "*We* were not born of fornication" (8:41). (I emphasize the word *we* because this is the force of the Greek, which here uses the pronoun *we,* which is normally omitted as the subject is already expressed in the verb ending.) This taunt would be meaningless on its own, if we did not know of the long-standing Jewish belief that Jesus was illegitimate. The force of the taunt is therefore clearly meant to be: "*We* were not born of fornication—but you *were!*"

In Mark we find Jesus described by his fellow townsmen of Nazareth in the following terms: "Is not this the carpenter, the son of Mary and brother of James and Joses and Judas and Simon, and are not his sisters here with us?" (Mark 6:3). The one name missing from this recitation of Jesus' relations is the most important one of all, that of Joseph. This cannot be because Joseph was not Jesus' "real" father, since those describing Jesus here, Nazarene Jews, would certainly not have believed any story of Jesus' miraculous birth (even if such stories were already being put about by his followers, which does not seem to have yet been the case).

Moreover, when this same scene is repeated in the other Gospels, Joseph's name does occur:

"Is not this the carpenter's son? Is not his mother called Mary? And are not his brothers James and Joseph and Simon and Judas? And are not all his sisters with us?" (Matt. 13:55-56)

"Is not this Joseph's son?" (Luke 4:22)

"Is not this Jesus, the son of Joseph, whose father and mother we know? How does he now say, 'I have come down from heaven'?" (John 6:42)

Why is Mark's account different from the rest? It may make more sense to turn the question about and ask: Why do all these later accounts differ from Mark? For Mark's statement not only is probably earlier than any of the others but it also is probably their source.

Before trying to explain this discrepancy, it would be best to understand its implications. Traditional Jewish nomenclature—still used in the synagogue service and on Jewish tombstones—refers to a person by his patronymic, thus "Joshua the son of Nun" or "Caleb the son of Jephuneh," the second name being that of father, never the mother—unless the name of the father is unknown! In other words, only someone of illegitimate birth would be referred to as "Jesus the son of Mary." The fact that his own contemporaries and fellow townsmen of Nazareth, who knew his family well, should refer to Jesus in this way is a clear indication that they regarded him as belonging to that category.

It would appear that the other Gospel writers changed the appellation of Jesus here precisely to avoid giving that impression. Some of the less authoritative manuscripts of Mark's Gospel also make a similar change, but the most reliable manuscripts have the version quoted above, which is also to be found in all the authorized translations of the Christian scriptures of the Western churches, Catholic and Protestant alike.

What is more, not only was there a long-standing Jewish and pagan tradition that Jesus was conceived in adultery but his natural father was even identified by name—as a Roman soldier called Panthera. According to Celsus, a pagan who wrote in about 180, not only was Mary guilty of adultery with Panthera but she was also convicted on this charge and driven out by Joseph, giving birth to Jesus secretly. (Origen, *Against Celsus* I. 28, 32, 69)

The Christian Gospels clearly are all acutely aware of the slur on Jesus' birth, and two of them do not even attempt to counter it. The other two, Matthew and Luke, who, as we have already seen in other connections, are not above fabricating stories for their own purposes, make a claim of divine birth for Jesus in order to deny the charge of illegitimacy. Seen in this light, the angel's reassurance to Mary that she was "full of grace" (Luke 1:28) and the story of Joseph's vision resulting in his forgiving Mary (Matt. 1:19-25) can easily be explained as a way of whitewashing Mary from what was considered to be a mortal sin.

Here we have the best motive in the world for inventing a story of a virgin birth—and therefore for following the Septuagint's mistranslation of the Isaiah prophecy. Such a story as that of Jesus' virgin birth is not at all in keeping with Jewish tradition. There are plenty of miraculous births related in the Jewish scriptures, but these miracles all stop well short of divine participation in the process. The usual type of Bible story involving a miraculous birth relates the birth of a son to a woman long past the age of childbearing (like Abraham's wife Sarah) or to one (like the mothers of Samson and the prophet Samuel) who had long given up all hope of ever bearing a child. The miracle consists in curing the woman of her infertility, but the birth still takes place in the normal fashion. Indeed, the suggestion that God had directly fathered a human child could only be regarded in Jewish religious belief as blasphemous.

The fact that Matthew and Luke were prepared to run the risk of being accused of blasphemy may well be an indication of the seriousness with which they viewed the alternative—the labeling of Jesus as a bastard.

Some Christian apologists have taken the line that the very improbability of a virgin birth should persuade us that the story is true. But, why then is it mentioned only by Matthew and Luke but not by Mark or John? Above all, why is it never mentioned by Paul, the Christian writer closest in time to Jesus? What is more, though a claim of divine birth would not favorably impress the Jews, Paul's writings—and the Gospels of Mark and John, for that matter—were directed more to pagan non-Jews, to whom the idea of divine birth was not at all strange and was indeed associated with the names of great rulers and heroes.

The Emperor Augustus, ruler of the Roman world during most of Jesus' life, called himself "son of a god," the god in question being his adoptive father, Julius Caesar. On his death Augustus himself was declared to be a god, as were most of his successors in turn. Greek and Roman mythology was full of stories of gods, notably Zeus or Jupiter, the chief of the gods, coming down to earth in disguise—two of Zeus' being those of a bull and, improbably perhaps, a swan—and impregnating a mortal woman, thereby fathering a demigod or hero.

In general, it may be said that to the Greeks and Romans the gap between man and god did not appear nearly so unbridgeable as to the Jews. But Matthew and Luke were not able or prepared to go over completely to the idea of divine paternity for Jesus. While making this claim, they cannot altogether relinquish the idea that his father was Joseph, which is reflected in the genealogies. As we have already seen, both genealogies, Luke's as well as Matthew's, are intended to be the lineage of Joseph, as both authors make quite plain. The only reason for suggesting, as some Christian apologists have done, that only one of the family trees is that of Joseph and the other Mary's genealogy is to get over the problem of the big discrepancies between them. In any case, of course, it would have been quite pointless for either Matthew or Luke to present Jesus' lineage through his mother, as Jewish inheritance laws were strictly patrilineal. The whole purpose of the genealogies was to claim for Jesus the title of Messiah, as the Messiah had to be of royal stock, a descendant of King David, a claim which could be made only through the male line, and therefore through Joseph.

According to John (1:43-46) the disciple Philip identified Jesus with the words: "We have found him of whom Moses in the law and also the prophets wrote, Jesus of Nazareth, the son of Joseph" (1:45). Though John is arguably the most anti-Jewish of all the writers of the Christian scriptures and though his book was evidently aimed at a non-Jewish readership, the thrust of this description is the identification of Jesus as the Jewish Messiah. So much so indeed that the name of Moses is thrown in to add to the authoritativeness of the identification, even though the five books of Moses say nothing about any Messiah.

But this gratuitous use of the name of Moses in the service of the Christian cause was not calculated to convince the Jews of John's day any more than the specific association of Jesus with Nazareth, as John knew only too well. As we have already noted, the very fact that Jesus came from Nazareth and not from Bethlehem is recorded by John as one of the taunts thrown in Jesus' face by the Jews of his own day, who were firmly convinced, on the basis of biblical evidence, not only that the Messiah could not possibly come from Nazareth, but even that no prophet could come from there (7:41 ff.). John's identification of Jesus as the Messiah was therefore one that could pass muster only with non-Jews, which was in any case the group for which he was writing. But here we come up against a paradox: the one feature of the birth story calculated to appeal to non-Jews and to repulse Jews is missing from John's Gospel but elaborately related in the work of Matthew, who *was* writing for Jewish readership. I refer of course to the story of the virgin birth.

An analysis of the paradox will finally dispel any doubts about the motivation behind the virgin-birth story. In the description of Jesus that John puts into the mouth of the disciple Philip there is nothing to alert us to the idea that there might have been anything at all unusual— whether good or bad—about Jesus' birth. He is named as "Jesus the son of Joseph" in the normal Jewish fashion, leaving us with the natural assumption that Joseph was nothing other than his father and the husband of his mother. John was writing outside Judea altogether, in the Greek world, and his original readers would have been most unlikely to have heard anything unfavorable about the birth of Jesus from any other source. So there was no need for John to resort to stories such as that of the virgin birth—unless he believed in its truth— which he evidently did not. Once again, therefore, we can see the virgin-birth story as a coverup, a fiction invented in order to conceal a most unpalatable truth, namely the true story of Jesus' illegitimate birth.

The unfortunate circumstances surrounding his birth may also explain Jesus' hostility toward his mother. In the story of the wedding feast at Cana, for example, Jesus gives Mary short shrift when she has the temerity to point out that there is no more wine left (John 2:3-4). Luke relates an incident in which a woman in the crowd calls out a blessing upon Jesus' mother: "Blessed is the womb that bore you, and the breasts that you sucked" (Luke 11:27). Jesus' response to this is curious: "Blessed rather are those who hear the word of God and keep it" (11:28). There is more than a hint here that Jesus did not consider his mother to belong to the category of "those who hear the word of God and keep it." Perhaps most striking of all is the incident related by all three of the synoptic Gospels, in which, when Mary and Jesus' brothers come all the way from Nazareth to Capernaum to visit him, he shows little enthusiasm to see them:

> And his mother and his brothers came; and standing outside they sent to him and called him. And a crowd was sitting about him;

and they said to him, "Your mother and your brothers are outside, asking for you." And he replied, "Who are my mother and my brothers?" And looking around on those who sat about him, he said, "Here are my mother and my brothers! Whoever does the will of God is my brother, and sister, and mother." (Mark 3:31-35) (cf. Matt. 11:46-50; Luke 8:19-21)

The Name Jesus

In the passage used as the basis for the virgin-birth theory, Isaiah is not content to predict the birth of a son to the young woman in question, but characteristically gives the exact name the unborn infant is to bear, Emmanuel, or "God is with us." If, as seems quite likely, the unborn child was in fact the later King Hezekiah, then it would appear that the boy's father, Ahaz, was unwilling to allow the prophet so easy a triumph by naming his son according to the prophecy.

In fastening on this prophecy as referring to Jesus, Matthew is clearly embarrassed by the lack of correspondence of the names. There obviously was no way of changing either Jesus' name or the name that Isaiah predicts will be borne by the unborn infant of his prophecy. but, to make the inconsistency less gross, Matthew rephrased the Isaiah quotation a little. Isaiah's prophecy says either "you shall call his name Emmanuel," the *you* referring to King Ahaz, the child's father, or else "she shall call his name Emmanuel," in which case the infant's mother is to name him so. This latter translation is the one normally given in modern versions, though the Septuagint has it as "you," but both these translations are equally acceptable renderings of the Hebrew as preserved in the Masoretic Text, the authorized Jewish Bible. A variant reading found in one of the Dead Sea Scrolls would present us with a third possibility: "his name will be called Emmanuel."

But Matthew departs from all of these translations in his version of the verse: "and they shall call his name Emmanuel" (1:23), which is not a correct translation of any known Hebrew text. Who are "they"? It is so vague as to create at least some doubt in the reader's mind that the name Emmanuel is meant to be the chld's actual given name; it leaves the impression that Emmanuel may be some sort of title or sobriquet given to the child by the general public. There can be little doubt that this departure from all biblical traditions on Matthew's part is deliberate.

At the same time, he makes the most of the name Jesus, first by including it in the statement made by the angel to Joseph and secondly by investing it with special prophetic significance: "She will bear a son, and you shall call his name Jesus, for he will save his people from their sins." (1:21). It is worth noting that here Matthew *does* adopt the phraseology that Isaiah used in speaking of "Emmanuel": "You shall call his name . . ."

Jesus is simply the Greek equivalent of the common Hebrew name Joshua, whose most famous bearer was Moses' lieutenant and successor, the conqueror of Canaan, Joshua the son of Nun. Matthew's explanation of its meaning is incorrect. "Jesus" does not indicate that the bearer of the name is to be a savior, but exactly the opposite—that he is to *be saved*. The literal meaning of the name is "saved by God" or "helped by God," which, unlike Matthew's fanciful translation, invests God, not the bearer of the name Joshua/Jesus, with special powers!

But we have not yet exhausted Matthew's stock of improbable birth stories. There remain what are the most unlikely stories of all: those of the star, the Magi, and the slaughter of the innocents.

The Star, the Magi, and the Slaughter of the Innocents

According to Matthew—and to him alone—Jesus' birth was heralded by the appearance of a star "in the East," which was followed by "wise men from the East," or Magi, who were led by the star to Jesus' manger in Bethlehem, where they prostrated themselves before the infant and presented him with rich gifts (Matt. 2:1-12).

Who were these mysterious exotic gentlemen, and why are neither they nor their star mentioned by any other source, not even the other Christian Gospels? There has been much discussion of the Magi, and their country of origin has been variously identified as Persia, Babylonia, and Arabia, to mention but three. The story improved in the telling. Before long, the three Magi were promoted to royal status and in time they developed names, biographies, and even relics, now housed in Cologne cathedral! Until as recently as about twenty years ago acceptance of the truth of the Magi story was a touchstone of orthodoxy in the Roman Catholic Church.

The star has also earned its fair share of speculation. Was it a comet, a nova, a supernova, a meteor, a meteorite, the conjunction of two planets? All such speculations are premature, as they presuppose that there could indeed have been a star of the sort related in the story. But *could* there have been? What we are dealing with here, after all, is a very unusual kind of heavenly body, one which was supposedly capable not only of moving across the sky but also of guiding travelers for miles and leading them to an exact spot. Once this is fully recognized for the impossibility that it is, it becomes clear just what an exercise in futility it is to try to identify the star with some actual astronomical phenomenon.

That Halley's comet probably appeared in 12 or 11 BC—a few years too early for Jesus' birth in any case—is quite irrelevant, because comets, like planets, rotate around the sun on a regular elliptical orbit which, in the case of Halley's comet, is a seventy-six-year cycle. When that comet last appeared, in 1910, it was visible from the earth for only a few days, hardly long enough for the three men to make their journey even from Arabia or Babylonia, let alone from Persia or further afield. What is more, neither a comet nor any other type of heavenly body could possibly guide travelers to a particular building. As for meteorites, or "shooting stars," which *do* fall to earth, it all happens so fast that the Magi would not have had enough time to pack their lunch, let alone follow the star to Bethlehem. What about a nova or supernova? This is a "new star," one which has not previously been discernible but which suddenly becomes very bright as a result of some internal explosion, the brightness lasting at times for a period of several weeks or even longer. But, once again, it could not act as an usher, moving along and then stopping over the exact spot where the baby Jesus was lying, as Matthew says it did (2:9). In addition, such a remarkable and rare astronomical event would certainly not have gone unnoticed by the astronomers of the day, at a time when astronomy was advanced.

For a long time a favorite explanation of the star was that it represented a conjunction of the two planets Jupiter and Saturn, which, it was calculated, would have taken place in 7 or 6 BC. But, besides the same objection as to the other types of phenomena, namely that it could hardly point to Jesus' crib, this planetary conjunction is unlikely to have been bright enough to be seen by the naked eye.

As usual, Matthew evidently got the idea from biblical prophecies, which he could now claim to have been fulfilled by the birth of Jesus. The chief text that Matthew is using here is the vision of the future of the Jewish people as seen by the pagan prophet Balaam in the book of Numbers. Hired by Balak, king of Moab, to curse the people of Israel, Balaam finds himself blessing them instead, and prognosticating a great future for them: "There shall come a Star out of Jacob, and a Sceptre shall rise out of Israel" (Num. 24:17).

Here we have a clear connection between the Messiah and the sign of a star. It is not surprising that this idea should have been attributed to a non-Jewish seer, as it was a commonplace amongst ancient pagans that great events, good and bad alike, were heralded by unusual astronomical phenomena. In Republican Rome, for example, a report of unfavorable omens in the sky was enough to stop all public business and postpone it to a more auspicious time.

But, though originally a pagan idea, this association of the coming of the Messiah with the appearance of a bright star was taken over by the Jews and incorporated into the messianic tradition—so much so that the leader of the Jewish revolt in the time of the Emperor Hadrian, about a century after the death of Jesus, changed his name from Bar Kosivah to Bar Kochbah ("son of a star") in claiming to be the Messiah.

So much for the star, but what about the Magi themselves? They too turn out to have biblical antecedents. In a famous passage in which Isaiah predicts the coming of the Messiah we read: "And nations shall come to your light, and kings to the brightness of your rising" (60:3). And then: "All those from Sheba shall come. They shall bring gold and frankincense, and shall proclaim the praise of the Lord" (60:6). A similar image is conjured up in the Psalms: "May the kings of Tarshish and of the isles render him tribute, may the kings of Sheba and Seba bring gifts! May all kings fall down before him, all nations serve him!" (72:10-11) Here we have all the elements so assiduously applied by Matthew to Jesus' birth story: foreign potentates bearing gifts of gold and incense coming to pay homage.

Why should we not believe Matthew's story? Because, not only is it implausible and vague—and a little too obviously modeled on the ancient prophecies, which, as we shall see, actually referred to a completely different scenario altogether—but it is totally unsupported by the other Christian Gospels, let alone by Jewish or pagan sources.

But Matthew caps this dizzy construction of imaginative fiction with a tour de force so daring as to dwarf all his previous tales. I refer to his story of the "slaughter of the innocents," according to which, when King Herod heard of the birth of the Messiah in Bethlehem, seeing this as a threat to his own position he ordered the death of all male children there under the age of two (Matt. 2:16). The ensuing massacre is, as usual, seen as the fulfillment of Jewish prophecy, on this occasion a passage from Jeremiah describing "Rachel weeping for her children" (31:15) taken completely out of context. For one thing, Rachel's voice is clearly stated in the passage—even as quoted by Matthew—as emanating from the town of Ramah, which is five miles *north* of Jerusalem, whereas Rachel's tomb, according to the book of Genesis (35:19 f. and 48:7), is on the road to Bethlehem, which is about five miles *south* of Jerusalem. In addition, Jeremiah's reference is clearly to the exile of Rachel's children, the Jewish people (or at least some of them) and his message to Rachel is a happy one:

> Thus saith the Lord: "Refrain thy voice from weeping, and thine eyes from tears: for thy work shall be rewarded," saith the Lord; "and they shall come again from the land of the enemy. And there is hope in thine end," saith the Lord, "that thy children shall come again to their own border." (Jer. 31:16-17)

Another biblical echo that is clearly discernible in the story of the massacre is that of the birth of Moses, who has to be hidden in the bulrushes in order to escape Pharoah's edict of death to all Jewish male children (Exod. 1:16 ff.). Matthew was also capitalizing on Herod's not altogether undeserved reputation for cruelty. But Herod's reign is anything but a closed book to history. He lived in one of the greatest ages of literature that the world has ever seen, and, though not at the center of the stage as far as world affairs were concerned, his reign is well documented. There is a full biography of him written by Nicholas of Damascus, plus the detailed account of Jewish history including his reign in Josephus' *Antiquities of the Jews,* to mention but two sources.

A massacre of all the male infants of Bethlehem—if true—could hardly fail to have been mentioned in these sources, and its total absence from them all can only point in one direction, namely to Matthew's having made the story up. His motive is quite plain. The story makes Jesus' birth, in Bethlehem, a matter of public knowledge at the time when it happened and it even manages to enlist King Herod's support for the belief that Jesus was the Messiah, for, after all, if Herod had not been convinced that the Messiah had indeed been born, why would he order the murder of all male infants in Bethlehem?

By contrast with all the heady excitement provided by Matthew's account of Jesus' birth, Luke's is positively dull. He offers us no star and no massacre, and his humble shepherds (2:8 ff.) are no match for the glamor and mystery of Matthew's Magi.

Conclusions

Matthew and Luke make the same three major claims about Jesus' birth: that it was a virgin birth, that it took place in Bethlehem, and that Jesus was of Davidic descent. But the evidence to back up these claims is quite different in the two accounts. In Luke, the annunciation of the birth is made to Mary; in Matthew it is made to Joseph. Matthew has Joseph and Mary marry; Luke does not. Both offer genealogies to prove Jesus' Davidic lineage, but there are more differences than similarities, especially in the names of the ancestors nearest in time to Jesus, notably Joseph's own father. Luke uses an elaborate story about a Roman census to explain the presence of Joseph and Mary in Bethlehem; Matthew gives the impression that they lived there permanently.

Then, as we have just seen, Matthew recounts stories of a star, three wise men, and a massacre, while all Luke offers are a few simple shepherds inspired by angelic visions. In addition, where Matthew has Mary, Joseph, and Jesus fleeing from Bethlehem to Egypt in order to escape Herod's death edict (2:13-14), Luke has them stay in Bethlehem for forty days and then return to Nazareth via Jerusalem (Luke 2:21-39). When Matthew brings them to Nazareth, it is (in keeping with his version of the birth story though at variance with all the other Gospels) as though they now go there for the first time (Matt 2:19-23). As usual, Matthew offers us a biblical text by way of corroboration: "And he [Joseph] went and dwelt in a city called Nazareth, that what was spoken by the prophets might be fulfilled, 'He shall be called a Nazarene'" (2:23).

This verse has attracted a good deal of attention, partly because for once Matthew is unable to find a biblical text which he can "apply." The supposed verse he "quotes" simply does not exist! Explaining *Nazarene* as a reference not to the town of Nazareth but rather to the special nazirite oath taken by such figures as Samson does nothing to save Matthew. Jesus clearly was *not* a nazirite, as he had not forsworn wine. But even reading the verse in that way would be of no assistance to Matthew, as no biblical verse can be called into service in that case either. From the context, though, it seems quite plain that what Matthew is trying to do is find some biblical justification for settling Joseph and his family in so unlikely a spot as Nazareth, a place with which, according to Matthew's birth story, they had had no prior association. The only way he can do so is to fabricate a biblical quotation.

In other words, Matthew and Luke share the conclusions that they want their readers to accept about Jesus' birth and infancy but neither share the factual evidence nor the reasoning from which those conclusions should have been derived. This shows that, instead of starting with the evidence and being led by it to the conclusions, they started with the conclusions and manufactured evidence to justify those conclusions. The three conclusions—that Jesus was born in Bethlehem, of Davidic descent, and by virgin birth—are improbable enough in themselves, but, as we have seen, the contortions into which Matthew and Luke are forced in order to "prove" them only gives the game away. And the fundamental factual disagreements between Matthew and Luke, on the one hand, and between them and the other Gospels and outside sources, on the other, only confirms our view that the claims made for Jesus' birth—which all add up to claiming for him the title of the Messiah in accordance with Jewish scriptural prophecy—are as false as the evidence used to support those claims.

To cap it all, two of the three claims are mutually exclusive. As we have seen, the claim to Davidic lineage depends upon accepting Joseph as Jesus' father, the very thing denied by the virgin birth theory.

II

Jesus the Jew

Though there are few, if any, Christians left who, like the Nazi-dominated Lutheran Church in Germany during the 1930s, would actually deny Jesus' Jewish origins, nevertheless it is a subject that many Christians prefer not to dwell on. Even Christian theologians often tend to stress the *differences* between Jesus' teachings and those of the Jewish rabbis of his day, the implication usually being that Christianity is not only very different from Judaism but also greatly superior to it.

For these reasons it is vitally important to find out just how Jewish Jesus was, both in himself and in his outlook on life.

Nazi anthropologists took some comfort from the fact that Jesus was a Galilean. Though originally part of David's kingdom, Galilee was given by King Solomon to the Phoenicians in payment of a debt. The area attracted a large non-Jewish population, resulting in its being called "Galilee of the Gentiles" by the prophet Isaiah (9:1). It became part of the Jewish state again by conquest only about a century before Jesus' birth. It is therefore quite possible that Jesus was not of Jewish blood, though, unfortunately for the Nazis, he is most unlikely to have been an "Aryan" either, as the Phoenicians were themselves of Semitic stock.

In terms of religion and identity, however, there can be no doubt whatsoever: Jesus was a Jew. In accordance with the general principle of the ancient world, all the inhabitants of a particular country were obliged to show their loyalty to the state, not only politically but also culturally and religiously. This principle is foreign to the modern Western world, but that has not always been the case. In Elizabethan England, for example, every Englishman was expected to be a member of the Church of England. If he was not, he was deemed to be a traitor to the state—and the same applied in Spain to anyone who was not a Roman Catholic. In fact, until very recently there was no freedom of worship in Spain for Protestant Christians, let alone for Jews or

Muslims, who had been forced to leave Spain in 1492.

Today we label this "religious intolerance," but its origin is quite different. There is plenty of evidence in the Bible that in early times each nation or tribe had its own religion, with its own god and its own cult. Capturing an enemy god was therefore believed to be much more than a symbolic gesture. The god, generally in the form of an idol, was now thought to be the prisoner of his captors and no longer able to protect his original tribe or nation. It is in this light that we must understand, for example, the Philistine capture of the ark, as described in the first book of Samuel (4:11).

The Jewish scriptures repeatedly attack idolatry and hammer home the lesson that pagan gods have no real power:

> Our God is in the heavens;
>   he does whatever he pleases.
> Their idols are silver and gold,
>   the work of men's hands.
> They have mouths, but do not speak;
>   eyes, but do not see.
> They have ears, but do not hear;
>   noses, but do not smell.
> They have hands, but do not feel;
>   feet, but do not walk;
>   and they do not make a sound in their throat.
> Those who make them are like them;
>   so are all who trust in them.
>
> (Ps. 115:3-8)

From time to time, however, traces are discernible of an older attitude: "For the Lord is a great God, and a great King above all gods" (Ps. 95:3). Though the Jewish God's supremacy is proclaimed here in no uncertain terms, it is equally clear that the existence of other gods is taken for granted. This is a reflection of a pluralistic view of the world. But the superiority of the Jewish God over all other gods is not used to convert non-Jews to Judaism.

Even when, as in the book of Jonah, a Jewish prophet is sent to preach to foreigners, his mission is most decidedly *not* to convert the people of Nineveh (in Assyria) to Judaism but merely to get them to repent of their sins. Jonah himself is reluctant to undertake this mission, understandably enough; to the Jews of antiquity Assyria was what Nazi Germany is to the Jews of today—the epitome of evil. Hence the setting of the Jonah story in Nineveh, even though it was written long after Assyria has ceased to exist. The whole story is clearly allegorical. Jonah—the name means "dove" in Hebrew—is not intended to be an historical personage but rather the personification of the Jewish people, and his famous misadventure in the belly of a whale (actually described simply as a "big fish") is the direct result of his recalcitrance. It is his reluctance to minister to the deadliest enemies of the Jewish people that impels him to run away. He boards a ship making for Tarshish, which is probably to be identified with Tartessus, a Phoenician colony in Spain, at the far end of the Mediterranean.

His first lesson, when thrown overboard and swallowed by the whale, is the omnipresence of God. The second lesson taught by this tiny gem of a book is that you do not have to be Jewish in order to earn God's mercy. Jonah is dejected to find that the dire warnings which he is eventually forced to proclaim to the people of Ninevah are taken seriously, that they repent with alacrity, and that their city is thereafter spared by divine favor.

The message of the book of Jonah is essentially therefore one of tolerance. Jonah's mission is to preach the impending destruction of Nineveh unless its people repent of their sins, which they do. There is no question of their converting to Judaism, the point being that non-Jews are just as eligible for God's grace as Jews.

Intolerance vs. Exclusivity

This is exactly the opposite of the Christian view, which sees divine grace and salvation as confined entirely to Christians (and often to the adherents of one particular denomination of Christianity). This view is well expressed in the verse which, for that very reason, is the one that has been translated into more languages than any other verse in the Christian scriptures: "For God so loved the world that he gave his only son, that whoever believes in him may have eternal life." (John 3:16). If the message is not clear enough from this, a subsequent verse leaves no doubt: "He who believes in him is not condemned; he who does not believe is condemned already, because he has not believed in the name of the only son of God." (John 3:18). This makes it quite plain not only that salvation depends on Christian belief but also that all non-Christians are automatically damned.

It is from this belief in a Christian monopoly on truth and salvation that intolerance sprang. In other words, it is the very fact that Christianity is based on a specific *belief*—namely, that Jesus was the Messiah or Christ or son of God—that made it intolerant from the outset. We might label Christianity a *creed* religion, as against Judaism, for example, for which the appropriate label would be *communal*. One is a Jew, not only by virtue of accepting some particular belief but through membership of a social group. That is not to say that Judaism is *not* associated with certain beliefs. Of course it is, but no belief or group of beliefs is the touchstone that determines whether one is a Jew or not. Some Jews accept a belief in the resurrection of the dead, for example, but not all. Some Jews take most of the Jewish Bible quite literally, others do not.

But, you may well ask, is this not also the case with Christianity? If there are fundamentalist Jews and liberal Jews, so are there fundamentalist Christians and liberal Christians. If there are disputed beliefs in Judaism, so are there disputed beliefs in Christianity: transubstantiation, predestination, and the nature of the Trinity being just a few random examples.

This is true enough, but there still is a fundamental difference in kind between the two religions. A Jew may reject as fictions Elijah's miracles, the existence of Moses, or even the story of the Exodus from Egypt, and still remain a Jew. A Christian who rejects Jesus as the Christ is no longer a Christian.

The Jews are often accused by Christians of arrogance on account of their exclusiveness: in claiming to be the Chosen People and in making it difficult for outsiders to become Jews. This is undoubtedly a form of arrogance, but how much less so and how much less dangerously so than the Christian claim to sole truth and salvation, resulting not only in intolerance but also in a long history of persecution— and not only of non-Christians but even of "heretical" Christians.

What is the definition of a heretic? Simply someone who disagrees with you on some matter of religious dogma. To those who believed, for example, that Father and Son in the Trinity were coeval (that is of the same age), anyone who came up with the commonsense observation that a son can hardly be of the same age as his father was making a heretical statement, to cite but one of the many heresies that have abounded in the history of Christianity.

Upon reflection it will become apparent that it is in the very nature of a creed religion to be intolerant. Once everything is seen as hinging on a particular belief—no matter what that belief may be—the belief must be carefully defined, and anyone not conforming to the belief *in that particular form of words* is automatically designated a heretic or an unbeliever.

This will be clear if we take a hypothetical example. Let us suppose that the belief which we have placed at the center of our new religion is that tortoises fly at night. This cardinal article of faith appears simple enough: tortoises fly at night. But that is only the most preliminary stage. Before long the terms *tortoise, fly* and *night* will have to be defined, and that is where disagreements are likely to arise. Tortoises will have to carefully differentiated from turtles on the one hand and terrapins on the other. There is bound to be some disagreement as to what exactly constitutes flying, to distinguish it from leaping or gliding, for instance. And what is the exact meaning of *night*? Is it night once the first star has appeared in the sky or only once a particular level of darkness has descended?

There has been no shortage of such disputations either in Judaism or in Christianity. But there is a crucial difference. In Judaism such disagreements, even when they concern fundamental concepts, can never threaten the essential fabric of Judaism, which does not depend upon any particular belief or set of beliefs. But in Christianity in the past, the least disagreement on even the most trivial belief has been enough to create a schism.

There could hardly be a greater contrast among religious leaders than that between Hillel and Shammai, two of the leading rabbis of the time of Jesus. In character, temperament, attitudes, and general outlook on life Hillel and Shammai were essentially at opposite poles, and they disagreed on practically everything. Their differences come out clearly in the well-known Talmudic story of the non-Jew who comes to Shammai offering to convert to Judaism provided the rabbi could teach him the whole of Jewish law while the convert stood on one foot. Shammai shoos the prospective proselyte away with his builder's yard, whereupon the same request is put to Hillel, whose response is quite different: "What is hateful to you, do not do to your neighbor: that is the whole Law; the rest is commentary; go and learn it" (Shabbath 31a). Hillel encapsulates the whole Torah in one brief precept, something which Shammai is not even prepared to countenance. Their attitudes to conversion are also in conflict, with Hillel encouraging conversion to Judaism and Shammai decidedly hostile to the idea.

Yet, despite the fundamental disagreements between Hillel and Shammai and their two respective schools, there was never any question of the one school labeling the other as heretics, infidels, or unbelievers, or of the one trying to excommunicate the other. They agreed to differ, with both schools remaining firmly Jewish and never questioning—or even discussing—the other's right to regard itself as such.

By contrast, disagreement over a single word has been enough to cause a schism in Christianity. In fact, the major conflict between the Roman Catholic and Eastern Orthodox churches *was* caused by just such a disagreement: over the word *filioque* in the Nicene Creed. The creed stated that the holy spirit emanated from the father *and from the son (filioque)*, the Eastern position being that the holy spirit came *only* from the father and not from the son at all. It has never occurred to either side that, as the disputed issue could never be finally resolved, the most sensible solution would be mutual tolerance. As usual in Christian sectarian disputes, the end result was conflict and repression—and a schism that has lasted for nearly a thousand years!

But Jesus himself was *not* a Christian; he was a Jew. He lived and died a Jew. This is an obvious and basic fact but still gives many Christians a jolt.

> "Think not that I have come to abolish the law and the prophets; I have come not to abolish them but to fulfill them. For truly, I say to you, till heaven and earth pass away, not an iota, not a dot, will pass from the law until all is accomplished. Whoever then relaxes one of the least of these commandments and teaches men so, shall be called least in the kingdom of heaven; but he who does them and teaches them shall be called great in the kingdom of heaven." (Matt. 5:17-19)

There can be no doubt about the meaning of this passage. It plainly asserts the validity of the Jewish Bible as binding on Jesus and his followers *in its entirety*. Yet this is exactly the opposite of the view taken by Christianity from an early date, which is all the more reason for believing that the statement recorded here by Matthew really *was* made by Jesus, showing just how Jewish he was in his general outlook.

Problems for the Early Jewish-Christian Church

The Book of Acts gives us some interesting glimpses of the conflicts within the infant Christian movement after Jesus' death. The conservative element within the movement, still regarding themselves as Jews, insisted that any non-Jew who joined the Christian movement had to become a Jew, that is, by circumcision (Acts 15:1). This was opposed by Peter and Paul, and it was eventually agreed that non-Jewish, or gentile, adherents of the Christian movement should not be bound by the full rigor of Jewish law but should only abstain from fornication and from eating blood, meat sacrificed to idols, and the meat of strangled animals (Acts 15:29). This introduced a double standard of behavior within the Christian movement, as Jewish members were still considered bound by every jot and tittle of Jewish law.

That is why even in the somewhat dubious case of Timotheus, whose father was a Greek but who had a Jewish mother (thus making him a Jew according to Jewish law), Paul himself circumcised him, evidently in order to placate the conservative wing of the Christian movement (Acts 16:1-3). These conservatives accused Paul of teaching the Jews in the Christian movement "to forsake Moses, telling them not to circumcise their children or observe the customs" (Acts 21:21). The "customs" referred to are clearly Jewish traditional practices.

The conservatives were quite right in identifying Paul's influence as leading to a drift from Jewish law and tradition in the Christian movement as a whole, affecting its Jewish members as much as its gentile ones. But, surprisingly perhaps, Paul did not attempt to challenge his conservative critics by coming out with a direct declaration that the Christian movement was no longer a branch of Judaism but a new and quite separate religion. It would have split the movement from top to bottom if he had taken such a stand, but even Paul himself does not appear to have viewed the movement as a new religion. So, to allay the conservatives' fears about his own Jewish identity, he agrees to take a Jewish oath of purification in the Temple (Acts 21:23-26).

Most revealing of all, when Paul is brought before the Sanhedrin, he appeals to the Pharisees in these words: "Brethren, I am a Pharisee, a son of Pharisees" (Acts 23:6). We may interpret this as a calculated and cynical appeal, and it was not unsuccessful, as the Pharisees present took Paul's part and cried out: "We find nothing wrong in this man" (Acts 23:9). But, upon closer examination, it would seem to be a less surprising self-description than we might have thought. Paul was, after all, a disciple of the famous Rabbi Gamaliel, himself a leading Pharisee (Acts 5:34; 22:3). What is more, even Jesus' position was probably closer to that of the Pharisees than is commonly believed.

For example, after telling his disciples to obey every "jot and tittle" of the Jewish law, to quote that beautifully picturesque phrase from the King James version (Matt. 5:18; see above for the whole passage), he goes on to warn them that "unless your righteousness exceeds that of the scribes and Pharisees, you will never enter the kingdom of heaven" (Matt. 5:20). Though Jesus here clearly excludes the Pharisees from his vision of "the kingdom of heaven," nevertheless the implication is that they *are* more righteous than their other rivals. In other words, what Jesus is essentially saying is that his disciples must be *super*-Pharisees, that they must out-Pharisee the Pharisees. Their obedience to the Jewish law must be even greater than that of the Pharisees. Jesus' objection to the Pharisees is not that they paid too much attention to the detail of Jewish law and custom but that they did not combine this minute observance—*which, as we have seen, Jesus commends to his own disciples* (Matt. 5:17-19)—with sufficient attention to the *spirit* of the law.

One area of conflict between Jesus and the Pharisees was the laws of the Sabbath, an institution of central importance in Jewish observance, particularly to the Pharisees, who are reported to have criticized Jesus on two occasions in this connection: once when his disciples were seen plucking ears of grain and the other time when Jesus supposedly healed a man with a withered arm on the Sabbath (Mark 2:23; 3:1-6; Matt. 12:1-14; Luke 6:1-11). The point about Sabbath observance is of course a prohibition on all forms of work:

> "Remember the sabbath day, to keep it holy. Six days you shall labor, and do all your work; but the seventh day is a sabbath to the Lord your God; in it you shall not do any work, you, or your son, or your daughter, your manservant, or your maidservant, or your cattle, or the sojourner who is within your gates." (Exod. 20:8-10)

It is in no small part to this law that the survival of Judaism is due. In times of great hardship and penury Jews have nevertheless forced themselves to set aside one day every week not only for rest but also for reflection, discussion, and religious learning, which would otherwise have been sacrificed to the all-pervasive search for a livelihood.

The Pharisees' alleged objection was to the fact that Jesus and his disciples were working on the Sabbath, but in fact Jewish law has always recognized that there were permissible exceptions to this rule. One fundamental rule of Jewish law is that *any* law may be broken, no matter how sacred, if the interests of human life are at stake. Thus, someone requiring constant medication is not only permitted but indeed obliged to continue taking his medicine and as much food as may be necessary to go with it, even on the Day of Atonement, the most solemn fast in the Jewish calendar.

Jesus obviously has this extremely important principle of Jewish law in mind in replying to his critics. He argues (somewhat obliquely) that his disciples were hungry when plucking the grain and, in connection with the healing incident, retorts: "Is it lawful on the Sabbath to do good or to do harm, to save life or to kill?" (Mark 3:4; Luke 6:9) Jesus' general point is summed up in the well-known saying, recorded only by Mark: "The Sabbath was made for man, not man for the Sabbath" (Mark 2:27).

But would the Pharisees not have agreed with this dictum? Of course they would; it is the whole essence of the Jewish law of the Sabbath. Then, what possible objection *could* the Pharisees have had against the Sabbath activities of Jesus and his disciples? Just this: that it was by no means clear to them that the two activities were emergencies—and one can hardly blame them for being dubious on this score. Jesus implies that his disciples were hungry, which Matthew, writing for a Jewish readership, correctly seizes on as the crucial point and emphasizes further himself (Matt. 12:1). But, were the disciples really so hungry as to need to break the ban on work? In other words, was it really a matter of life and death, or were the disciples just a little peckish and having a midmorning snack? Similarly with the healing incident, Jesus makes sure to use the words "to save life," but is that really what he was doing by healing a withered hand? In other words, was it really an emergency operation? It is easy to see why the Pharisees would not have thought so, and that must have been their objection.

It would seem, therefore, that our reports of these incidents are somewhat distorted, the Pharisees being portrayed as inhumanely enforcing the letter of the law in all circumstances. Jesus' airy statements of humane principles, though reported by the Gospels as if in conflict with Jewish law, are nothing other than statements of that very Jewish law—thus creating a fog in which the realities of the facts of the case are lost from view. For the fact is that, though Jewish law makes provision for a genuine case of need, the two breaches of the Sabbath law concerned do not appear to have been in that category. Once the varnish is removed, what we are left with is a very unprepossessing picture indeed: Here we have Jesus, the self-styled upholder of "every jot and tittle" of Jewish law breaking the law and then desperately trying to hide his breach under a blanket, but fairly clear-cut, exception within the law itself, but sniping at his critics all the while.

This gives us a pretty good idea of Jesus' attitude to Jewish law in practice. He is so anxious not to break it that he wishes to appear even more law-abiding than the Pharisees, though it is clear that his disciples were not always as observant of Jewish law as Jesus would have liked them to be.

As a communal religion Judaism is concerned with every aspect of social life, not only those areas which would today be recognized as embraced by the term *religion*. Among the areas seemingly extraneous to religion is that of hygiene, which plays an important part in Jewish law and tradition. One basic rule is to wash one's hands before eating, a rule which, it seems, Jesus' disciples did not always observe. When upbraided by the Pharisees on this score, Jesus, contrary to all his own teachings, acts on the principle that attack is the best defense and duly lambasts the Pharisees for supposedly breaking a different law altogether, that of respect for parents, and then proceeds to enunciate a general principle of cleanliness, which is presumably meant to exculpate his disciples' failure to wash their hands before eating (Mark 7:1-23; Matt. 15:1-20).

Why can't Jesus simply admit that his disciples were wrong to do so? There is certainly no way he can satisfactorily justify their action, given his own principles. Perhaps no verse puts his position in relation to the Pharisees more succinctly than this one: "The scribes and the Pharisees sit on Moses' seat; so practice and observe whatever they tell you, but not what they do; for they preach, but do not practice." (Matt. 23:2-3). Here once again we find praise of the Pharisees coupled with blame. What is particularly noteworthy is that there is a blanket approval of Pharisatic teachings (which only confirms what I said above about the Pharisees not being ignorant that "the Sabbath was made for man, not man for the Sabbath").

This makes Jesus' reaction to the criticism over the lack of handwashing all the more puzzling. He says: do what the Pharisees say. The Pharisees say: wash your hands before eating. There should be no problem.

There clearly *is* a problem, but what exactly is it? Jesus, the self-styled super-observant Jew has been caught out. His disciples are found failing to observe a basic Jewish rule of hygiene, which by dint of repetition day in and day out should have been second nature to them. This is why an admission of guilt on Jesus' part was out of the question, and the same applies to any attempt to shift the blame onto the disciples' shoulders, for this would reveal that his disciples were not as steeped in Jewish law and lore as Jesus would have liked his audience to believe. This explains the belligerent tone he adopts against his critics and also the disquisition which he launches into to demonstrate that "not what goes into the mouth defiles a man, but what comes out of the mouth, this defiles a man" (Matt. 15:10). If all Jesus meant was that "what comes out of the mouth" defiles *more* than "what goes into the mouth"—which is not what he says—then the Pharisees would have been most unlikely to take exception to it as we were told they did (Matt. 15:12). If, on the other hand, Jesus really intended to reject the hand-washing rule outright, then he is acting contrary to his own injunction "practice and observe whatever they [the Pharisees] tell you" (Matt. 23:3).

Nevertheless, in the process of defending his disciples against the charge of failing to wash their hands, Jesus actually rejects not only that rule but also the prohibition on the eating of certain foods (Mark 7:19). Was this radical rejection of Jewish rules of conduct merely the result of overreaction on Jesus' part to those who dared criticize his disciples? Or is the incident of the hand-washing just the vehicle for enunciating a new doctrine? The doctrine put forward here *as if new* may be summarized as follows: externals are of no significance; spiritual concerns alone matter. This doctrine, variously interpreted over the centuries, has become a central pillar of Christian belief, especially when contrasted with Judaism portrayed—as it usually has been by Christians—as superficial and ritualistic.

As so often, however, doctrines or beliefs claimed as Christian are in reality much older Jewish inventions. The passage of Isaiah quoted by Jesus in this connection brings this out, although, as is so often the case, the Gospels do not quote it quite correctly:

> "This people honors me with their lips,
> but their heart is far from me;
> in vain do they worship me,
> teaching as doctrines the precepts of men."
> (Mark 7:6-7; Matt. 15:8-9; cf.Isa. 29:13-14)

This is a common theme among the Jewish prophets. Isaiah has a long invective on the subject in his very first chapter (Isa. 1:10-17), and similar sentiments are expressed by Ezekiel, Jeremiah, Hosea, Amos, and Micah. Isaiah was writing some seven centuries before Jesus' birth—so this idea can hardly be claimed as a Christian innovation. Moreover, as we have seen, Jesus was constantly going out of his way to show what an observant Jew he was. An observant Jew, however, as Jesus recognized, would not dispense with a "jot or tittle" of the Jewish law, yet here he was himself setting aside some basic rules of conduct!

Which is the true picture? Was Jesus the observant Jew that he was anxious to portray himself as being? Or was he the reformer, the innovator, smiting Judaism hip and thigh? Or was he a mixture of the two? Despite his protestations to the contrary, Jesus clearly did depart from accepted Jewish belief and practice in a number of significant ways. It may not be entirely coincidental that it is in Matthew, that most Jewish of the Gospels, that the picture of Jesus, the pious Jew, comes out most clearly.

The injunction to obey punctiliously everything that the Pharisees say (Matt. 23:2-3) occurs *only* in Matthew, though the warning against changing a "jot or tittle" of the Jewish law is found in Luke (16:17) as well as in Matthew (5:18), but the version of this verse found in Mark, the oldest Gospel, is quite different: "Heaven and earth will pass away, but my words will not pass away" (Mark 13:31). There is no reference here at all to Jewish law, only to Jesus' own words. Did Matthew and Luke embroider this saying to such an extent as to introduce a wholly new dimension into it? Matthew would have had a motive for doing so, as his Gospel is essentially addressed to a Jewish readership, but what about Luke? It is of course possible that Matthew and Luke drew their saying from another source altogether, and not from Mark.

But, whatever the explanation, there is no way of reconciling the "jot and tittle" saying with the extremely free and easy reinterpretation of Jewish law that we so frequently find Jesus indulging in in the pages of the Gospels. The original Greek of the phrase *jot or tittle* actually refers to the minutest markings in the Jewish Torah, the Jewish tradition then as now being that even an obvious mistake in the grammar or spelling of the Torah must be left as it is. This may smack of extreme literal-mindedness, but it has a practical purpose. The slightest textual variant, it was long ago recognized, could give rise to dispute. Therefore there is only one authorized text of the Jewish Bible, namely the so-called Masoretic Text (Hebrew: *masorah,* tradition). For the same reason, even today not a single deletion or correction of any kind is allowed in a Torah scroll, which has still to be written by hand by a professional scribe.

The point though is that in his "jot or tittle" remark, far from attacking Jewish literal-mindedness, Jesus endorses it wholeheartedly. The very difficulty of reconciling this position with that of the Christian church by the time the Gospels were written makes it all the more likely that it is genuine, and its retention by Luke especially points to its authenticity.

If so, then Jesus was rather inconsistent, as there can be no doubt that he did depart from Jewish law and tradition in many important ways, though these departures were undoubtedly magnified in the Christian church after his death, and it is not inconceivable that some later innovations were fathered on Jesus in the interests of respectability.

Jesus certainly seems to have delighted in discomfiting other Jewish groups by pointing out how they fell short of their own criteria of moral and religious excellence. For example, he launches into a diatribe against the Pharisees for their supposed hypocrisy over the law to honor father and mother (Mark 7:10-13; Matt. 15:3-6). What Jesus seems to be accusing them of doing is using the fiction of an offering (*korban*) in the Temple as a way of evading responsibility to aged parents. The details of the use of the *korban* in this way are unfortunately not known, but the Hebrew word *korban* merely means a present or offering. Perhaps money or valuables could be dedicated to the Temple in such a way as to make them unavailable for other uses, such as support of needy relations, though quite how the original owner could still retain control over his "offered" possessions—if at all—is by no means clear.

But, whatever the truth behind these allegations, the law in question was a strange one for Jesus to choose, for, as we have already had occasion to notice in another connection, he himself appears to have been anything but a model son. Except at the crucifixion, Jesus is reported as reproaching his mother every time they met, namely at the marriage of Cana and when she came together with his brothers to see him. John's description of the scene at Cana is very lifelike (John 2:1-4). The catering at the wedding feast is inefficient and there is no more wine left. This was no more Jesus' responsibility than Mary's, who, making small talk, remarks on the fact that the wine has run out. Taking this as a personal attack on himself, possibly on his miracle-making properties, Jesus rounds on his mother and lets fly: "O woman, what have you to do with me? My hour has not yet come" (John 2:4). As punctuation marks formed no part of the original Gospel texts, it would be quite possible to take this last sentence to mean: "Has my hour not now come?" This translation, favored among others by the fourth-century Church Father, Gregory of Nyssa, would seem to make better sense, especially in the light of the rest of the story, in which Jesus proceeds to replenish the stocks by miraculously turning water into wine. His retort to Mary would then mean something like this: "Stop fussing. Don't you know that I am now ready to perform miracles?"

Not surprisingly, this incident has attracted a good deal of attention from commentators, many of whom have tried their best to smooth over any signs of conflict between Jesus and Mary. But even his form of address to her, equally unusual in Greek and in Hebrew for a son addressing his mother, bespeaks the rage he feels against her.

The other incident is equally revealing, if not more so. Mary and Jesus' brothers specially come to see him while he is preaching to a large crowd, but they are rudely rebuffed. The story is told in all three of the synoptics (Mark 3:31; Matt. 12:46; Luke 8:19). Here is Mark's version:

> And his mother and his brothers came; and standing outside they sent to him and called him. And a crowd was sitting about him; and they said to him, "Your mother and your brothers are outside, asking for you." And he replied, "Who are my mother and my brothers?" And looking around on those who sat about him, he said, "Here are my mother and my brothers! Whoever does the will of God is my brother, and sister, and mother. (Mark 3:31-35)

Jesus' audience clearly sees nothing wrong with Jesus' family's obvious concern about him. In fact, the audience seems quite ready to allow Jesus to interrupt his preaching to go and talk to his mother and brothers. But Jesus is not content merely to rebuff them. Adding insult to injury, he launches into a ringing renunciation of family ties in general—a far cry indeed from "honor thy father and thy mother"!

Nor is this an isolated remark. We find the same idea expressed several times:

> "If any one comes to me and does not hate his own father and mother and wife and children and brothers and sisters, yes, and even his own life, he cannot be my disciple." (Luke 14:26; cf. Matt. 10:35-38 and Luke 12:52-53)

The alarming message here is plain: ties of blood count for nothing as against loyalty to Jesus and his movement. What is demanded here is a type of totalitarian loyalty that has become all too familiar in modern times! But the point we are concerned with is that it is completely at loggerheads with the family-based kind of loyalty that is so central to Judaism and that finds expression in the Fifth Commandment.

Jesus and the Gentiles

That Jesus was a Jew is a fact that Christians generally accept, however reluctantly. The notion that Jesus saw his movement as a purely and exclusively Jewish one would be received with even less favor, but there is evidence that points in that direction. Jesus' speech speeding his twelve apostles on their mission is as good a starting point as any: "Go nowhere among the Gentiles, and enter no town of the Samaritans, but go rather to the lost sheep of the house of Israel" (Matt. 10:5-6). What exactly does this mean? The word translated as *Gentiles* is, in the Greek as in Hebrew, literally *the nations,* a reference to all the peoples of the world with the sole exception of the Jews. As for the Samaritans, they were chiefly the descendants of the Assyrian, Babylonian, and Cuthaean settlers sent to the northern kingdom of Israel after its conquest by Assyria seven hundred years before the birth of Jesus. The Samaritans' own intermittent claims to Jewish blood were always totally rejected by the Jews.

In other words, Jesus' statement confines his apostles' mission strictly to the Jewish people. Some have seen the phrase "lost sheep of Israel" coupled with the fact that the apostles were twelve in number as a reference to the ten lost tribes together with the two surviving Jewish tribes, but this seems unlikely. Not only does Jesus want his apostles to avoid any contact with Gentile *people* but he also orders them to stay away from Gentile *areas* (literally, "Do not go into the way of the nations"), which would make it somewhat difficult for them to track down the ten lost tribes!

Does the injunction imply, as some scholars have suggested, that the mission was to be the Jews *first* but subsequently followed up by a mission to the Gentiles? The peremptory wording of the instruction is against this, as is the report of another incident, also by Matthew. This is the case where Jesus is approached for help by a Canaanite woman whose daughter is "severely possessed by a demon" (Matt. 15:22). Jesus roughly turns her away, his explanation being: "I was sent only to the lost house of Israel" (Matt. 15:24). This categorical statement, this time in reference to Jesus' view of his own mission, is supplemented by his further explanation: "It is not fair to take the children's bread and throw it to the dogs." (Matt. 15:26).

The Jews are commonly referred to in Hebrew as the "children of Israel," Israel originally being another name for the third Jewish patriarch, Jacob. As for *dogs,* this is evidently an unflattering reference to Canaanites or, perhaps more likely, to Gentiles in general. The implication is clear: any help given to a non-Jew is a waste. Nevertheless, Jesus is eventually softened by the Canaanite woman's faith in him, and he duly relents (Matt. 15:28).

In Romans, however, Paul is quoted as saying: "For I am not ashamed of the gospel: it is the power of God for salvation to every one who has faith, to the Jew first and also to the Greek" (Rom. 1:16). Is this a "revised version" of the original conception of the mission? Or is it Matthew who is leading us up the garden path?

Then we have the evidence of Acts, a record of what the apostles were doing, as it were, "in the field," according to which, despite Jesus' injunction as quoted by Matthew, they *did* evangelize amongst the Samaritans (Acts 8:25). In Luke's Gospel we even have a report of Jesus himself sending messengers to a Samaritan village to prepare the way for him. When he is rebuffed by the villagers, two of his disciples are anxious to bring fire down from heaven to consume the intransigent Samaritans but Jesus restrains them (Luke 9:51-55).

Another picture of Jesus as favorably disposed towards the Samaritans occurs in John, in the story of the much-married Samaritan woman at the well (John 4:7-26). In the confrontation between Jesus and the Pharisees a few chapters further on we find Jesus actually called a Samaritan by the Pharisees, presumably to signify their displeasure at his association with Samaritans (John 8:48).

Finally, we have in Luke the best-known reference of all to a Samaritan, namely the story of the good Samaritan, put into Jesus' own mouth, the whole point of the story being to accuse the Jews of his day of inhumanity, using the Samaritan as a foil. Samaritans were held in very low esteem by their Jewish contemporaries, so to paint a Samaritan in a better light than a Jewish priest and Levite was clearly intended to be shocking, and of course in the story the priest and Levite "pass on the other side" of the street when they see a man lying half dead on the roadside after being attacked by robbers, but it is the Samaritan who stops and takes care of the man, who is presumably a Jew (Luke 10:30-36). The story makes no pretence to be a true account but is frankly offered as a parable explaining the meaning of the term *neighbor*. Who is a man's neighbor? asks Jesus. Not necessarily his kith and kin, is the answer, but "the one who showed mercy on him" (Luke 10:37). But we cannot help asking nevertheless: Why should Jesus have chosen a parable in which the Jews were the "bad guys" and the Samaritan the "good guy"? There is clearly some hostility here, but is it hostility on the part of Jesus or Luke? For it is exactly the opposite of the bias that we encountered in Matthew. There is no easy answer, unless it is that Jesus' attitude to Judaism and his fellow Jews was so inconsistent as to be ambivalent or that different writers wished to portray Jesus in different lights.

III

Jesus and the Messianic Idea

The Gospel accounts of the life of Jesus have long been a source of acute embarrassment to many Christians, and no part of those accounts more so than the episodes describing Jesus' birth, his miracles, and his resurrection, which make up the bulk of the biographical sections of the Gospels. Particularly with the rise of the Rationalist movement of the eighteenth century there was increasing skepticism about miraculous and supernatural events previously accepted without query as historically true. This skepticism was applied not only to the Christian Gospels but to all works of history, ancient and modern alike. One influential school of thought cut the Gordian knot by pronouncing that all the narratives of Jesus' life were fictitious, or at least symbolical or mythical, and that no such person as Jesus of Nazareth had ever existed. This position was held not only by many rejectors of Christianity but also by many influential Christian theologians and commentators, who advocated accepting the stories not literally but figuratively, not as history but as theology and philosophy.

But there is a fundamental flaw in such a view of the Gospel accounts. After all, Christianity centers about one single figure as no other religion does. Islam certainly places a great deal of emphasis on the life and teachings of Muhammad, but, reverenced through he is, he is no more than a prophet nevertheless, albeit *the* prophet outranking all others and the last one, according to Muslims. His position is clearly expressed in the basic Islamic credo as proclaimed by the muezzin from the minaret of every mosque in calling the faithful to prayer five times each day: "There is no god but Allah, and Muhammad is the prophet of Allah." (This, incidentally, is why Muslims object strenuously to being called "Mohammedans" and having their faith referred to as "Mohammedanism," as used to be done routinely in the West, on the Christian analogy.)

In Judaism there is and has always been a multiplicity of important figures: the patriarchs Abraham, Isaac, and Jacob; prophets

49

such as Elijah, Isaiah, Jeremiah, and Ezekiel; and, probably most notably of all, Moses. But none of these even begins to assume the role that Muhammed plays in Islam, let alone Jesus' role in Christianity. The Jewish patriarchs and prophets, not to mention the kings and priests, are all portrayed in the Bible as eminently fallible and flawed human beings, leaders to be emulated in some respects and criticized in others. Even if it could be proved that, say, Abraham never existed but that he is merely a mythical or legendary figure with no foundation in historical truth, that would not affect the truth or acceptability of Judaism. Judaism does not stand or fall even by the existence of Moses, arguably—though not indisputably—the greatest of the Jewish biblical figures. Moses' importance stems not from his biography, remarkable though that is, but from the laws and teachings attributed to him. Whether they were *his* laws and *his* teachings or not is irrelevant.

But, you may object, does this not also apply to Christianity? It is Jesus' teachings and injunctions that matter, you say, regardless of whether they really are his teachings and injunctions or not, and, for that matter, regardless even of whether he existed or not.

No. Such an argument, plausible enough on the surface, represents a serious misunderstanding of the fundamental differences between Judaism and Christianity. To accept Jesus' teachings without regarding Jesus himself as anything more than an ordinary human being, possibly with some sort of prophetic gift, would not be Christianity in the sense that Paul, Mark, Matthew, Luke, and John preached it. For the Gospels and Epistles to portray Jesus as a teacher would have been much easier than the task they undertake, which is to portray Jesus as *the Christ.*

Christ is the English form of the Greek word *Christos,* which is the direct translation of the Hebrew *Mashiach,* anglicized as Messiah. The original meaning of the word *Christ* was therefore no more and no less than "Messiah." As we saw in the previous chapter, the whole thrust of the Gospel birth-narratives is to claim for Jesus the title of Messiah. But what exactly does this claim entail? What is meant by the term *Messiah?*

The Messianic Idea

Literally, *Messiah* or *Mashiach* simply means "anointed" (with oil), and in the Pentateuch the only people described as anointed or instructed to be anointed are the priests (for example, see Exod. 29:7). In fact, anointing a priest by pouring oil on his head formed part of the ceremony of consecrating him to divine service. The reason for its appearance in this religious ceremonial is probably to be traced to the traditional use of oil as part of the bathing and cleansing process in a number of ancient civilizations. In Greece, for example, athletes would pour oil over their bodies after exercising and then scrape it off their skin with a strigil or scraper. But, unlike the Greeks, the Jews extended this use of oil in ordinary physical cleansing to ritual and ceremonial cleansing, the idea being that a priest had to be clean and pure in order to officiate at the altar.

The first person mentioned in the Bible as ceremonially anointed without being a priest is Saul, the first king of Israel. The prophet Samuel is specifically instructed by God to anoint Saul (1 Sam. 9:16) and the ceremony is described as follows: "Then Samuel took a vial of oil and poured it upon his head, and kissed him and said, 'Has not the Lord anointed you to be prince over his people Israel?'" (1 Sam. 10:1)

It may be easier to understand why a priest should be anointed with oil than a king. But the reason for it is given by Samuel in the quoted verse: the job of a king, like that of a priest, is seen as a divine trust. So, when Saul fails to obey completely the divine command as relayed to him by Samuel to destroy utterly the Amalekites and all their possessions, the prophet informs him that he is deposed from the throne. (1 Sam. 15). In other words, Saul has failed in the divine mission entrusted to him and must therefore be punished.

It may appear strange that the divine command in question was to commit what might well be condemned today as an act of brutality and Saul's "failure" was his refusal to obey this command fully. For what he was expected to do was not only to defeat the Amalekites but also to "kill both man and woman, infant and suckling, ox and sheep, camel and ass." (1 Sam. 15:3). In fact, Saul did not fail to *defeat* the Amalekites; he even took their king, Agag, captive. His failure consisted in sparing the king's life and also in preserving the best of the Amalekite cattle, instead of destroying them all as instructed (1 Sam. 15:7 ff.).

There are two very important points that emerge from an analysis of this episode. The first is that a Jewish national leader is seen as an agent of the divine will and must obey it to the letter at all times. The other point is that this God is very closely identified with the people of Israel, their successes and failures not only in matters of the spirit but in *all* matters. Though these principles happen to emerge particularly clearly in this rather unsavory episode, they are fundamental principles running right through the Jewish Bible. To put it in a nutshell, biblical

Judaism sees no dividing line between religion and society or between "church and state."

To the modern way of thinking, the position of king is a secular or temporal one, not a religious or spiritual one. In the Bible, however, a king's functions straddle these two seemingly separate areas. When David is anointed king, for example, we read: "Then Samuel took the horn of oil, and anointed him in the midst of his brothers; and the Spirit of the Lord came mightily upon David from that day forward" (1 Sam. 16:13).

What is the relevance of all this to the Messianic idea? Just this: the Messiah is none other than the anointed one of God. Saul was therefore a Messiah, David was a Messiah, Solomon was a Messiah, every anointed Jewish king was a Messiah. After some four hundred years the House of David ceased to rule, and their kingdom ceased to exist. The Jewish people had lost their independence. It was this cataclysmic event that gave rise to what can truly be called the messianic idea: the hope and the belief that the Jewish people would regain their freedom. And how else could that freedom be envisaged except in terms of a revived Jewish kingdom under a scion of the House of David, a family that had held power for longer than most dynasties in history? Hence the persistent tradition that the Messiah be of Davidic lineage (and hence too the much less persistent idea that the Messiah should be born in Bethlehem, David's place of origin).

Above all, the Messiah was to be a king, an earthly king ruling over an earthly Jewish kingdom. Thus the prophet Amos:

"In that day I will raise up the booth of David that is fallen and repair its breaches, and raise up its ruins, and rebuild it as in the days of old; that they may possess the remnant of Edom and all the nations who are called by my name," says the Lord who does this. (Amos 9:11-12)

That Amos is referring to an actual territorial kingdom is made particularly clear by the mention of Edom, the area just south of the Dead Sea whose inhabitants actively assisted Nebuchadnezzar to destroy the Jewish state, looting and pillaging Jerusalem and killing its inhabitants (see Psalm 137). According to tradition the Edomites were the descendants of Esau, thus personifying the age-old hostility that existed between them and the Jews, who of course traced their descent from Esau's brother and rival, Jacob. The territory of Edom was conquered by the Jewish state under Kings Saul and David, but the Edomites subsequently regained their independence. This is the point of Amos' reference. He is looking forward to a time—which *did* in fact come—when Edom would once again be incorporated into a Jewish state.

But, though Amos here speaks of a renewed Jewish state which he identifies with David, there is no specific mention of a king or Messiah. This omission is made good by Isaiah in what is undoubtedly his most famous prophecy, beginning with the words: "There shall come forth a shoot from the stump of Jesse, and a branch shall grow out of his roots" (Isa. 11:1). After the charming vision of wolves dwelling in peace together with lambs and leopards lying down with kids, we come to this passage: "In that day the root of Jesse shall stand as an ensign to the peoples; him shall the nations seek and his dwellings shall be glorious" (Isa. 11:10). Here we have two unmistakable references, not only to a renewed Jewish state but also to a Jewish king, a descendant of David (Jesse being King David's father).

The cosmopolitan tone suggested by phrases such as "an ensign to the peoples" has been taken by some Christian commentators as a reference to the spread of Christianity beyond the confines of the Jewish people, but it is clear from the context that what Isaiah is really trying to describe here is the great power and prestige of the new Jewish ruler, which he expects to be so great that foreign powers will flock to him. The references become more specific in the next few verses:

> In that day the Lord will extend his hand yet a second time to recover the remnant which is left of his people, from Assyria, from Egypt, from Pathros, from Ethiopia, from Elam, from Shinar, from Hamath, and from the coastlands of the sea. He will raise an ensign for the nations, and will assemble the outcasts of Israel, and gather the dispersed of Judah from the four corners of the earth. The jealousy of Ephraim shall depart, and those who harass Judah shall be cut off; Ephraim shall not be jealous of Judah, and Judah shall not harass Ephraim. But they shall swoop down upon the Philistines in the west, and together they shall plunder the people of the east. They shall put forth their hand against Edom and Moab, and the Ammonites shall obey them. (Isa. 11:11-14)

These verses contain two related prophecies: the return of the people of Israel from exile and the rise of a new reunited Jewish state. The two Jewish kingdoms of Judah and Israel, here referred to as Ephraim, will be reunited and will conquer their hostile neighbors. It is important to notice that the messianic kingdom is to be a purely

Jewish state.

The Messiah, according to Isaiah, is to usher in an era of peace and harmony, but this is not to be done in any mystical fashion but by means of a restoration of a strong and united Jewish monarchy under the house of David. We have already seen how desperately the Gospel writers tried to claim for Jesus a Davidic pedigree, but what of the substance of the prophecy?

Here those championing Jesus' claim to be the Messiah were confronted by an immovable obstacle. There was no way that they could falsify the evidence so as to suggest that the Jewish people had regained their freedom, as they most patently had not. They had in fact lost what little independence they had had, and, though the reign of the Emperor Augustus did introduce an era of peace, the blessings of peace did not extend to Judea. To the bulk of the Jews Roman rule was just another in a long series of foreign yokes under which the people of Israel had suffered oppression.

What were the Christian scripture writers to do? They could not claim that those key hallmarks of the messianic age—peace and freedom—had come, so how *could* they establish Jesus' claim to the messianic title? They still try to associate Jesus with the coming of peace, but they conveniently put off its arrival until after a time of war and general upheaval:

> "And when you hear of wars and rumors of wars, do not be alarmed; this must take place, but the end is not yet. For nation will rise against nation, and kingdom against kingdom; there will be earthquakes in various places, there will be famines; this is but the beginning of the birth-pangs." (Mark 13:7-8)

The bad times ahead are therefore explained away as an elaborate metaphor representing the labor pains giving birth to the eventual age of peace. A similar view of the future is to be found in the writings of the Jewish sect that produced the Dead Sea Scrolls. Here, for example, is a quotation from one of their hymns:

> Yes, I am in distress
> as a woman in travail
> bringing forth her firstborn,
> when, as her time draws near,
> the pangs come swiftly upon her
> and all the grievous throes

that rack those heavy with child.

For now, amid throes of death,
new life is coming to birth,
and the pangs of travail set in,
as at last there enters the world
the man-child long conceived.

Now, amid throes of death,
that man-child long foretold
is about to be brought forth.

Now, amid pangs of hell,
there will burst forth from the womb
that marvel of mind and might,
and that man-child will spring from the throes!

Delivery comes apace
for him that now lies in the womb;
as the hour of his birth draws near,
the pangs begin!
(Hymn 5 [III, 3-18] *The Dead Sea Scriptures,*
ed. T. H. Gaster, New York, 1956, pp. 135-6)

This somewhat repetitive hymn, hammering home the imagery of labor pains coupled with the coming of a Messiah, shows that the cataclysmic vision represented by the Gospels was not unique to Christianity. This is by no means the only parallel between the Christian scriptures and the writings of the Dead Sea sect, which is believed by some scholars to have been a Jewish group known as the Essenes. It is possible, as has been suggested by some, that Jesus and his followers may also have belonged to some such group, though this is debatable and not really important for our purposes. The fact that both the early Christians and the Dead Sea sect expected the prophesied age of peace to be preceded by a period of general upheaval and conflict shows that this idea was current among at least *some* Jews at the time.

As usual there is an obvious biblical source lying behind all this, in this case, as so often, a quotation from Isaiah. But what is striking is that Isaiah's prophecy says exactly the opposite:

Before she was in labor she gave birth:

before her pain came upon her she was delivered of a son.
Who has heard such a thing?
Who has seen such things?
Shall a land be born in one day?
Shall a nation be brought forth in one moment?
For as soon as Zion was in labor
she brought forth her sons.
(Isa. 66:7-8)

It is clear from this that we are not dealing with a Messiah as such but rather with a much more impersonal Jewish national rebirth, as can be seen not only from the use of the words *land* and *nation* but also from the fact that it is *sons* in the plural that Zion is to give birth to. But the main point that Isaiah is making here is that the rebirth of Israel is to take place *without* the expected birth-pangs, that is, *without* the intervention of a time of troubles and tribulation—in other words, exactly the opposite of what the Dead Sea Scrolls and the Christian Gospels tell us.

Why did the writings of these two groups make this radical change in the prophecy which Isaiah made? The reason is not hard to find. Christianity was not alone in claiming to have found the Messiah. The Dead Sea sect similarly seems to have identified the Messiah with their own leader, called by the title "Teacher of Righteousness of the End of the Days," as we know from their writings entitled the Damascus Document and a Commentary on the prophecy in the Old Testament book of Habakkuk.

The dire straits in which the Jewish people found themselves under Roman rule—the worst since the days of the Maccabees nearly two centuries earlier—were an obvious breeding ground for the sprouting of messianic hopes and therefore of messianic claims. And we know from the Christian book of Acts, as well as from the writings of the Jewish historian Josephus, that there was no shortage of claimants for the messianic title at this time. But, though the bad times undoubtedly predisposed the Jews to seek a Messiah, this did not square with biblical prophecy. Hence the departure from Isaiah's prophecy about birth-pangs.

Another of Isaiah's prophecies, however, suited the bad times much better and was, not surprisingly, eagerly seized upon by the Christian writers. I refer of course to the so-called "suffering servant" prophecy, the most famous quotation from which was set to music by Handel in *The Messiah* oratorio: "He is despised and rejected of men;

a man of sorrows, and acquainted with grief." (Isa. 53:3). So confident were Christian theologians of the identification of this suffering figure with Jesus that in old editions of the King James version the chapter heading inserted here reads: "The vicarious sacrifice of Christ, Jehovah's Servant."

But, if this quotation seemed promising from a Christian point of view, then the first mention of the "suffering servant" was even more so: "Behold my servant, whom I uphold, my chosen, in whom my soul delights; I have put my Spirit upon him, he will bring forth justice to the nations" (Isa. 42:1).

Is this not a reference to the spread of Christianity to the nations of the world and therefore to Jesus as the "light of the world"? Such is the interpretation placed upon this passage by many Christian commentators. Closer scrutiny of the whole prophecy to which this extract belongs reveals a quite different understanding of it.

Who, for a start, *is* this "servant"? It is quite clear from other parts of the same prophecy that the "servant" is not a single individual but a whole nation: the Jewish people. Isaish makes no secret of this, but actually puts these words into God's mouth: "You are my servant, Israel, in whom I will be glorified." (Isa. 49:3). The whole people of Israel is therefore God's "servant," a very close metaphorical rendering of the idea of the chosen people. As for the suffering and indignities that the servant has to endure, these conform only too closely to the history of the Jewish people. But, as always, Isaiah's ultimate vision is one of hope: the hope of a restored Jewish state respected by the rest of the world.

This brings us back to our starting point, namely that the salvation as envisioned by Isaiah and the other Jewish prophets is at least partly a political phenomenon, though they would not have recognized "religion" and "politics" as separate spheres of activity. What it means, though, is that the Messiah would be expected to overthrow the foreign yoke and become the ruler of the Jewish people. This of course was why the Messiah was seen as a descendant of King David rather than of Moses, Samuel, Elijah, or any other "holy" man. David certainly does not fall into that category, despite being credited with authorship of the Psalms. Not only was he something of a lecher, but he was also quite capable of sending a man into the front line of battle purely for the purpose of taking over his widowed wife. It was for reasons such as this that, according to the biblical account, God refused to allow the temple of Jerusalem to be built by David, an honor reserved for his son and successor, Solomon. David's most memorable achievements were military: killing Goliath, taking Jerusalem, and establishing a stable and powerful Jewish state.

But this posed a serious problem to the Christian Gospel writers: How were they to square their candidate for the messianic title with the military and political image required of a scion of the house of David? John's Gospel cuts the Gordian knot in the famous phrase, "My kingdom is not of this world" (John 18:36). Here at a single stroke Jesus is made to claim and at the same time to disclaim the monarchical title.

It is perhaps worth pointing out in this connection that the word traditionally translated here as *kingdom* is a Greek word, *basileia,* which in this context should rather be translated *kingship*, as some modern versions do. The reason for moving away from the older rendering is that we may get the quite wrong idea that what is being referred to is the geographical area or region over which Jesus claimed to rule, whereas what he is talking about is something quite different, namely the quality of being a king.

Nowhere else in the Christian scriptures does this extremely memorable phrase recur, which may perhaps mean that it was the product of John's imagination. "My kingdom is not of this world" is John's version of Jesus' answer to Pontius Pilate's question: "Are you the king of the Jews?" (John 18:33). So, in this Gospel Jesus is made to *deny* that he claimed to be the Jewish Messiah, who, as we have seen, was expected to win back Jewish independence and set up a reborn Jewish state under his rule. John's Gospel was aimed at non-Jewish converts, who would not have cared whether Jesus was or was not the Jewish Messiah. On the whole, as we have seen, John does support the view that Jesus was the Messiah, but it is not nearly as important to him as to the writers of the synoptic Gospels, Mark, Matthew, and Luke. Here John has hit upon a formula that combines a vague monarchical claim for Jesus with a disclaimer of the messianic title, a superlative combination that gives Jesus the aura of royalty without too much of a Jewish association. It is in this Gospel, it must not be forgotten, that Jesus is made to refer to the Jewish race as descendants of the devil (John 8:44)—a taunt that would of course taint Jesus himself and all his disciples, as well as the Pharisees whom he was supposedly addressing.

In the synoptic Gospels the whole portrait of Jesus centers on his depiction as the Jewish Messiah, so it would never do for the authors of those works to allow Jesus to disclaim that title in *their* pages. On the other hand, however, if they quoted him as defying the Roman governor by claiming to be the rightful ruler of the Jewish people, which, after all, is what the messianic claim meant, then the conclusion would be inescapable that he was rightly put to death for treason against the Roman government, an impression the Gospels are anxious to avoid.

In Mark alone do we have Jesus postively claiming to be the Messiah (Mark 14:62), though this claim is made only in his examination by the high priest and is not repeated in his trial before Pilate. To Pilate's question, "Are you the king of the Jews?" Jesus' answer, according to Mark, was a noncommittal and mystifying "You have said so" (Mark 15:2), which has baffled generations of commentators and shows no sign of losing its ambiguity even now. In Matthew and Luke this same answer is attributed to Jesus in reply not only to Pilate but also to the high priest (Matt. 26:64; 27:11; Luke 22:70; 23:3). Translators have agonized over this phrase, some offering "the words are yours," which gives it a vaguely negative connotation, others venturing "it is as you say," which is tantamount to an affirmative answer (NEB). The King James version is "thou has said," of which the RSV's "you have said so" is merely a modern rephrasing. This is literally what the Greek text says, and it may possibly have been *intended*—either by Jesus (if he really said it) or by the Gospel writers— to be ambiguous.

But, before trying to decide what Jesus' real answer is most likely to have been, we must analyze the meaning of the phrase "you have said so." Does it mean yes, no, both, or neither? There is certainly no unanimity among commentators. Those who take it to mean yes, or at least as an essentially affirmative reply, cite as a parallel to it a passage in Matthew in which Judas asks Jesus whether he is to be the one to betray him. Jesus' answer is once again, "You have said so" (Matt. 26:25). Other similar parallels from Jewish writings have been adduced. The implication of the phrase "you have said it" seems to be: "*You* have said it—not I," with more than a hint of agreement however. If this explanation is correct, as seems most likely, then Jesus' reply is in the affirmative throughout, even if more evasively so in the other Gospels than in Mark.

It is easy enough to understand why one would be hesitant to make a claim that would automatically lead to one's execution. But, did Jesus really claim to be the Messiah, and, if so, what was his understanding of that concept?

Mark, followed by Matthew and Luke, relates an incident in which Jesus asks his disciples who people say he is. (Mark 8:27-30;

Matt. 16:13-20; Luke 9:18-21). They rattle off a list of identities, none of which appears to please him: John the Baptist, Elijah, Jeremiah, or simply a prohet or someone like one of the prophets of old. In all three of the synoptic Gospels Peter is made to give the answer "You are the Christ" (Mark 8:29). As we have seen, *Christ* is nothing other than the anglicized Greek for *Messiah*, and in the accounts of Matthew and Luke the word *Christ* is further explained so as to leave no doubt whatsoever about the equation between *Christ* and *Messiah*. In Matthew Peter describes Jesus as "Christ, the Son of the living God" (Matt. 16:16), this latter phrase being one closely associated with the king of Israel, and therefore with the Messiah. In the second book of Samuel we find a specific statement of this in the phrase, "I will be his father, and he shall be my son" (2 Sam. 7:14), referring to each and every king of Israel of the house of David, which is promised eternal rule: "And your house and your kingdom shall be made sure for ever before me; your throne shall be established for ever" (2 Sam. 7:16). A similar reference may be found in the second Psalm, where a messianic vision is vividly portrayed. At first we are told that foreign nations and their rulers plot in vain "against the Lord and his anointed" (Ps. 2:2), that is, against God and the king of Israel. God laughs these vain hostile attempts to scorn and then turns to the king of Israel and addresses him in the following words:

> "You are my son, today I have begotten you.
> Ask of me, and I will make the nations your heritage,
> and the ends of the earth your possession.
> You shall break them with a rod of iron,
> and dash them in pieces like a potter's vessel."
> (Ps. 2:7-9)

Not only, therefore, is the designation "son of God" a messianic title, but it is associated with a very down-to-earth, political view of the Messiah.

In Luke, the answer that Peter gives to Jesus is "the Christ of God" (Luke 9:20), that is, the anointed of God, which again, as we have had occasion to notice, is a description of the Messiah as king of Israel.

In all three of the synoptic Gospels therefore Peter is made to describe Jesus as the Messiah. Moreover, all these accounts intend us to believe that this was regarded by Jesus as the "right" answer to the question of his identity. In Matthew this is made clear by Jesus' special blessing on Peter (Matt. 16:17-19), but in all three accounts it is abundantly clear that Jesus finds Peter's answer satisfactory, and he immediately swears his disciples to silence on this score, as well he might, knowing that any claim to be the Messiah would be viewed with hostility by Roman and Jewish authorities alike (Mark 8:30; Matt. 16:20; Luke 9:21).

So far so good. Jesus clearly views himself as the Jewish Messiah—in the canonical Christian scriptures. But, by contrast, in the so-called *Gospel According to Thomas,* one of a collection of religious writings produced by a Christian sect declared to be heretical in ancient times—namely the Gnostics—we find ourselves in quite a different situation altogether. Here, when Jesus asks his disciples to describe who he is, the replies he gets are as follows:

> Simon Peter said to him: you are like a righteous angel. Matthew said to him: You are like a wise man of understanding. Thomas said to him: Master, my mouth will not at all be capable of saying whom you are like. Jesus said: I am not your master, because you have drunk, you have become drunk from the bubbling spring which I have measured out. And he took him, he withdrew, he spoke three words to him. Now when Thomas came to his companions, they asked him: What did Jesus say to you? Thomas said to them: If I tell you one of the words which he said to me, you will take up stones and throw at me; and fire will come from the stones and burn you up. (#83, log. 13, ed., A. Guillaumont et al., 1959).

In this account, therefore, neither Peter nor even Thomas, the central figure of this Gospel, identifies Jesus as the Messiah. This immediately raises the question: Did the historical Jesus claim to be the Messiah or not? In view of the importance attached to this claim by the writers of the Christian scriptures, it is surprising how very little evidence they provide that Jesus actually saw himself in this role.

In an incident related in all three synoptic Gospels, Jesus is at pains to deny that the Messiah would be a descendant of David:

> And as Jesus taught in the temple, he said, "How can the scribes say that the Christ is the son of David? David himself, inspired by the Holy Spirit, declared, 'The Lord said to my Lord, sit at my right hand, till I put thy enemies under they feet.' David himself calls him Lord; so how is he his son?" (Mark 12:35-37; cf. Matt. 22:41-46; Luke 20:41-44)

This is an extremely bad piece of biblical exegesis and does Jesus' logical powers no credit. The point he is making is that David, the assumed author of the quoted Psalm (No. 110), addresses the Messiah as "my Lord," which he would hardly do if the Messiah were his own descendant. Besides the fact that it is by no means certain that David *was* the author of the Psalm or that it *is* the Messiah who is being addressed here, why should David not address his own messianic descendant as "my Lord"? The Hebrew word in question, *adoni*, is not nearly so respectful and self-abasing a form of address as its English translation. In fact, the word *adon* is simply the ordinary equivalent of *Mister* in modern Hebrew. The story illustrates Jesus' intense desire to dissociate the Messiah from Davidic descent. But, why should he resort to such quibbling in order to make this seemingly unimportant point, unless he was himself planning to claim the messianic title knowing that he did not possess the required Davidic descent?

Another pointer to the authenticity of this incident is the contrast between Jesus' own approach to the question of Davidic descent and that of the Christian scripture writers. The Gospels, as we have already had occasion to see, will stop at nothing in order to secure the title of Messiah for their candidate, even where this results in contradictory or even mutually exclusive claims. But Jesus himself, according to this incident at any rate, is not prepared to make the patently false claim of Davidic descent in order to lay claim to the messianic title, though he is forced instead into a petty and illogical quibble.

But, it must be stressed, Jesus' special pleading over his interpretation of Psalm 110 does not need to mean that he was already claiming to be the Messiah, only that it was likely that he was at least paving the way for a future claim. The acid test of Jesus' attitudes is of course to be found in his trial and execution. Would a man on trial for his life allow accusations to go unchallenged if they were totally false and if he could escape death simply by denying them? The chief accusation leveled against Jesus was evidently that he claimed to be the Jewish Messiah. Such a claim would have been as offensive to the Roman authorities as to the Jewish ones, for, as we have seen, the Messiah was expected to be as much a political as a religious leader, and any messianic claim was therefore a rebuttal of Roman rule over the Jewish people. Clearly this was well understood by the Jews of the day, and Jesus must have known that he was doomed once he confessed to claiming the messianic or kingly title.

From the Roman point of view this was not just a religious dispute within the Jewish community but something much more serious: treason against the Roman Empire. If he was not guilty of claiming to be king of the Jews, there could have been no point in Jesus' suddenly making this claim at his trial for the first time. On the other hand, his extremely indecisive behavior at his trial would appear to confirm that he *was* guilty as charged, in other words, that he *had* been claiming to be the Jewish Messiah. That is presumably why he gave the rather ambiguous reply that all four of the Gospels record him as giving to Pontius Pilate. He did not want to say, "Yes, I *am* king of the Jews," because saying that to the Roman governor of the province of Judea could only be taken by the Roman authorities as an admission of guilt: a confession of treason.

But, why then did he not play safe by denying the charge and replying, "No, I am not king of the Jews"? If he really had not been making messianic claims, that is surely the answer he would have given. The fact (if it *is* a fact) that he does *not* deny the charge outright is probably indicative of two things: one, that he knew that there would be witnesses able to testify that he *had* claimed to be the Messiah; and secondly, that he himself probably believed that he was indeed the Messiah.

But this runs us straight into a very serious dilemma. There was only one possible basis for a Jew to claim to be the Jewish Messiah, and that was the Jewish scriptures, most notably the prophecies of Isaiah and the other Jewish prophets. Now, according to these prophecies the Messiah had to meet certain criteria, such as Davidic descent and birth at Bethlehem. But Jesus must have known full well that he was not a descendant of King David and had not been born in Bethlehem. Therefore if he claimed to be the Messiah he must have done so with an awareness that he was putting forward a false claim.

The only way for him out of this impasse is his reinterpretation of Psalm 110. But, to dismiss all the crystal-clear prophetic references to Davidic descent in favor of one self-serving illogically reinterpreted verse in a Psalm is not the sign of a great mind or a great religious leader but is rather the badge of a narrow, intolerant mind.

This does not leave us with a very attractive choice. We are presented with a choice between Jesus, the deliberate fraud, and Jesus, the self-serving, arrogant bigot—unless of course the Gospels are wrong in portraying Jesus as himself claiming to be the Messiah. Perhaps the messianic claim was made by his followers only after Jesus' death. But, if *that* is correct, though it lets Jesus himself off the hook so to speak, it confronts his followers or the Gospel writers with a serious charge of deliberate falsehood.

On balance, it seems more likely that the messianic claims *were* originally put forward by Jesus himself and not simply fabricated by his followers. There are several reasons for believing this. One is the incident of the reinterpretation of Psalm 110, flying in the face, as it does, of the Gospels' own claims of Davidic descent for Jesus. Second is the very fact of Jesus' execution at the hands of the Romans, who are most unlikely to have resorted to this unless convinced that he represented a positive threat to Roman power in Judea, which could only mean that he *was* claiming to be the Messiah.

Perhaps most significant of all is the fact that in Mark, probably the oldest of the Gospels and the one from which the others evidently derived most of their information, Jesus *does* come out with a direct admission of a messianic claim when questioned by the Jewish high priest, though not in his actual trial before Pontius Pilate. (Mark 14:61-62; 15:2). This inconsistency itself—duly "corrected" in the other synoptics, which make Jesus give the same evasive reply to the high priest as to the Roman governor (Matt. 26:64; 27:11; Luke 22:70; 23:3)—lends credibility to Mark's account and is not difficult to understand. When questioned by the Jewish authorities in what was clearly just an informal enquiry, Jesus was emboldened to utter his messianic claim unequivocally. However, when actually put on trial for his life before the Roman governor, such an approach would clearly have been inadvisable. Hence his much more reticent and ambiguous reply to Pontius Pilate by comparison with his bold and defiant tone when answering the high priest. The truth may well be that when questioned by the Jewish authorities Jesus had no inkling that he was to be handed over to the Roman governor and tried on a capital charge.

What sort of person would claim to be the Messiah knowing that he did not meet the specific scriptural criteria that were held to be inviolable? Could such a person possibly be the personification of humility that Jesus is invariably represented as being?

Humility and Arrogance

Even those who find themselves quite unable to accept Jesus as anything more than a mere human being would generally regard him as a particularly admirable human being, with humility as one of his chief praiseworthy qualities. But even this must come under scrutiny.

The renunciation of all family ties in favor of single-minded personal loyalty to himself that, as we have seen, he demanded of his followers can hardly be characterized as humility on his part. In fact, his injunction extends even further than renouncing one's blood-ties: he also demands that a disciple of his "hate . . . even his own life" (Luke 14:26), requiring therefore a subordination of the individuality of the convert to the will of the group as personified by its leader—a phenomenon not unknown in the modern world, in which cult leaders have arisen who have stripped their followers of their own individuality to the extent even, in one notorious case, of persuading them to commit mass suicide. Jesus of course did not demand anything harmful of his followers, but the message of disciples being subservient to the master is plain enough, and does not depend upon this one verse alone. After condemning the Pharisees for loving display and titles of honor, such as *rabbi* (literally, master), Jesus addresses these remarks specifically to his own disciples:

> "But you are not to be called rabbi, for you have one teacher, and you are all brethren. And call no man your father on earth, for you have one Father, who is in heaven. Neither be called masters, for you have one master, the Christ." (Matt. 23:8-10)

It is noteworthy that this picture of fellowship and brotherhood in Jesus' movement is to apply to everyone—*except himself*. There is to be a leveling among his disciples, but he himself is to tower above them all as rabbi and master. "You," says Jesus (not "we") "are all brethren," clearly implying that *he* is more than a mere brother to his disciples, though he stops short of claiming to be their father and indeed forbids them to offer this appellation to any human being (*pace* the many Christian clergymen who claim this title as of right).

After loftily setting himself on a pedestal in this way, his next words ring rather hollow: "He who is greatest among you shall be your servant; whoever exalts himself will be humbled, and whoever humbles himself will be exalted. . ." (Matt. 23:11-12)

Self-descriptions such as "I am the light of the world" (John 8:12) are not easily seen as marks of humility. But perhaps the most instructive text in this connection is the famous: "I am the way, and the truth, and the life; no one comes to the Father, but by me" (John 14:6). Needless to say, this verse has aroused endless discussion and controversy, mostly on the interpretation of the three words *way, truth,* and *life,* but what cannot be doubted is that we have here an assertion that there is only *one* way, even if we cannot be sure where that way leads. But it is yet another example of intolerance: there is only one way and that way leads through acceptance of Jesus as Christ. The second half of the verse actually places Jesus as an intermediary between the individual worshiper and God, which has resulted in the fact that the Christian, unlike the Jew, cannot approach God directly but only through Jesus; hence the formula "through Jesus Christ our Lord" routinely tacked onto so many Christian prayers. This sort of thing is totally alien and indeed repugnant to Judaism and Islam, in which the worshiper is always in direct contact with his Maker.

This elevation of Jesus as an intermediary between man and God may also be taken as the first step towards regarding him as part of the Godhead itself, something that can only be seen as marking a very radical departure from the struct monotheism of Judaism. There is nothing in the Jewish messianic tradition to give the Messiah anything even remotely approaching the position that Jesus arrogates to himself according to the Gospel records, let alone a basis for him to claim to be a divinity—which however *he* never did. For, whatever the much-discussed terms "Son of God" and "Son of Man" may mean, whether they are intended as messianic titles or not, there is nothing to suggest that either of them could possibly constitute a claim to being divine. There is still a huge chasm between "the Son of God" and "God and the Son," and, though many strenuous efforts have been made by Christian theologians to trace the idea of the Trinity back to the Gospels and the Epistles, no convincing evidence has forthcoming.

Where then, you may well ask, *did* the idea of Trinity come from? One source is clearly the very self-magnification of Jesus that we have just been examining. But, however much exaggerated, that should have led to no more than a double Godhead, hardly a threefold one. A persistent ancient tradition, however, imbued the number three with special mystical properties. Not only is it the first truly plural number (two, in Greek and some other ancient languages, is not plural but "dual," having its own special forms that are neither singular nor plural), but it also happens to be the number of the male generative organs. The special significance of the number three had been trans-lated into worship many centuries before Christianity, most notably in the form of the three Egyptian gods, Isis, Osiris, and their child Horus. It was probably this cult, extremely popular and widespread (particu-larly in the eastern Mediterranean where Christianity arose), which is chiefly responsible for the ultimate development of the Christian Trinity. There are statues of Isis clutching the baby Horus to her breast, which are to this day worshiped as images of Mary and Jesus.

IV

Miracles and Faith

Miracles are not confined to the Christian scriptures. They are just as much—or at least, nearly as much—in evidence in the Jewish Bible. Even if we confine ourselves to the miracles associated with Moses, we quickly begin to compile an impressive list: the burning bush, the serpent rod, the plagues, the parting of the Red Sea, the manna, the uplifted hands, the striking of the rock. In addition to these, there are numerous other miracles attributed to other biblical figures, most notably perhaps to the prophet Elijah and his successor Elisha.

The purpose of the miracles in the Jewish Bible is essentially to demonstrate in a graphic way the power of God. Upon reflection, miracles may well be thought to be a trivial, inappropriate or even a wholly fallacious way of proving this. After all, if God is seen as creator of the universe, then clearly the whole of nature, including all the laws of science, were ordered by Him. Newton's law of gravity is really God's law; Boyle's law of pressure is God's law; and Archimedes' principle is just another glimpse of the infinite wisdom and cosmic order created by God.

But in addition to being the omniscient creator of the universe, God must by definition be regarded as the omnipotent ruler of that universe. At first sight there may not appear to be any contradiction between these two divine attributes. But what if God decided to suspend the operation of the law of gravity for a while? If we believe that He cannot do so, then what we are saying is that He has not the *power* to do so, which is the same as saying that He is *not* omnipotent after all. God's position then becomes reduced merely to that of someone who, so to speak, wound up the universe like a clock at the beginning of time and has no further control over it. If, on the other hand, God is believed to retain control over the universe, then He *must* be able to suspend the operation of gravity or of any other "law" of nature whenever He likes. It would certainly trivialize our view of God if we believed that He would tamper with His own natural "laws" just for the fun of it, and it is essentially at this point that those who believe in miracles part company with those who do not.

Those who are skeptical of miracles but nevertheless accept the omnipotence as well as the omniscience of God might say that though God is of course able to reverse or suspend the operation of any "law" of nature, He would not want to do so because His omniscience enabled Him to create the optimum universe at the outset. It would therefore be an admission of failure for God to tamper with His creation in any way. And, if the object of the miracle was, as so often, taken to be an attempt on God's part to win over a particular human being or group of people, then this would appear to be lowering God to the level of man. If He is omnipotent, He would not need to resort to a stratagem to impress the wayward.

In short, belief in miracles may create more problems than it solves. Nevertheless, it is to be found in Judaism as well as in Christianity. (Although Islam believes God is omnipotent, the Qur'an does not dwell on the miraculous apart from the original creation.) But there are some significant differences between Judaism and Christianity. In the Jewish Bible miracles are attributed to a number of different agents, whereas in the Christian writings the only performer of miracles is Jesus. This is of central significance, and once again underlines what I said earlier about the dominance of Jesus over his disciples.

But there is an even more crucial difference between the Jewish miracles and those of Jesus. In the case of the Jewish miracles, whoever the human agent may be the miracle is always essentially attributed to God. Often the miracle is performed on direct and specific divine instructions and the human agent is no more responsible for the miracle than the person who turns on the ignition of an automobile is the inventor of the internal combustion engine. Most of Moses' miracles fall into this category. He is simply ordered by God to lift up his hands or to strike a rock and all the rest is taken care of by God. Moses is merely "turning on," as it were, a preprogrammed machine whose workings he does not in the least understand. But even where the human agent has a more active role to play in the making of a miracle, as for example in the cases of Elijah and Elisha, it is still God's miracle and not that of the human agent. In the contrast between Elijah and the prophets of Baal, Elijah's success in getting *his* altar to burst into flames when the prophets of Baal had tried all day unsuccessfully to do the same was not seen as a sign of Elijah's power but of God's, as the text demonstrates quite clearly:

And at the time of the offering of the oblation, Elijah the prophet came near and said, "O Lord, God of Abraham, Isaac, and Israel, let it be known this day that thou art God in Israel, and that I am thy servant, and that I have done all these things at thy word. Answer me, O Lord, answer me, that this people may know that thou, O Lord, art God, and that thou hast turned their hearts back." (1 Kings 18:36-38)

That this message was not lost on the assembled throng is evident from their response to the miracle: "And when all the people saw it, they fell on their faces, and they said, 'The Lord, he is God; the Lord, he is God'" (18:39).

The contrast with the Christian miracles could not be greater. Matthew's account, it is true, of Jesus' healings ends with the remark that the enthusiastic crowd "glorified the God of Israel" (Matt. 15:31), the only time that this phrase occurs throughout the Christian scriptures. The original version of this passage in Mark differs from it in several important ways. First, and not for the first time, Matthew has clearly embroidered Mark's account (Mark 7:32-37). Where Mark has only one miracle and a fairly low-grade one at that—the curing of deafness coupled with a speech impediment—Matthew has a whole list of healings ranging from blindness to dumbness and lameness (Matt 15:30-31). Secondly, while Matthew describes the whole thing as happening in public, Mark specifically tells us that Jesus took his patient aside from the crowd and saw him privately, and that he "charged them to tell no one" (Mark 7:36). Thirdly, when the news does get out, Mark's crowd gives no credit to God but only to Jesus: "And they were astonished beyond measure, saying, 'He has done all things well; he even makes the deaf hear and the dumb speak'" (Mark 7:37). The credit given to "the God of Israel" in Matthew's account is therefore clearly an addition made by him to bring the story more into line with the Jewish miracle tradition.

In the episode of the walking on the water, the reaction of the boatful of bemused disciples is not gratitude to God or recognition of His power but direct tribute to Jesus: "And those in the boat worshipped him, saying, 'Truly you are the Son of God'" (Matt. 15:33).

But, how much credence should we give the miracles? In John's Gospel we are specifically informed that the miracle of the water and the wine performed at the wedding of Cana was Jesus' first miracle: "This is the first of his signs, Jesus did at Cana in Galilee, and manifested his glory; and his disciples believed in him" (2:11). As usual, all credit for the miracle is given to Jesus himself. But, what is remarkable is that there is no mention of this miracle in any of the other Gospels. This would not matter so much if it were not specifically labelled by John as the *first* miracle, which we would expect to be better remembered than any other.

In addition, there is no mention of Jesus' miracles by any Jewish or pagan source. What *is* mentioned in pagan writings is much less picturesque, merely that he was the leader of a troublesome Jewish sect. Yet the Romans had as hearty an appetite for miraculous tales as anyone. And hostility is not enough to explain away the lack of reference to Jesus' supposed miracles in non-Christian sources. What one's admirers call miracles, after all, may be fastened onto by one's detractors and labelled as magic, wizardry, or sorcery, which were regarded in a very sinister light indeed. *If,* therefore, reports of Jesus' supernatural powers had been as current in his own lifetime as the Gospels give us to believe, then it is highly unlikely that his enemies would have allowed such an opportunity to attack him to slip by.

And even if there *were* such reports, how much conviction would they carry? There is no shortage of reports of miraculous, supernatural, or simply preternatural events in the modern world; yet, despite concerted efforts to verify such occurrences, there is still no conclusive evidence to support any of them either, be it a reported miraculous healing, claims of fortune telling, or a supposed encounter with visitors from another planet.

The Resurrection

Of all the miracles associated with the name of Jesus none is more crucial—or more problematical—than the Resurrection. As usual, Mark provides us with a less extreme picture than the other Gospels. In fact, the best texts of Mark's Gospel do not include any reference to Jesus' appearing to any of his disciples after his death but merely mention that he has been raised from the dead. There is now a consensus among scholars that the accounts of Jesus' posthumous appearance and ascension (Mark 16:9-20) formed no part of Mark's Gospel at all but were added later by someone else.

This in itself is most peculiar. If Jesus *had* been raised from the dead and *had* appeared to some of his disciples, then surely Mark could not have failed to record it. The fact that this had to be tacked on later by someone else indicates that Jesus' appearances and ascension were *not known* to Mark, whose Gospel, it is generally agreed, was written about thirty years after Jesus' death. In other words, the story of a raised Jesus appearing to his disciples and then ascending to heaven was only invented a generation or more after the events were supposed to have happened.

Moreover, the different accounts of Jesus' appearances are hopelessly confused and contradictory, both in respect of the identity of those by whom Jesus was seen and of the locations of the visions. One account, however, was penned by someone who himself claimed to have seen a vision of Jesus, namely Paul. This claim is made in his first Epistle to the Corinthians in the course of a discussion on the bodily resurrection of the dead, a doctrine which was particularly repugnant to the Greeks of that day. Paul's argument runs as follows:

> Now if Christ is preached as raised from the dead, how can some of you say that there is no resurrection of the dead? But if there is no resurrection of the dead, then Christ has not been raised; if Christ has not been raised, then our preaching is in vain and your faith is in vain. We are even found to be misrepresenting God, because we testified of God that he raised Christ, whom he did not raise if it is true that the dead are not raised. (1 Cor. 15:12-15)

This somewhat sophistic argument makes acceptance of Jesus' resurrection the basis for belief in resurrection of the dead in general, and the basis of belief in Jesus' resurrection is in turn faith in the creed enunciated by Paul as follows:

> For I delivered to you as of first importance what I also received, that Christ died for our sins in accordance with the scriptures, that he was buried, that he was raised on the third day in accordance with the scriptures, and that he appeared to Cephas, then to the twelve. Then he appeared to more than five hundred brethren at one time, most of whom are still alive, though some have fallen asleep. Then he appeared to James, then to all the apostles. Last of all, as to one untimely born, he appeared also to me (1 Cor. 15:3-8)

Later on in the same chapter, in response to the question, "How are the dead raised? With what kind of body do they come?" (15:35) Paul is at pains to draw a clearcut distinction between a living human body and that of a resurrected dead person. "You foolish man!" he berates his imaginary questioner, going on to point up the contrast, which is perhaps best summed up in the following verses:

> The first man was from the earth, a man of dust; the second man

is from heaven. . . . I tell you this, brethren: flesh and blood
cannot inherit the kingdom of God, nor does the perishable inherit
the imperishable. (1 Cor. 15:47, 50)

From this we can only conclude that the *risen* Jesus was *not* a being of
flesh and blood but a spiritual being of some sort. The danger of that
doctrine, though, is that it can easily slide into the belief that Jesus was
not raised from the dead at all but that those who saw him merely saw
a vision or imagined it in a dream. This would be much easier for a
believer to accept than a completely physical resurrection, but despite
this, the Gospels, and especially those of Luke and John, do insist on
tangible physical resurrection.

John tells the story of Thomas doubting the resurrection until he
has seen and felt Jesus' wounds from the cross (20:25-27), and Luke
specifically rejects the idea that the risen Jesus is a spirit:

As they were saying this, Jesus himself stood among them. But
they were startled and frightened, and supposed that they saw a
spirit. And he said to them, "Why are you troubled, and why do
questionings arise in your hearts? See my hands and my feet, that
it is I myself; handle me, and see; for a spirit has not flesh and
bones as you see that I have." (Luke 24:36-40)

It must be remembered that Paul's first Epistle to the Corinthians was
probably written about the year 50, which makes it earlier than *any* of
the Gospels. The fact that their physical view of the resurrection flew
in the face of the already established authority of Paul makes their
position appear all the more puzzling.

But the explanation is not hard to find. The central claim throughout the Gospels, as we have seen, is that Jesus was the Jewish Messiah.
But Jesus had failed, as he himself recognized in his dying words on
the cross (whose authenticity may well be vouched for by the fact that
they are quoted in Aramaic, the only occasion on which this is done):
"My God, my God, why has thou forsaken me?" (Mark 15:34; Matt.
27:46; with a slight variation in the two versions). Here we have the
authentic voice of a human being in profound agony. Would he have
accused God in this way if he had really believed that his death was to
be not the end of living but the beginning of glory? Surely not. And
the point is that in the Jewish concept of the Messiah there *was* (and,
for that matter, is) no suggestion that he would suffer a martyr's death
and be reborn. The passages in Isaiah dealing with the so-called "suffering servant" are clearly not intended to refer to the Messiah at all but

rather to the Jewish people as a whole, of whose subsequent history these prophecies have proved only too accurate a prediction.

Jesus' death clearly placed his followers in a dilemma. His ignominious death would be taken by others, as it had been by himself, as a sign of failure and, above all, as proof that he was not the Messiah. If only his death could be reinterpreted in a positive way. Hence the desperate need to call into service any biblical verse which might remotely suggest the need for the Messiah to suffer and die. But the leaders of the movement must have realized that that would not be enough to persuade doubters.

If only Jesus had *not* died at all! The Jewish doctrine of the resurrection of the dead was ready to hand. Rejected by the aristocratic Sadducees and as enthusiastically supported by the populist Pharisees, the doctrine could now be interpreted in a literal sense, thus at once giving hope of eternal physical life to believers and establishing Jesus as alive and well, triumphant over death.

It was clearly, therefore, in order to safeguard Jesus' claim to the title of Messiah/Christ that the Gospel writers felt compelled to part company even with Paul on the question of the resurrection.

And it was this physical view of resurrection which held the field for hundreds of years, with speculation on whether a child who died in infancy would be resurrected as a child or as an adult and even whether a woman might not be resurrected as a man—on the principle that one should be resurrected in one's most perfect form and that a woman was really an imperfect man!

But, regardless of the *nature* of Jesus' resurrection, whether fully physical or essentially spiritual, can one believe that it occurred at all? Besides the evidence already mentioned, all four Gospels have an account of it. As usual, Matthew adds a lot of detail which is not to be found in Mark, or for that matter in Luke or John:

> Next day, that is, after the day of Preparation, the chief priests and the Pharisees gathered before Pilate and said, "Sir, we remember how that impostor said, while he was still alive, 'After three days I will rise again.' Therefore order the sepulchre to be made secure until the third day, lest his disciples go and steal him away, and tell the people, 'He has risen from the dead,' and the last fraud will be worse than the first." Pilate said to them, "You can have a guard of soldiers; go, make it as secure as you can." So they went and made the sepulchre secure by sealing the stone and setting a guard. (Matt. 27:62-66)

Excellent evidence that the tomb could not have been tampered with by human hands—*if it were true.* But, if it *had* been true, would the other Gospels not have made a point of mentioning it too? Matthew also tells us that "there was a great earthquake" when the stone sealing the tomb was rolled back by an angel (28:1-3), a cataclysmic event that could hardly have gone unnoticed but is recorded only by Matthew.

The Empty Tomb

Another suspect report is that of the discovery that the tomb was empty. All four Gospels contain an account of this, but there is a good deal of disagreement as to when the tomb was first seen to be empty, by whom this was noticed, and the circumstances surrounding the discovery. Thus, for example, Matthew has it discovered by only two women whose purpose in going to the tomb was merely to "see" it (28:1), whereas both Mark and Luke have more women making the discovery (three in Mark, more in Luke) and having a more specific motive for visiting the tomb, namely to anoint the body with oil, an odd thing to do on a body fully two days dead and buried. (Mark 16:1-8; Luke 24:1-3).

In the conversation that supposedly took place between the Jewish leaders and Pontius Pilate, the fear is expressed that if Jesus' body were removed from the tomb by his disciples, they would then go about proclaiming his resurrection. Yet, when, according to Christian tradition, the tomb *was* found to be empty, no such proclamation was made. Why not? Presumably because the tomb was *not* empty—that is, if there was a tomb to begin with. Jesus was, after all, executed as a criminal, which would not have entitled him to an individual grave at all (See Deut. 21:23; Gal. 3:13). The Gospel writers must have been aware of this; hence the appearance of a *deus ex machina* in the shape of Joseph of Arimathea, who is allowed by the Roman authorities to carry off Jesus' body and bury it. But in the report in Acts of the sermon that Paul gave in Antioch, Jesus is said to have been buried by those very Jewish authorities who were responsible for bringing him to trial (13:29).

The embarrassment which Jesus' death occasioned his disciples must have been acute, and it comes through very clearly in Paul's creed as quoted above, in which he *twice* specifically links Jesus' death with Jewish prophecy: "Christ died for our sins *in accordance with the scriptures*" and "he was raised on the third day *in accordance with the scriptures*" (my emphasis; 1 Cor. 15:3-4; cf. Acts 13:27-29). Which scriptures is Paul referring to? There is this verse of the prophet Hosea: "After two days he will revive us; on the third day he will raise us up, that we may live before him." (Hosea 6:2). But the reference here is not to resurrection at all, but rather to God's reconciliation with the Jewish people after punishing them. Hosea, it must be stressed, was writing some *seven hundred* years before the time of Jesus, and his prophecy must be understood in terms of the circumstances of his own day, a time when there were still two independent Jewish kingdoms, Judah and Israel, but when their independence was threatened from without by powerful foreign states and, as the prophet saw it, by moral and religious decay from within.

The alacrity with which early Christianity fastened onto such unpromising biblical texts as this only underlines their desperate concern to link the career of their founder with Jewish prophecies. It may not be too much to suggest that the tradition that it was on the *third* day that Jesus was raised from the dead may owe its origin to the desire to latch it onto the Hosea text!

The Shroud of Turin

Because of the need for Christians to believe in the superhuman nature of Jesus, more and more demands were made on the believer's credulity. Before long, not only Jesus but also a whole host of saints were believed to be capable of miracles. Shrines were erected on the site of these supposed miracles, and saints were often worshipped in their own right. Furthermore, any physical object associated with Jesus, Mary, or any of the saints, likewise became an object of reverence. This resulted in a widespread medieval trade in relics. Several repositories claimed to have Jesus' foreskin; saintly bones are widely dispersed throughout the Christian world; and even the three Magi eventually acquired relics, now lodged in Cologne cathedral.

Perhaps the most topical of all relics is the so-called Shroud of Turin, believed by some to be Jesus' winding-sheet. The cloth bears two images, back and front, of a naked man with the wounds of crucifixion. Some believe this is the imprint of Jesus' body, and it has something of the appearance of a photographic negative.

Yet, no such "relic" was even known to exist before the fourteenth century, when the shroud made its first appearance and was put on display in France. The Bishop of Troyes, his suspicions aroused, investigated the matter: "Eventually, after diligent inquiry and examination, he discovered the fraud and how the said cloth had been cunningly painted, the truth being attested by the artist who had painted it, to wit, that it was a work of human skill and not miraculously wrought or bestowed."[1]

This passage is quoted from a report on the matter by a subsequent Bishop of Troyes later in the same century, who, among other things, adds that "further to attract the multitude so that money might cunningly be wrung from them, pretended miracles were worked, certain men being hired to represent themselves as healed at the moment of the exhibition of the shroud, which all believed to be the shroud of our Lord."[2]

The two fourteenth-century bishops were not taken in by this attempt to batten on the contemporary vogue for relics and miracles, proving themselves less credulous than many of their modern counterparts who continue to insist on the authenticity of the shroud despite all the evidence against it: the "blood" is far too red to be real but is clearly painted; the weave of the cloth does not conform to the pattern of the time of Jesus; and it is not the right shape for a Jewish shroud of the period.

In 1978 the cloth was subjected to a detailed microscopic examination conducted by the McCrone Research Institute in Chicago, which only confirmed the opinion of the fourteenth-century bishops:

> The entire image is . . . the work of a skillful, well-informed artist . . . It seems reasonable that the image was painted on the cloth shortly before the first exhibition, about 1357 . . . We have concluded that the image on the cloth is at least as old as about 1350, that it was done by an artist and that if all iron-earth pigment plus tempera medium were removed there would be no image on the "Shroud."[3]

Even this categorical statement based on close scientific analysis has not dispelled the belief in many quarters that this is Jesus' windingsheet. Why not? Because, if the shroud is genuine, it somehow verifies Jesus' superhuman claims and, most of all, the resurrection. Any other shroud would surely have disintegrated together with the flesh that it embraced, but only the body of the risen Christ could leave an imprint such as appears on the Turin Shroud. So, at any rate, might it be assumed.

Once again, it is the need for Christianity to "prove" the validity of the special claims made for its founder that leads it into such preposterous contortions as belief in the authenticity of the Turin Shroud.

Jewish vs. Christian Miracles

That, of course, is why there is no cult of relics or miracles in Judaism. There *are* very ancient remains that have been found in Israel, including pieces of genuinely old cloth, but there has never been the slightest tendency to reverence them in any way. Even if Moses' magic rod turned up in an archaeological excavation, or David's shield, these would be only of antiquarian interest—very great antiquarian interest undoubtedly, but interest different in kind from the adulation accorded a relic.

And the same applies to miracles. The miracles related in the Jewish Bible are no easier to accept than the Christian miracles. Now that the parting of the Red Sea is performed in Hollywood on a daily basis, *that* miracle at least may appear less difficult to accept as an historical event. But what of the others? What of the ten plagues, the burning bush, the manna, and all the miraculous healings, to mention but a few?

The whole point in this question as in every other is that the validity of Judaism or one's identification with it do not depend on accepting either miracles or any other Bible stories as factual. As we have had occasion to observe before, herein lies one of the most basic differences between Judaism and Christianity. Reject the truth of the miracle at Cana and you are challenging the claim that Jesus was no mere mortal but a divine being invested with unique powers. Reject the miracle of the resurrection and you are rejecting the most central tenet of Christian belief.

Without Christian belief you cannot claim Christian identity. But without acceptance of the miraculous, you cannot have Christian belief. In this simple pair of sentences are summed up one of the central problems of Christianity, for they place the Christian believer in an impasse. If he accepts the miraculous against his better judgment, he becomes the dupe of prejudice. On the other hand, if he merely pretends to accept the miraculous while not really doing so, he is a hypocrite. And if he rejects the miraculous out of hand, he can claim to be a Christian as it is officially defined only by self-deception.

NOTES

1. Memorandum of Pierre d'Arcis, Bishop of Troyes, to Pope Clement VII, written in 1389, quoted in full by H. David Sox, *The Image on the Shroud*, Appendix A, p. 148.

2. Ibid.
3. Walter C. McCrone, McCrone Research Institute, Chicago, *Microscopic Examination of the "Shroud" II,* abstract quoted by Sox, *The Image on the Shroud,* Appendix B, pp. 153 ff.

V

Trial and Crucifixion: Jewish or Roman?

Jesus died at the hands of the Romans—or was it the Jews? According to the Gospel of John, Pontius Pilate, the Roman governor of Judea, found Jesus innocent of any crime. "I find no crime in him" are the words John puts into his mouth at the end of the trial (18:38). Pilate then allows "the Jews" (there is no further description) to ask for the release of either Jesus or a certain Barabbas, described by John as "a robber" (18:40). When the Jewish crowd clamors excitedly against Jesus and in favor of the release of Barabbas, Pilate scourges Jesus, and goes out again to the crowd and once again affirms his belief in Jesus' innocence: "Behold, I am bringing him out to you, that you may know that I find no crime in him" (19:4). Then "the chief priests and the officers" cry out for Pilate to crucify Jesus, but he remains obdurate and for the third time delcares his belief in Jesus' innocence: "Take him yourselves and crucify him, for I find no crime in him." (19:6). After further questioning of Jesus, Pilate "sought to release him" but is met by Jewish indignation, whereupon, the governor "handed him over to them to be crucified." (John 19:16). The word *them* here is of course a reference to "the Jews," who, we are next informed, then proceeded to crucify Jesus:

> So they took Jesus, and he went out, bearing his own cross, to the place called the place of a skull, which is called in Hebrew Golgotha. There they crucified him, and with him two others, one on either side, and Jesus between them. (John 19:17-18).

With the subtlety of a sledgehammer John pounds home two related points: the guilt of the Jews and the blamelessness of the Romans for Jesus' death. Not only are the Jews portrayed here as clamoring for Jesus' execution but they are described as actually carrying out the crucifixion themselves.

Luke's account also gives this impression, except that, after three times expressing his belief in Jesus' innocence, Pilate is described as giving in to the Jews to the point of actually passing the death sentence on him, before turning him over to the Jews for execution (23:24-26).

In the other two synoptics, Mark and Matthew, we find a rather different situation described. In both these Gospels it is Roman soldiers who carry out the crucifixion and not the Jews (Mark 15:16, 24-25; Matt. 27:27, 31, 35).

Does this mean that the accounts of Mark and Matthew blame the Romans for Jesus' death? Not at all. Mark explains that it was only because Pilate wished "to satisfy the crowd" of Jews that he released Barabbas instead of Jesus and delivered Jesus for crucifixion (15:15). Matthew as usual goes further. To underline Roman innocence and Jewish guilt he (and he alone) offers us the story, which has now become proverbial, of Pilate washing his hands of the whole thing:

> So when Pilate saw that he was gaining nothing but rather that a riot was beginning, he took water and washed his hands before the crowd, saying, I am innocent of this man's blood; see to it yourselves. (Matt. 27:24)

As if this was not enough to ram home his point, Matthew has the Jewish crowd cheerfully claiming responsibility themselves: "His blood be on us and on our children!" (Matt. 27:25)—a phrase which has been used down to the present day to indict on a charge of "deicide" not only the Jews of Jesus' day but the Jewish people as a whole throughout history. In case we still have not got the message, Matthew adds yet another little episode: the dream of Pilate's wife:

> Besides, while he was sitting on the judgment seat, his wife sent word to him, "Have nothing to do with that righteous man, for I have suffered much over him today in a dream." (Matt. 27:19)

All four Gospel accounts agree in pinning the blame on the Jews and in exonerating Pontius Pilate, but disagree on practically everything else. In other words, their conclusions agree, but not the evidence adduced in support of those conclusions. The words Mark uses of the "false witnesses" who testified against Jesus actually apply perfectly to the Gospels themselves: "For many bear false witness against him, but their witness agreed not together" (14:56). In short, it would appear that the Gospel writers first reached their conclusion (namely, that the Jews were guilty of Jesus' "murder") and only afterwards put together a story to support that conclusion.

These stories are so full of contradictions, inconsistencies, and illogicalities as to leave the whole question of Jesus' arrest, trial and death in a morass of doubt. It may help at this stage to isolate the main questions in this quagmire:

1. By whom was Jesus arrested and for what purpose?
2. By whom was Jesus tried, and on what charge?
3. How many trials did Jesus have? (Possible answers range from one to three!)
4. What was the verdict or verdicts, if any?
5. By whom was Jesus crucified?

Though practically everything to do with the trial and crucifixion is surrounded by doubt of one kind or another, one fact is undisputed, and that is that *Jesus was crucified.* Let us therefore take that as our starting point and proceed from one certainty to another as in a mathematical proof.

Who Crucified Jesus?

1. Given that Jesus was crucified, he must have been crucified by *someone.* Who? The choice is between the Romans (as Mark and Matthew say) and the Jews (as Luke and John maintain). The fact is that crucifixion was never a Jewish form of execution, therefore it could only have been done by the Romans. Moreover, there are telltale signs in John's account to show that he knew this. In fact, after specifically describing Jesus' crucifixion at the hands of the Jews (19:18), John forgets himself and says: "When the soldiers had crucified Jesus they took his garments and made four parts, one for each soldier" (19:23). But, who were these soldiers? The only soldiers mentioned—and, for that matter, the only ones there would have been in Judea at that time—were *Roman* soliders. So, even John clearly knew that it was by the Romans and not by the Jews that Jesus had been crucified.

Oddly enough, John even makes the Jewish authorities say: "It is not lawful for us to put any man to death" (18:31). This was not actually the case, as we know from Talmudic sources, which makes it all the more strange to find it in John's account. The Greek literally means "it is not permitted for us *to kill* anyone," which would seem to refer to the physical act of execution rather than the passing of a death sentence, which is evidently what John wants it to mean. But, even then, it is very odd, for, if the Jews could not pass the death sentence, it seems quite unbelievable that they would be allowed to execute (in both senses of the word) someone else's death sentence.

2. Given that Jesus was crucified by Roman soldiers (as Mark and Matthew also say), it is clear that this was no mob lynching but a formal Roman execution, crucifixion being in any case the usual Roman form of execution.

The Trial and Verdict

3. Given that Jesus was executed by the Romans, we must conclude that this was the sequel to the verdict of a judicial trial, and clearly a verdict of guilty. As it was a Roman execution, as we have already established, the verdict must have been that of a Roman, and not a Jewish, court. This means that we can only conclude that Pontius Pilate, who as Roman governor of the province was in change of judicial as well as of administrative and military matters, had pronounced a verdict of "guilty" over Jesus. Once again, though the Gospels do their best to fudge the issue and make Pilate out to be convinced of Jesus' innocence, the truth does shine through in places. In John, for example, after three times declaring Jesus' innocence Pontius Pilate is suddenly described as sitting on the "judgment seat" (Greek: *bema*) and, though John studiously avoids giving us the verdict that Pilate had clearly taken up his position to do, the next thing we know is that Jesus is handed over for crucifixion (19:13-16). So, even from this extremely tendentious report it is clear that Pilate found Jesus guilty and sentenced him to death.

Mark and Matthew are equally careful not to report the actual sentence but it is there by implication: "Then he released for them Barabbas, and having scourged Jesus, delivered him to be crucified" (Matt 27:26; see also Mark 15:15). Even if these were the only sources we had, it would be quite clear enough that Pilate *did* find Jesus guilty. But, as it happens, Luke actually gives us the verdict in so many words, though, needless to say, not before stressing that Pilate had stated for the third time that he had "found in him no crime deserving death": "But they [the Jews] were urgent, demanding with loud cries that he should be crucified. And their voices prevailed. So Pilate gave sentence that their demand should be granted" (23:23-24).

The Charge

4. Given that Jesus was found guilty by Pilate, on what charge had he been indicted? All the Gospels agree in describing the trial before Pontius Pilate as centering on the question of Jesus' monarchical, that is, Messianic, claims, the crucial question being: "Are you the King of the Jews?"—which all four Gospels record Pilate as putting to Jesus (Mark 15:2; Matt. 27:11; Luke 23:3; John 18:33). In Luke we have the nearest thing to a modern charge-sheet: "We found this man perverting our nation, and forbidding us to give tribute to Caesar, and saying that he himself is Christ a king" (23:2). Of these charges the last is the most serious and it is this one alone which, in accordance with Roman practice, was inscribed over the cross: "Jesus of Nazareth, the King of the Jews" (John 19:19). Once again, all four Gospels agree (with minor variations of wording) that this was the charge on which Jesus was publicly announced to have been crucified (Mark 15:26; Matt. 27:37; Luke 23:38).

In what exactly did Jesus' crime consist? Why, after all, should the Romans trouble themselves over Jewish Messianic claims? Precisely because, as I have already explained, the Messiah was seen not only in purely religious terms but also in a political role: the Messiah was to be the savior of the Jewish people, reestablishing an independent Jewish kingdom under his own rule. How else could the Romans interpret this than as a challenge to their rule over Judea? In short, *it was on a charge of treason that Jesus was charged and convicted.*

Romans or Jews?

5. Given that Jesus was tried and convicted by a Roman court, is it possible that he had already been tried by a Jewish court, as Mark and Matthew make out? (Mark 14:53-65; Matt. 26:57-68). There certainly was provision for the Sanhedrin, the Jewish Council, to act as a court of law. In practice there seem to have been two types of Sanhedrins. One, sometimes termed the "Great Sanhedrin," had seventy-one members drawn from the priesthood, the elders, and the scholars or rabbis, but this body seems to have confined itself to legislative and administrative functions. Judicial functions were exercised by the so-called "Small Sanhedrin" of twenty-three members, presumably also drawn from the same groups as the larger body (see Mishna Sanhedrin I:4-5).

But, despite this, there are quite a few difficulties in connection with the accounts in Mark and Matthew of Jesus' trial before any such body. For one thing, we know that no valid meeting of any kind of Sanhedrin could be held except within the precincts of the Temple (Babylonian Talmud, Avodah Zarah 8b; Shabbbut 15a; Sanhedrin 41b, based on Deut. 17:10). But, say Mark and Matthew, it was in the high priest's house that Jesus was tried by a council of priests, elders, and scribes (Mark 14:53-54; Matt. 26:57-59). Secondly, it was specifically laid down by Jewish law that criminal cases had to be tried during the day and never at night. Even if a case was still proceeding when night fell it had to be adjourned to the following day (Mishna Sanhedrin IV:1). Yet Jesus is said to have been tried not only at night but indeed on the very night of the Passover feast (Mark 14:17; Matt. 26:2, 20), which, if true, would have contravened not only the specific prohibitions on trials at night and on festivals but also the general prohibition on work on a sabbath or festival, since, according to the Jewish calendar, a day is regarded as beginning not at dawn or even at midnight but at sunset the previous evening.

The Jewish authorities are said by Mark and Matthew to have engaged in a fruitless search for evidence against Jesus. But, according to Mark, though there was no shortage of "false witnesses" to testify against him, in the picturesque King James phrase "their witness agreed not together" (14:56). Yet, in the very next verse, we read:

> And some stood up and bore false witness against him, saying, "We heard him say, 'I will destroy this temple that is made with hands, and in three days I will build another, not made with hands.'" (14:57-58)

To which Mark then confusingly adds: "Yet not even so did their testimony agree" (14:59). In which respect did their testimony fail to agree? Mark does not tell us. Matthew's account is obviously drawn from Mark's but is a slightly streamlined version of it, and there is no mention of the evidence not agreeing (Matt. 26:59-61). Both Mark and Matthew label as false the testimony that Jesus made the quoted remark about the Temple, yet a very similar statement is placed by John in Jesus' own mouth in the story about the money-changers in the temple:

> "Destroy this temple, and in three days I will raise it up." The Jews then said, "It has taken forty-six years to build this temple, and will you raise it up in three days?" But he spoke of the temple

of his body. (2:19-21)

John's interpretation of Jesus' remark is extremely odd, to say the least, especially in view of the fact that the whole discussion up to that point had to do with the actual Temple building. John's interpretation is clearly an attempt to "explain away" Jesus' remark, either because it betrays a hostile attitude to the Temple, the center of Jewish worship, or, more likely precisely because Mark and Matthew deny that he ever made any such remark.

Whom do we believe? If John's account is true, then the "false witnesses" in Mark and Matthew are nothing of the kind: they are speaking nothing but the truth. On the other hand, if Mark and Matthew are right, then John is himself a false witness!

But why exactly was it considered so damning if Jesus *did* make the remark? It was certainly an arrogant enough claim to profess to be able to restore the Temple (however interpreted) in three days, but that does not make it criminal. This was well-recognized by the high priest in the accounts that we have, for he is quoted as asking Jesus a rather strange question: "What is it that these men testify against you?" (Mark 14:60; Matt. 26:62). If the remark about the Temple which the witnesses had attributed to Jesus *in itself* constituted a criminal offence, then the high priest would not have needed to ask this question; it would have been obvious what crime the witnesses were imputing to Jesus. But of course the high priest is right: the remark itself is *not* criminal. What the high priest is asking Jesus is essentially this: "What offence is to be *inferred* from your remark about the Temple?"

The high priest is in little doubt as to what that offence might be, as he reveals in his next remark: "Are you the Christ, the Son of the Blessed?" (Mark 14:61; see also Matt. 26:63). The implication is that anyone claiming to be able to rebuild the Temple in three days was making so extreme a claim that such a person was also likely to profess to be the Messiah. In Mark 14:62 (though not in Matthew, 26:63-64) Jesus gives an unequivocal answer: "I am; and you will see the Son of man sitting at the right hand of Power, and coming with the clouds of heaven." Whereupon the high priest tears his tunic and says: "Why do we still need witnesses? You have heard his blasphemy. What is your decision?" (Mark 14:63-64). Mark then adds: "And they all condemned him as deserving death" (14:64).

Mark's account is very confused indeed. First there is the confusion over the evidence to which I have already referred. Then there are two serious mistakes. One is that an accused can be convicted on the evidence of his own confession alone; the other that Jesus' reply to the high priest constituted blasphemy.

In Jewish law blasphemy is a very specific charge as well as being a very serious one. It arises from an infringement of the third of the Ten Commandments: "Thou shalt not take the name of the Lord thy God in vain" (Exod. 20:7). But this refers to the *name* of God, the tetragrammaton or four-letter name, which only the high priest was permitted to pronounce and even he only on the solemn Day of Atonement. The use of this holy name by anyone else was blasphemy. What then does one do when reading a biblical text containing the divine name? Jews long ago got into the habit of substituting for it some other word altogether, usually the word normally translated as "Lord." In fact, even this word became so closely associated with the divine name that it was considered wrong to use it in ordinary speech, being replaced in practice by such terms as "the place," or simply "the name." The two terms quoted by Mark are both evidently meant as equivalents for the divine name: "the Blessed" and "Power," the latter still being used, perhaps most notably on the Mezuzah, or prayer scroll attached to every Jewish doorpost.

In short, Jesus was *not* guilty of blasphemy, since he had not uttered the divine name but, according to Mark, had clearly used the alternative term, "Power." Yet he was found guilty by the Jewish court and sentenced to death—at least, according to Mark and Matthew.

What do we make of all this? The whole proceedings have been characterized as follows by a Canadian Chief Justice:

> The Hebrew Trial . . . steeped as it was in illegality . . . had been a mockery of judicial procedure throughout. Jesus was unlawfully arrested and unlawfully interrogated . . . The court was unlawfully convened by night. No lawful charge supported by the evidence of two witnesses was ever formulated . . . As he stood at the bar of justice, he was unlawfully sworn as a witness against himself. He was unlawfully condemned to death on words from his own mouth.[1]

The trial before the high priest and the Sanhedrin clearly made a mockery of justice. Or did it? We have to come to that conclusion if we accept Mark's and Matthew's account of it—but must we? The fact that a Canadian Chief Justice has done so without reservation is hardly to his credit.

It is easy to understand that a hostile court might relax the laws of evidence in order to convict a particularly hated accused. But why should the Sanhedrin have breached not only the laws of justice and humanity but even the detailed provisions of Jewish religious observance and their own rules in order to do so—holding the trial at night, on an important festival, and in the high priest's house? These technical infringements would have invalidated the proceedings just as certainly as ignoring the rules of evidence. So, even if we can believe that all the members of the Sanhedrin were unprincipled bloodthirsty criminals, they would also have had to be totally brainless to fly so completely in the face of legality—for one very good reason: namely, that if they flouted legality as completely as we are given to believe, then Pontius Pilate would have been able to set aside their verdict. What we have in Mark and Matthew is clearly therefore a grossly exaggerated and distorted picture of the whole proceedings.

Some Christian commentators have realized the extreme improbability of such a pile-up of illegalities and have tried to get rid of the more formal illegalities by redating the trial, so as to have it spread over no fewer than three days, thus avoiding any evening sessions or infringement of a Jewish festival. The fact that one has to resort to such contortions at all is surely itself indicative of the insuperable nature of the problem.

Mark and Matthew give us the impression that it was on a charge of blasphemy that Jesus was found guilty by the Sanhedrin and sentenced to death. Yet, as we have seen, the words he is quoted as speaking did not constitute blasphemy and could not have been so regarded by any Jewish court. A Jewish court that so perverted justice as to convict a man of blasphemy who had uttered words which were patently not blasphemous would quickly have lost all credibility. After all, the supposedly blasphemous words were not a secret, and both Mark and Matthew report them. But, whether Jesus spoke those words or not, it is quite inconceivable that a Jewish court could have found him guilty of blasphemy on that basis.

What about Jesus' claim to be the Messiah? Here we have the real objection that the Jewish authorities had against Jesus. *But claiming to be the Messiah was not a crime in Jewish law.* This must have been known to Mark and Matthew, who have therefore, probably quite deliberately, conflated the Messianic question and a charge of blasphemy to obtain the best effect. Mark and Matthew must have known that Jesus had not been charged with or found guilty of blasphemy; but they also knew that claiming to be the Messiah was not a crime in Jewish law. It is clear, though, that they wanted to put the Jewish authorities in the very worst possible light, so this was done by making the Sanhedrin condemn Jesus to death for blasphemy, which obviously could not have been the case.

John, less concerned with the niceties of Jewish law and tradition, cuts the Gordian knot and simply has the Jews saying: "We have a law, and by that law he ought to die, because he has made himself the Son of God" (19:7). There was of course no such law, but putting it like this not only simplified matters and avoided the necessity of introducing such thorny and irrelevant questions such as that of blasphemy; it also enabled Christians to accuse the Jews of killing Jesus for claiming to be the Messiah—his chief claim.

What then is the true story behind all the confused tangle? In John's Gospel there *is* no Sanhedrin trial at all, only an informal examination by the high priest's father-in-law, himself a former high priest (18:13, 24). If we take *this* as being the true story, the most glaring inconsistencies and falsehoods in the synoptics' accounts can be eliminated. For a start, if it was just an informal questioning session that would explain why it was held at night, on a festival, and in the high priest's private house. It may also explain why there was no formal charge lodged against Jesus. Above all, it explains what is perhaps the most serious anomaly in the accounts of Mark and Matthew, which is that after supposedly sentencing Jesus to death the Sanhedrin hands Jesus over to Pontius Pilate—who proceeds to try him all over again!

This nonsensical sequence of events is avoided if Jesus was *not* sentenced by the Sanhedrin or even tried by it at all but merely *questioned* by the high priest or, as it seems, by his father-in-law and predecessor and *then* handed over to Pilate for his one and only trial, a Roman trial. That is evidently the true sequence of events. But why are Mark and Matthew so insistent on our believing that Jesus was tried, convicted, and sentenced to death by the Sanhedrin if nothing of the kind happened? As usual, it is part of their attempt to shift the blame for Jesus' death from the Romans to the Jews. As we have seen, John does this by making the Jews perform the actual crucifixion. So, once again, all the Gospels agree on their conclusion—that the Jews were to blame for Jesus' death—but the evidence upon which that conclusion supposedly rests differs widely in the different accounts.

It is interesting to reflect on the contrast between the supposed two trials in Mark and Matthew. In Jesus' *actual* trial, that is, the Roman trial, these Gospels go out of their way to paint Pilate as well-disposed to Jesus, even if this makes him ultimately appear an extremely weak and indecisive character—exactly the opposite of what he was like according to non-Christian sources. They also make a point of not recording Pilate's verdict—which could only have been "guilty"— but are not slow to attribute a verdict of guilty to the supposed Jewish trial. In other words, by means of suppression on the one hand and invention on the other they create the impression that the "Jewish trial" was the real trial!

John offers us only one trial: the Roman one before Pontius Pilate. Mark and Matthew regale us with two. But Luke outdoes them all and provides no fewer than three for our delectation and enlightenment, the third (or the second, chronologically speaking) is one before Herod Antipas, tetrarch of Galilee: "When Pilate heard this, he asked whether the man was a Galilean. And when he learned that he belonged to Herod's jurisdiction, he sent him over to Herod, who was himself in Jerusalem at that time" (23:6-7). Herod is conveniently situated in Jerusalem so as to be able to give Jesus an extra little trial, during which, we are told, "Herod with his soldiers treated him with contempt and mocked him" (23:11). Then, unaccountably and without coming to any decision, "arraying him in gorgeous apparel, he sent him back to Pilate" for a continuation of his Roman trial (Luke 23:11).

The story has an implausible ring to it from the start. If Jesus fell under Herod's jurisdiction, then why did Herod send him back to Pilate without reaching a decision? And if Jesus did *not* fall under Herod's jurisdiction, why was he sent to him in the first place? It is nonsense to suppose that just because Jesus was a Galilean his case had to be referred to Herod. That is not the way Roman law operated, for, as had been explained to Pilate, Jesus' activities were spread throughout the Jewish area: "He stirs up the people, teaching throughout all Judea, from Galilee even to this place" (Luke 23:5). The whole little episode is evidently a fabrication—but for what purpose? Quite likely in order to "fulfill" a biblical prophecy, this time one from the Psalms: "The kings of the earth set themselves in array, and the rulers were gathered together, against the Lord and against his Anointed" (2:1-2).

This passage is not quoted in Luke's Gospel but in the Acts of the Apostles, which is generally recognized as written by the same person who wrote "Luke's" Gospel and which specifically relates these verses to a supposed "conspiracy" against Jesus by Herod Antipas and Pontius Pilate (Acts 4:26). This also explains the rather strange remark we find at the end of the story about Herod Antipas in Luke's Gospel: "And Herod and Pilate became friends with each other that very day, for before this they had been at enmity with each other" (23:12).

6. Given that there was no trial before the Sanhedrin but only an informal examination by the high priest or his father-in-law followed by a Roman trial before Pontius Pilate, by whom had Jesus been arrested and on what grounds? All four Gospels relate the story of Jesus' arrest, all of them attributing the arrest to the Jewish authorities (Mark 14:43; Matt. 26:47; Luke 22:47, 52; John 18:3, 12). Though some modern commentators have sought to deny that this could have been so, there is really no reason to reject it. There was a sort of police force attached to the Temple, and it is this body that was probably responsible for the arrest. The Jewish authorities, alarmed at what they had heard about Jesus, and, not least no doubt, reports that he was claiming to be the Messiah, evidently had him brought to the high priest's house for questioning so as to get to the bottom of all the rumors that were probably going the rounds. When Jesus confirmed the Jewish authorities' worst fears by not only admitting to have uttered Messianic claims but by actually repeating those very claims before the high priest (or his father-in-law, the former high priest), it was decided to hand him over for trial to Pontius Pilate. This was necessary because, however much Jesus' Messianic claims may have been resented by the Jewish authorities of the day, putting forward such a claim was not a crime under Jewish law—but, paradoxically perhaps, was a capital offence under Roman law: that is, it was treason against the Roman state.

Guilty or Not Guilty?

Anyone in any way responsible for Jesus' death is automatically considered blameworthy. Jesus himself is taken to be quite blameless and innocent. To Christians he is the "Lamb of God" and many Jewish writers on the subject have been anxious to exculpate the Jews of the blame attaching to Jesus' death. But blame for what? Was Jesus murdered? That is certainly the impression that one gets from a lot of the literature. In 1965, for example, the Second Vatican Council passed a resolution which has often been hailed as marking a new tolerance toward Jews on the part of the Roman Catholic Church. The resolution reads as follows: "Even though the Jewish authorities and those who followed their lead pressed for the death of Christ, neither all Jews indiscriminately at that time, nor Jews today, can be charged with the crimes committed during his Passion."[2]

Is this really the magnanimous statement that it is generally regarded as being? The only question at issue is whether *all* Jews everywhere and for all time should be held guilty, or only the Jews of Jesus' own day or some of them. But I say again, guilty of what?

If, as the Roman Catholics (together with many other Christian denominations) believe, Jesus was not a mere mortal at all but part of the Godhead who came down to earth in human form for the precise intention of dying for the sins of his believers, then how could anyone be held "guilty" of his "murder"? Can one "murder" God?

If, on the other hand, we simply view Jesus and his trial in ordinary human terms, is it not possible that he *was* guilty and was quite justly punished under the laws of his era, a possibility which does not appear to have occurred to many (if any) commentators to date!

Jesus' trial, as we have seen, was on a charge of treason against Rome. The evidence of the so-called "false witnesses" is corroborated for all to see by John's Gospel. Though the incriminating element of the statement attributed to Jesus by these witnesses is a little opaque, the typical "reasonable man" invoked as the interpreter of intention in modern judicial practice would have little difficulty in identifying Jesus' statement as embodying a Messianic claim. Moreover, Jesus is reported in the Gospels as unequivocally voicing such a claim before the high priest, and even in his actual trial before Pilate he is not recorded as making any attempt to deny the charge, let alone to refute the evidence brought against him. And, whereas Jewish courts were bound by the strict rule, based on a biblical injunction (Deut. 17:16; 19:15), that the testimony of two independent eyewitnesses was the minimum prerequisite for any criminal conviction, no such rule exists in Roman law.

We do not normally consider the Romans and the Jews to have had very much in common, yet there was one central respect in which the two peoples shared a similar outlook. However different the Jewish and Roman religions may have been—and it would be hard to think of two religions *more* different in most respects—both were what I have termed "communal" religions.

Religion was seen as being inseparable from government and society. In early Rome the king had been the head of the state religion as well as of the state, a conjunction of powers re-created when the Emperor Augustus eventually took over the position of high priest *(pontifex maximus)* after the death of his erstwhile triumviral colleague Lepidus. From then on every Roman emperor automatically assumed this position upon accession. The Jewish high priesthood had been similarly united with monarchical power in the Hasmonaean dynasty, the successors of Judah the Maccabee, who had successfully championed the cause of Jewish independence resulting in the reestablishment of a Jewish state, usually referred to as the Second Commonwealth.

The Messiah was *not* normally expected to be a priest, as he was to be a descendant of David, who was not of priestly stock. But, as ruler of the Jews under a new divine dispensation, his functions were clearly to be very much a blend of the sacred and the secular.

This would not have been at all strange to the Romans. What *would* have been difficult for them to understand was any attempt to separate these two types of function, which is clearly what John's Gospel is trying to do in putting into Jesus' mouth the words: "My kingdom is not of this world" (18:36). There are at least two implications here. One is spelled out explicitly in the remainder of the verse: "If my kingship were of this world, my servants would fight, that I might not be handed over to the Jews; but my kingship is not from the world." This is clearly meant to combat one of the earliest taunts by non-Christians, which is reflected in the synoptic Gospel accounts of the crucifixion:

> And those who passed by derided him, wagging their heads, and saying, "Aha! You who would destroy the temple and build it in three days, save yourself, and come down from the cross!" So also the chief priests mocked him to one another with the scribes, saying, "He saved others; but he cannot save himself. Let the Christ, the King of Israel, come down now from the cross, that we may see and believe." Those who were crucified with him also reviled him (Mark 15:29-32; Matt. 27:39-44; Luke 23:35-39).

The second implication is that if Jesus was claiming an otherworldly kingdom he could scarcely be a threat to the Romans. "My kingdom is not of this world" then takes on the appearance of a plea of "not guilty" to treason. As John's account is the only one to mention this crucial point, it is unlikely that Jesus ever uttered those famous words. Moreover, had he done so, Pilate would probably not have known what to make of it, a reaction which John actually represents very graphically by making the bluff Roman governor repeat his question: "So you are a king?" (18:37). To Pilate's way of thinking, then, a person either was or was not claiming to be a king. Any qualifying phrases are dismissed as special pleading and disregarded.

"My kingdom is not of this world" is also a plea that does not square with the Jewish Messianic concept. For, as we have seen, it was believed that the Messiah would literally restore the Davidic kingdom—an earthly kingdom in a very real sense, embodying regained Jewish independence. If Jesus was claiming to be the Messiah, which he does appear to have been doing, then a declaration that his kingship was "not of this world" would have amounted to a repudiation of this claim.

For all these reasons, it is highly unlikely that Jesus actually did use special pleading of the type represented by these words. It is not hard to see, however, why the early Christians would have *liked* him to have done so. Unlike the Jews, who formed a distinct nation with its own history, culture, and language—and, above all, with a separate identity—those non-Jews who joined the Christian movement were otherwise indistinguishable from their pagan neighbors. Most of them were Greek-speaking, poor, and tended to live in towns rather than in the countryside. But they had no distinctive social or cultural identity to mark them off from all the other Greek-speaking poor town-dwellers in the Roman Empire—the overwhelming majority—who did *not* become Christians. Above all, whereas the Jews had a strong national identity that made them regard Roman rule as a foreign yoke, the (non-Jewish) Christians, having no other national identity, wished to remain loyal subjects of the Roman emperor.

But here there arose a serious obstacle. The Romans, having a communal conception of religion, could not understand how a person could reject the Roman (pagan) religion—as the Christians did—and still claim to be loyal to the Roman state. To the Roman way of thinking, political and religious loyalties were one. If you were loyal to the Roman Empire you must automatically be loyal to the Roman gods, who were seen as the tutelary deities of the Empire. Rejection of those gods could only be construed as rejection of the state—namely as treason. It was for this reason that the early Christians were persecuted by the Romans.

But what were the Christians to do about it? They clearly could not find room in their religion for the pantheon of pagan gods, but at the same time they obviously did not want to be treated as traitors, especially if they were not. All they could do was to keep stressing their loyalty to Rome and the emperor, and "my kingdom is not of this world" is one of the earliest manifestations of this attitude but probably has nothing to do with Jesus or his trial.

A more direct statement of loyalty to the emperor is also attributed to Jesus: "Render to Caesar the things that are Caesar's, and to God the things that are God's" (Mark 12:17; Matt. 22:21; Luke 20:25). This was supposedly Jesus' reply to a question put to him by some of his Jewish opponents on whether it was lawful for Jews to pay taxes to the Romans. Jesus is represented as rightly regarding this question as a trap (Mark 12:15; Matt. 22:18; Luke 20:23).

It is unlikely to be coincidental that we find an allusion to this very matter in Jesus' charge sheet, in which his accusers describe him as "forbidding us to give tribute to Caesar" (Luke 23:2). Though this accusation appears only in Luke, it is answered by implication by the "render to Caesar" dictum, which is reported by all three synoptics.

Which of the two diametrically opposed statements is true? Did Jesus expressly declare the paying of Roman taxes to be wrong, or did he enjoin cooperation? The fact that he regarded the question as a trap may be a clue here. Why should his enemies have chosen that particular topic to trap him with, unless he was already known to have expressed dangerous (that is anti-Roman) sentiments on the subject? So both reports may be true. Jesus may well have given his enemies the cagey but essentially "safe" answer the synoptics all record—*after* having taken an anti-Roman attitude in his preaching. Nor would it be surprising if someone claiming to be the Messiah should encourage Jews to resist Roman rule, at least to the extent of withholding taxes. In fact, it would have been strange had a Messianic claimant *not* taken such action but had enjoined meek subservience to Rome.

Of course, in view of the circumstances in which the early Christians found themselves, it was obviously more prudent to paint Jesus as a law-abiding subject of the Roman Empire than as preaching resistance to Rome, however peacefully.

There is little to suggest that Jesus was primarily a political rebel against Rome, as he has sometimes been portrayed by certain modern writers. Nevertheless, in putting forward Messianic claims for himself he was necessarily challenging Roman rule over the Jewish people even if this was not his chief objective. But, in doing so, he was guilty of treason under Roman law and was therefore justly executed.

Barabbas

Just how much of a real threat, if any, Jesus posed to the Roman administration is another question, and of course it relates very closely to his level of popularity and the size of his following in the population of Judea. Here, as so often, the Gospels are inconsistent and contradict themselves. On the one hand they carefully build up an image of Jesus as the leader of a mass movement, whose following is so great that the Jewish authorities are afraid his arrest may lead to a popular disturbance (Mark 14:2; Matt. 26:5; Luke 22:2). Yet, when the opportunity is given for Jesus to be released, the Jews loudly call for his crucifixion and for Barabbas to be released instead (Mark 15:11; Matt. 27:21; Luke 23:18; John 18:40). And even the Gospels make it quite plain that this preference for Barabbas over Jesus was not confined to the Jewish authorities, whether priests or Pharisees, but was the express wish of the whole Jewish crowd gathered outside the courtroom, though Mark and Matthew are quick to point out that the crowd was "persuaded" by the priests to press for the release of Barabbas and for Jesus' execution (Mark 15:11; Matt. 27:20). It is hard to imagine how the priests would have "persuaded" an excited crowd to reverse their feelings so completely and so suddenly.

Mark and Matthew were obviously conscious of the dilemma into which their exertions had driven them and, not for the first time, they tried to have their cake and eat it, wanting to combine an assertion of Jesus' popularity with total rejection at the end so as to conform to the image of the "suffering servant" who is "despised and rejected of men" (Isa. 53:3). It was for this latter purpose that the Barabbas incident came in handy.

John simplistically describes Barabbas as "a robber" (John 18:40), thus painting the Jewish crowd in the worst possible of colors which so vociferously favored him and reviled Jesus. But it is clear from Mark and Luke that Barabbas was no ordinary criminal: he was a rebel against Roman rule who had been involved in an insurrection, during which he had evidently killed some Romans (Mark 15:7; Luke 23:18). In fact, political rebels throughout history have often been labelled by their enemies as criminals, and we happen to know that the so-called Zealots, who formed a Jewish resistance movement against Roman rule in Jesus' time, were commonly termed "robbers" *(lestai)* even by the pro-Roman Jewish historian Josephus.

It is not difficult to see why a Jewish crowd would have favored an active resistance fighter against Roman rule in preference to someone who, while claiming to be the Messiah, had never done anything to help the Jews throw off the foreign yoke.

It is quite possible, however, that the whole Barabbas incident is fictitious. Nothing is known in Jewish sources of the supposed "custom" of freeing a prisoner at Passover, which is the whole basis of the Barabbas episode (Mark 15:6; Matt. 27:15; John 18:39).

But, even if the Barabbas story is totally fictitious, the whole crucifixion scene gives no indication whatsoever that Jesus had much of a popular following. Contrary to the supposed expectations of his enemies, Jesus' trial and public crucifixion did not lead to any mass turbulence or disturbance of any kind. Indeed, if the Roman historian, Tacitus, writing about 85 years later, can be believed, the Christian movement was quiescent for some time after Jesus' death (Annals 15:44). This is hardly surprising, as Jesus' death could have done nothing to persuade Jews that he had been the Messiah: there was no tradition that the Messiah would die at the hands of his enemies, despite the capital later made of this very fact. And, until considerably later, there *were* no non-Jews in the Christian movement.

Indeed, Jesus' lack of popular support by comparison with Barabbas (if he existed) may also explain why Pilate was keen to release Jesus rather than the "notorious" rebel against Roman rule.

NOTES

1. H. Cohn, *The Trial and Death of Jesus* (London, 1972).

2. *Nostra Aetate* (CTS Do 360), cited in *The Church and the Jews: Declaration of the German Bishops* (London: Catholic Truth Society, Publishers to the Holy See, 1980), p. 16.

VI

Fulfillment of Prophecy?

One of the chief concerns—if not *the* chief concern—of the Gospels is to "prove" that Jesus was the Messiah *as prophesied in the Jewish scriptures.* There are essentially two ways in which they set about doing this, depending of the needs of the case, and we have already encountered examples of both. In fact, there is even a case in which *both* are used. This is the case of the Davidic descent. Jesus himself, it seems, knowing full well that he was *not* of royal descent and realizing how unlikely it was that any of his contemporaries would believe him if he claimed that he *was,* made no attempt to do so.

What he did instead, it may be recalled, was to try to argue, by means of a verbal quibble in the interpretation of Psalm 101, that the Messiah was *not* meant to be a descendant of King David. Even if this reinterpretation had been convincing—which it is not—it would still have had no effect on the numerous remaining biblical texts describing the Messiah in direct terms as of Davidic descent. It was probably at least partly for this reason that Matthew and Luke decided to adopt a different approach. Cutting the Gordian knot, they both quite categorically asserted that Jesus *was* of Davidic descent and each proceeded to produce a family tree to "prove" the point, with the disastrous results discussed in Chapter 1.

The two ways of "proving" the fulfillment of prophecy are, then, either to bring your story into line with the prophecy or to interpret the prophecy in such a way as to bring *it* into conformity with the story.

The Anointing at Bethany

The one indispensable ingredient in the biography of someone claiming to be the Messiah or Christ was anointing. For, after all, as we have seen, the literal meaning of both these terms, in Hebrew and Greek respectively, is nothing other than "the anointed." The modern mind might be inclined to understand this in a metaphorical sense and not to insist upon it as a physical act. But, so anxious are the Gospels to *prove* that Jesus was the Messiah that they all relate an incident in which Jesus is actually anointed with oil. Mark, Matthew, and John place the incident in Bethany, a village on the road between Jerusalem and Jericho, while Luke sets it in Galilee (Mark 14:3-9; Matt. 26:6-13; Luke 7:36-38; John 12:1-8). John, however, joins Luke in describing it as an anointing of Jesus' feet, while Mark and Matthew have him anointed on the head, the usual place for a kingly anointing. Mark, Mathew, and John all make a specific reference to burial in connection with the anointing, and Luke, by having the oil applied to the feet, also makes an indirect allusion to it, as feet would not normally be anointed except in the process of embalming a corpse. Because of the two settings, commentators have expended much ink on the question of whether Jesus experienced only one anointing or two. In reality he probably experienced none. Each of the Gospels may have constructed a suitable anointing episode deliberately intended to combine the elements of a royal anointing with the more usual type of anointing performed at the time, namely that associated with death.

To deny the royal implications of the anointing—even though performed in anything but royal circumstances and by someone who would never have been regarded as a suitable person to officiate at a royal investiture, namely a woman—would seem to be missing the point. Moreover, it can hardly be coincidental that in John the very next scene describes Jesus' triumphal entry into Jerusalem where he is hailed by the crowd as "King of Israel" (John 12:12-14).

The same scene is also related by the synoptics and it affords yet another example of our first category of "proving" the fulfillment of prophecy by making the story fit the prophecy, no matter how ludicrous the result. In Matthew's account, for example, we find Jesus riding into Jerusalem not on one ass but on two. (Matt. 21:1-7). What is the reason for this uncomfortable ride? Matthew himself tells us by quoting the biblical prophecy (Zech. 9:9) of which the two-ass ride was supposedly the fulfillment:

> Tell the daughter of Zion,
> Behold, your king is coming to you,
> humble, and mounted on an ass,
> and on a colt, the foal of an ass.

In fact, Matthew had misunderstood Zechariah's prophecy, in which the device of parallelism common to Hebrew poetry is employed.

Zechariah clearly did *not* mean to suggest that the Messiah would ride on two animals any more than the Pentateuch had two animals in mind in the following verses: "Behold, a people! As a lioness it rises up and as a lion it lifts itself" (Num. 23:24) or "He couched, he lay down like a lion, and like a lioness; who will rouse him up?" (Num. 24:9).

The point of the parallelism appears to be emphasis through slightly varied repetition. So, all Zechariah is saying is that the Messiah, if this is a Messianic reference at all, will ride on a young ass, which is evidently an oblique reference to a verse from Jacob's blessing upon his son Judah, who was to be the father of the royal tribe of that name:

> The scepter shall not depart from Judah,
> nor the ruler's staff from between his feet,
> until Shiloh comes; and to him shall be the
> obedience of the peoples.
> Binding his foal to the vine
> and his ass's colt to the choice vine,
> he washes his garments in wine
> and his vesture in the blood of grapes. (Gen. 49:10-11)

Jacob's blessing is itself a prophecy, though its interpretation has been much debated, especially the phrase "until Shiloh comes," the only Shiloh known to the Bible being the town where the ark of the covenant was kept during the period of the Judges (Josh. 18:10; Judg. 18:31; Isa. 4:3). It is clear though that the verse essentially prophesies the accession of the house of David, who indeed was of the tribe of Judah, whereas Saul, the first King of Israel, was of the tribe of Benjamin. If modern scholars are right in dating the passage to the time of Solomon then at least part of the prophecy had already happened by the time it was written. But Jacob's vision sees the descendants of David ruling in unbroken succession "until Shiloh comes," an apparently meaningless phrase which, by changing two letters of the Hebrew text, can be made to read "until he comes to whom it [the scepter] belongs," which indeed is the way the Revised Standard Version translates it. Even this is not exactly crystal clear, but is generally understood as a Messianic reference.

It is hard to understand why this rewriting of the verse has commended itself to so many Christian scholars, who of course take it as a reference to Jesus as the Messiah. For, besides doing violence to the Hebrew, it also patently fails to make sense. Jacob sees an unbroken succession of Davidic kings sitting on the throne right up to the time of "Shiloh," yet not by any stretch of the imagination could Jesus be portrayed as coming at such a time. On the contrary, a period of nearly six hundred years had elapsed between the deposition of the last Davidic king and the birth of Jesus.

But, though the blessing could not possibly refer to Jesus, this does not of course rule out the possibility that it is a Messianic prophecy. Indeed, it clearly *is*, the Messianic king being described as a man of peace in contrast to someone like King David himself, who was very much a man of war. Hence the references to his riding on an ass, an ordinary peaceful mode of transport, rather than on a warhorse; to his tethering his ass to an insubstantial vine rather than to something more solid; his clothes are soaked in wine, "the blood of grapes," rather than in actual blood, which one might have expected in the case of a warrior-king. All in all, therefore, what we have here is evidently a prophecy of an age of peace, quite possibly a reference to King Solomon, whose kingdom may indeed be described as having "the obedience of the peoples" and whose reign was essentially a period of peace and prosperity. In addition, the name Shiloh could quite easily refer to Solomon, who was the youngest son of King David. The youngest son of Judah, upon whom the benediction is pronounced, had the name Shelah (Gen. 38: 5, 26). This is written in the Hebrew alphabet (which of course lacks vowels) as SHLH, which is also one of the spellings used for Shiloh, the more usual spelling being SHYLH. If this association between the youngest son of Judah and the youngest son of David is right, it gives us an additional reason for seeing the blessing as referring to Solomon.

Jacob's blessing on Judah, then, is the passage that the prophet Zechariah evidently had in mind in his famous verse about the ass. To return to our original point about parallelism, it will be clear from the verses quoted from the blessing in Genesis that there are no fewer than five sets of parallels in this brief extract alone: scepter/ruler's staff; foal/ass's colt; vine/choice vine; garments/vesture; wine/blood of grapes. The Hebrew word translated as "foal," incidentally, refers specifically to a young donkey and not to a horse. So, there are not two animals referred to here any more than there are two scepters, two vines, two sets of clothing, or two dippings in wine.

The reason that this is significant is that it reveals the motivation behind Matthew's ludicrous picture of Jesus riding into Jerusalem on the backs of *two* asses. So intent is he on "proving" that it is Jesus who is referred to in the Zechariah prophecy that he feels obliged to portray Jesus as fulfilling the most crass literal understanding (or misunderstanding, in this case) of the prophet's words. In this, Matthew, always the most preoccupied of the Gospel writers with biblical prophecy, differs from Mark, Luke and John, all of whom have Jesus seated on only *one* ass (Mark 11:1-10; Luke 19:28-35; John 12:12-15). That Matthew's comical portrait is *not* just the result of a misunderstanding and ignorance of the convention of Hebrew parallelism is clear from the fact that he had Mark's single-ass account, yet chose to depart from it in the interests of a *literal* "fulfillment" of the prophecy.

We have seen that "Shiloh" in Jacob's blessing could not possibly refer to Jesus, but what of the Zechariah prophecy itself? Zechariah lived in the period of Persian domination in the sixth century BC, but the prophetic book which has come down to us under his name appears to contain some much later material, including the prophecy we are concerned with, which may well refer, like the foregoing verses, to Alexander the Great, who subdued Phoenicia and gave the Jews a privileged position.

The cities of Tyre and Gaza, which offered Alexander the fiercest resistance, are mentioned by name, together with several others in the same general area (Zech. 9:1-8). It is immediately after this warlike picture that we read:

> Rejoice greatly, O daughter of Zion!
> Shout aloud, O daughter of Jerusalem!
> Lo, your king comes to you;
> triumphant and victorious is he,
> humble and riding on an ass, (and)
> on a colt the foal of an ass.
> I will cut off the chariot from Ephraim
> and the war horse from Jerusalem;
> and the battle bow shall be cut off,
> and he shall command peace to the nations;
> his dominion shall be from sea to sea,
> and from the River to the ends of the earth.
> (Zech. 9:9-10)

Once placed in its context, the prophecy of the humble king riding on an ass can more easily be identified as a prophecy of peace following the victories of a great conqueror, and there are few conquerors whose empires could more accurately be described as stretching "from sea to sea, and from the River to the ends of the earth" than that of Alexander the Great. Above all, this, like all the other biblical Messianic prophecies, is concerned with a real human king ruling over actual territories. Another such is the one associated with the name of Melchizedek, King of Salem.

Melchizedek

Once again, the Christian claim is based on a biblical text referring to another biblical text. The Christian claim, found in the Epistle to the Hebrews, is essentially that, though not a priest in the ordinary sense, Jesus was "a high priest after the order of Melchizedek" (Heb. 5:10).

Melchizedek first appears in the story of Abraham, where he has only a "walk-on" part:

> And Melchizedek king of Salem brought out bread and wine; he
> was priest of God Most High. And he blessed him and said,
> "Blessed be Abram by God Most High,
> maker of heaven and earth;
> and blessed by God Most High,
> who has delivered your enemies into your hand!"
> And Abram gave him a tenth of everything.
> (Gen. 14:18-20)

Despite this extremely brief mention, Melchizedek clearly was no ordinary pagan king. The tithe which Abraham (or Abram, as he was called at this stage) gave him must clearly be understood to be a tenth of the booty captured in the war, and this is in fact the way the New English Bible translates it. On the authority of Psalm 76 it is thought that Salem, the name of Melchizedek's kingdom, is simply another version of the name Jerusalem, but this is not quite certain. If Melchizedek *was* king of Jerusalem, it might perhaps explain his next appearance in the pages of the Bible, in a psalm evidently composed for recital at coronations in which the king is told: "You are a priest for ever after the order of Melchizedek" (Ps. 110:4).

Jerusalem was captured by King David and was immediately made the capital of his kingdom. Associating the Jewish kings with Melchizedek in the coronation service was a way of corroborating their claim to the city. It no doubt also suited them to lay claim to Melchizedek's priestly title, which might come in handy in any conflict with the actual Jewish priesthood, the descendants of Moses' brother Aaron, who not only officiated in the Temple service but essentially formed an aristocratic class. To this day, incidentally, a priest (*Kohen,* hence the name Cohen and other similar surnames) is called up first to the reading of the Law in the Jewish synagogue service and has a more stringent set of rules to obey than other Jews.

The word *order* in the phrase "a priest after the order of Melchizedek" is misleading. It implies that this shadowy figure, Melchizedek, belonged to some sort of organized priesthood which continued to exist after his time. If he did, there certainly is no evidence of it, and the word *order* should rather be translated by a term such as *type, kind,* or *style,* thus: "a priest after the style of Melchizedek."

The Christian claim that Jesus was a priest of this type, explicitly based as it is on Psalm 110 (which is quoted at Heb. 5:5-6), can rest on only one foundation, namely Jesus' claim to be the Messiah, king of Israel, and descendant of David, to none of which, as we have seen, was he in the least entitled.

But why should the book of Hebrews single out the Melchizedek-type priesthood as it does? A clue is given in the way in which Jesus is quietly promoted from "a priest after the order of Melchizedek" (Heb. 5:6), as quoted from the psalm, to "a *high* priest after the order of Melchizedek" (Heb. 5:10, my emphasis). Neither Melchizedek himself nor any of the Jewish kings is ever described as a high priest, only as a priest. But the central point of the Epistle to the Hebrews is to assert Jesus' superiority to any previous Jewish figure and even to the angels. He is superior, we are told, to the prophets (Heb. 1:1-3), to Moses (3:1-6), and also to the high priests (5:1-6). For this assertion to carry any weight it was clearly not enough for Jesus to be a mere priest of the type of Melchizedek but a "high priest" of that (non-existent) "order."

But, why should the author of this Epistle have been so concerned in the first place to assert Jesus' superiority to the high priests, on which he spends over three chapters by comparison with the few paltry verses given to claiming Jesus' superiority over Moses and the prophets?

Here the Dead Sea Scrolls come to our aid. In the so-called Manual of Discipline we read that the members of the Dead Sea sect would be governed by their original rules "until the coming of a prophet and the Messiahs of Aaron and Israel" (1QS 9:10-11). There could be no mistaking it: *two* Messiahs are clearly mentioned. When this text was first discovered it caused a sensation. Orthodox Jewish tradition had always thought in terms of only one Messiah, a descendant of King David. But it is clear that the Dead Sea sect, thought to belong to the group of Jews known as Essenes, did not share this tradition. What is more, the "Messiah of Aaron," namely a priestly Messiah, was considered by them to be more important than the

"Messiah of Israel" (1QSa 2:12-17). That the idea of two Messiahs was not confined to the Dead Sea sect is indicated by the noncanonical Jewish book known as the *Testament of the Twelve Patriarchs,* which speaks of a Messiah from the tribe of Levi—the tribe of Aaron and his descendants—and of a Messiah of the tribe of Judah, to which the royal house of David belonged. Once again, it is the priestly Messiah who is given the first place (Test. Rub. 6:7-12). From this it is clear that the "Messiah of Israel" of the Dead Sea scrolls is to be identified as the royal Messiah of the tribe of Judah and the house of David, who in the mainline tradition of Judaism was the only Messiah. But, where the expectation is of two Messiahs, it would seem that the royal Messiah is stripped of his spiritual leadership and relegated to a purely secular position—hence his inferiority to the priestly Messiah, who is to be the spiritual leader.

Christianity has always claimed Jesus as the one and only Messiah, but it was precisely in Jesus' time that the idea of two Messiahs was current, at least in certain Jewish circles. The problem therefore was how to claim for Jesus *both* Messianic titles at once. The difficulty was that, in the ordinary way of thinking, the two were not only different but also mutually exclusive. The royal Messiah, as a descendant of David, had to be of the tribe of Judah; the priestly Messiah, as a descendant of Aaron, could only be of the tribe of Levi. The problem seems insoluble, but suddenly there is a fanfare of trumpets and on comes Melchizedek, who manages to combine priesthood and royalty in his own person. But Jesus goes one better than Melchizedek, or at least the author of Hebrews makes him go one better, because, while Melchizedek was king and priest, Jesus is said to be a king and a *high* priest, a complete nonsense, as by definition, there could be only *one* high priest and that was most certainly not Jesus, who was not a priest of any description. But, why was this nonsensical claim to the high priesthood made for Jesus in the first place? Because Melchizedek's priesthood did not represent anything in addition to the monarchical title. All the Jewish kings claimed to be Melchizedek's heirs and in so doing regarded themselves as priests as well as kings— but not as *high* priests. But, unless Jesus was said to be a high priest, he could easily be outflanked by someone claiming to be the priestly or Aaronic Messiah.

It is important to realize that Jesus was by no means the only candidate for the Messianic title. Indeed, the troubled times in which the Jewish people then found itself proved particularly fertile soil for the proliferation of such claims, just as political or economic malaise in modern times has tended to throw up charismatic leaders offering hope to the desperate.

The Book of Acts itself names some previous Messianic pretenders, Theudas and Judas the Galilean (Acts 5:36-37), both of whom were probably Jewish resistance leaders against Roman rule. Theudas' name recurs in the writings of the pro-Roman Jewish historian Josephus, who gives us more information about him (*Antiquities* 20:97-98).

He is unflatteringly described as a *goēs*, a Greek word variously translated as "magician," "wizard," "sorcerer," "cheat," or "impostor," the implication being that he claimed to be something that he was not. According to Josephus, Theudas claimed to be a prophet endowed with supernatural powers, including the ability to part the waters of the River Jordan, and his following included "the majority of the masses," the word for *masses* being the Greek word *ochlos,* which refers to a mob of poor people. Luke, in the Book of Acts, seems to be deliberately taking issue with this picture of Theudas as the leader of a mass movement by specifying that he had "about four hundred" followers and by being studiously vague about Theudas' claims (Acts 5:36). Theudas was eventually killed on orders from the Roman governor, another point which Luke glosses over. Perhaps the parallels between Theudas and Jesus were just a little too close for comfort!

Some commentators are reluctant to identify the Theudas mentioned in Acts with the one who appears in the pages of Josephus, on the grounds of chronology: Josephus' Theudas was killed in the year 44, a good decade *after* Jesus' execution, whereas Acts makes Theudas predate the census of the year 6. If we take this seriously, there may appear to have been *two* risings more than a generation apart both led by men called Theudas. This, however, is highly unlikely. What is much more probable is that Luke's dating is wrong; Josephus' account is too solidly embedded in a detailed historical narrative to be forty years off.

Indeed, Luke's mistake can be traced directly to his careless use of Josephus. Since Luke gives an actual (if approximate) figure for Theudas' following while Josephus does not, Luke could not have been drawing on Josephus, some have argued. But they have evidently been duped by Luke for the motive I have just mentioned: his concern to minimize the amount of support Theudas had. There are too many correspondences between the two accounts for Luke *not* to have been using Josephus. In any case, there are no other accounts of this period of Jewish history known to us, and it is likely that there never were.

The telltale clue comes in what both Luke and Josephus have to say just after their Theudas episodes. *Both* mention the name of Judas the Galilean, who led a rebellion against the Romans at the time of the census of the year 6. Luke relates this as happening *after* Theudas' revolt. But what Josephus tells us is that shortly after the Theudas revolt Jacob and Simon, the *sons* of Judas the Galilean, were brought to trial and crucified (*Antiquities* 20:102). Luke evidently misunderstood the Josephus passage. Seeing the mention of Judas and the census *after* the mention of Theudas, he assumed (since Josephus' *Antiquities* is essentially a chronological narrative) that Theudas' revolt occurred *before* the census, not noticing that the reference to Judas was in fact a flashback brought in at this point only to link up with his sons' execution.

This is a most interesting slip on Luke's part, since for once we undoubtedly have his source. But though the mistake is not in itself very important, it reveals Luke as adopting a somewhat slipshod method of handling historical truth—quite apart from the deliberate distortions and fabrications of which he is guilty in other cases.

There were therefore no fewer than three Jewish risings against Roman rule in the period between the years 6 and 44: those of Judas the Galilean, of Theudas, and of Judas' sons Jacob and Simon. Even though Jesus' own movement may not have been primarily anti-Roman in intent, his Messianic claims could only stamp him as guilty of treason in Roman eyes—exactly the same offence of which Judas, Theudas, Jacob and Simon were evidently held to be guilty. Moreover, it must never be forgotten that, by contrast to modern Western ways of thinking, neither the Romans nor the Jews at that time made any distinction between politics and religion. Theudas and Judas and his sons may have stressed what we would call the "political" rather than the "religious" aspects of their leadership while in Jesus' case it was the other way round; but all of them evidently used similar Messianic claims to achieve their respective goals, and the Roman authorities viewed them all in the same light and punished them accordingly.

John the Baptist

It is not known whether Theudas or the family of Judas the Galilean were of priestly stock, but there was one Messianic contender—and a contemporary of Jesus into the bargain—who most certainly *was* a priest: John the Baptist. This we know from the detailed narrative surrounding his birth as described by Luke, who informs us not only that John's father Zechariah was a priest but also that his mother was "of the daughters of Aaron" (Luke 1:5). What is more, the annunciation of John's birth is said to have been made to his father Zechariah while he was officiating at the Temple service (Luke 1:9-12).

Though we may well doubt the historicity of the annunciation itself, we can readily accept the description of John the Baptist as coming of priestly stock. For, though there were no surnames of the modern type in use among the Jews of the time, there was a clear distinction drawn between priests, Levites, and other Jews (termed "Israelites"). The normal form of nomenclature was of the type "Simon the son of Joseph," but a priest (or a Levite) would have his status tacked on additionally, thus: "Simon the son of Joseph, the priest." So, there would be no doubt in anyone's mind as to who was a priest and who was not.

Another reason for believing Luke's classification of John the Baptist as a priest is the very fact that it was not in Luke's interest to do so. The last thing that Luke wanted was to give anyone the idea that John was the priestly Messiah expected by the Essenes and others. Indeed, all the Christian Gospel writers are at pains to deny any Messianic title to John the Baptist, though Luke is the only one to reveal directly that he was ever considered a Messianic candidate:

> As the people were in expectation, and all men questioned in their hearts concerning John, whether perhaps he were the Christ, John answered them all, "I baptize you with water; but he who is mightier than I is coming, the thong of whose sandals I am not worthy to untie; he will baptize you with the Holy Spirit and with fire. (Luke 3:15-16)

The Baptist is here made expressly to deny any Messianic claim on his own part, depicting himself rather as simply the harbinger of good tidings preparing the way for the coming of the Messiah.

We are clearly meant to assume from this passage that it was Jesus for whom John the Baptist saw himself as preparing the way. Yet even the Gospels tell how John sent two of his disciples to ask Jesus, "Are you he who is to come or shall we look for another?" (Luke 7:19; Matt 11:2-3). This is not particularly flattering to Jesus, as the true Messiah should surely be clearly visible to all and sundry and not have to announce his identity himself—as Jesus is ignominiously obliged to do. Not surprisingly, perhaps, he then rounds on the Baptist in addressing his audience: "I tell you, among those born of women none is greater than John; yet he who is least in the kingdom of God is greater than he." (Luke 7:28; Matt. 11:11)

The implication here is that, though the harbinger of the new era, the Baptist is not privileged to enter it and to be part of it. This is brought out very clearly in the next two verses in Matthew's account:

> From the days of John the Baptist until now the kingdom of heaven has suffered violence, and men of violence take it by force. For all the prophets and the law prophesied until John; and if you are willing to accept it, he is Elijah who is to come. (11:12-13)

It is of course very convenient for Christianity to have the Baptist himself disclaim any Messianic title for himself, although by no means can we be sure that he *did* disclaim any such role. And the obvious need discernible in the Gospels to deny him the Messianic title and to cast him in the greatly inferior and, from the Christian point of view, much safer role of Elijah only makes us all the more curious about the relationship between John the Baptist and Jesus.

John the Baptist comes closer than anyone else in the pages of the Christian Gospels to sharing the limelight with Jesus, but, as we have just seen, even he is kept at arm's length. This is apparent throughout. Perhaps the best example is the different Gospels' treatment of the famous baptism scene.

> In those days Jesus came from Nazareth of Galilee and was baptized by John in the Jordan. And when he came up out of the water, immediately he saw the heavens opened and the Spirit descending upon him like a dove; and a voice came from heaven, "Thou art my beloved Son; with thee I am well pleased." (Mark 1:9-11)

It is not enough for Jesus simply to be baptized by John, for that might place John in a superior position to Jesus. Hence the vision, which leaves us in no doubt that it is Jesus who is the more important figure. Luke goes a bit further. Though setting Jesus' baptism against a general background of John's baptizing activities, he does not specifically tell us that Jesus was baptized *by John*. In the fact, the baptism itself is played down and the vision becomes the central feature.

> Now when all the people were baptized, and when Jesus also had been baptized and was praying, the heaven was opened, and the Holy Spirit descended upon him in bodily form, as a dove, and a

voice came from heaven, "Thou art my beloved Son; with thee I am well pleased." (Luke 3:21-22)

As usual, Matthew's version outdoes the rest. Just in case we might get the wrong idea about the relative importance of Jesus and John, Matthew actually makes John utter words to set our minds at rest. So, when Jesus comes to be baptized, John tries to dissuade him.

> Then Jesus came from Galilee to the Jordan to John, to be baptized by him. John would have prevented him, saying, "I need to be baptized by you, and do you come to me?" But Jesus answered him, "Let it be so now; for thus it is fitting for us to fulfill all righteousness." Then he consented. And when Jesus was baptized, he went up immediately from the water, and behold, the heavens were opened and he saw the Spirit of God descending like a dove, and alighting on him; and lo, a voice from heaven, saying, "This is my beloved Son, with whom I am well pleased." (Matt. 3:13-17)

Here, with his usual sledgehammer subtlety Matthew recruits the Baptist himself to put himself down. But, if John the Baptist is modest in the synoptic Gospels, in John's Gospel he is positively masochistic. Now not only does he deny that he is the Messiah; he even denies that he is Elijah or "the prophet" but says that he is merely "the voice of one crying in the wilderness" (John 1:23).

In Matthew and Luke, as we have seen, John the Baptist is so uncertain of Jesus' identity that he has to ask him whether he is the Messiah or not. This embarrassing scene is quite absent from the Fourth Gospel, where the Baptist has suddenly become quite acutely aware that Jesus *is* the Messiah and does not miss an opportunity of telling us so (John 1:15, 29-34). This time, not only is there no mention of Jesus' baptism by John but the dove scene is now put into the mouth of John the Baptist, who concludes with the words: "And I have seen and have borne witness that this is the Son of God" (John 1:34).

But the author of this Gospel is clearly still worried. After all, even though John the Baptist has now demonstratively abased himself before Jesus in the pages of his Gospel, there is still a nagging doubt, which is put into the mouths of Pharisees who, when the Baptist utters his blanket disclaimer and describes himself merely as "the voice of one crying in the wilderness," retort: "Then why are you baptizing, if you are neither the Christ, nor Elijah, nor the prophet?" (John 1:25). The

Baptist's answer is essentially that though he baptized with water, Jesus baptized with the Holy Spirit (John 1:26-33). In other words, if baptizing is seen as conferring high status on John, then Jesus must have even higher status, because he also baptizes—and with a superior product to boot!

But even after this exercise in me-tooism, the mind of the Gospel writer is not quite at rest. He is worried that the fact that Jesus came onto the scene *after* the Baptist may be thought to indicate that he was inferior to him. To this the Baptist is himself made to give the lie: "After me comes a man who ranks before me, for he was before me." (John 1:30), which is a piece of pure sophistry.

But the author of the Fourth Gospel is still not happy. John the Baptist cannot be allowed simply to *deny* that he is the Messiah:

> And this is the testimony of John, when the Jews sent priests and Levites from Jerusalem to ask him, "Who are you?" *He confessed, he did not deny, but confessed,* "I am not the Christ." And they asked him, "What then? Are you Elijah?" He said, "I am not." "Are you the prophet?" And he answered "No." (John 1:19-21, italics added)

Notice the extreme care with which this passage is constructed. Instead of the vague denials that we find in the synoptics, what we have here is a detailed and unequivocal rejection of anything approaching prophetic status let alone Messianic pretensions. First, the "witnesses" to John's "confession" are named as priests and Levites sent from Jerusalem, the center of Jewish worship. Then comes the contorted phrase which I have italicized, which, in the Greek as in the English translation actually repeats the word *confessed* (Greek: *hōmologēsen*). Why? The word literally means to assent or agree and is therefore a *positive* word, whereas "deny" (Greek: *arneomai*) is of course wholly negative in its associations. Simply to deny something probably carries less weight than to *assert positively* that something is not so—or so the author of this Gospel would have us believe. The whole object of the exercise is to impress upon us indelibly John the Baptist's total rejection of a Messianic claim or any other title of honor or distinction.

The tone here is so shrill as to verge on the hysterical. Why? The motive is clearly anxiety, a dread on the part of the Christian author that John the Baptist might upstage Jesus. Every possible precaution is taken to prevent this. If John the Baptist baptizes (and he really did), then so does Jesus—only better. And, moreover, if John the Baptist is a priest (and he really was), then so is Jesus, only he is a *high* priest! Such, at any rate, is the message the Gospels are so anxiously trying to stamp on our minds.

The importance of the priesthood, as I have already explained, was all the greater to the Dead Sea sect, who believed in a separate—and superior—priestly Messiah; it is not at all impossible that John the Baptist belonged to some such sect himself. His wild outfit and rough living, coupled with his asceticism and Messianic preaching all point in that direction.

So, Melchizedek to the rescue—of Jesus, that is, from the threat of John the Baptist!

"For Unto Us a Child Is Born"

So far we have been concerned with cases where the story has been adjusted so as to fit a biblical prophecy. But, before moving on to the opposite process, in which biblical texts are reinterpreted to bring them into line with certain awkward facts of Jesus' life (for example, his execution), there is another important example of the first kind of adjustment that we must look at.

The ninth chapter of the prophet Isaiah contains what is perhaps the most famous of all prophecies:

> For to us a child is born,
>   to us a son is given;
> and the government will be upon his shoulder,
>   and his name will be called
> "Wonderful Counselor, Mighty God,
>   Everlasting Father, Prince of Peace."
> Of the increase of his government and of peace
>   there will be no end,
> upon the throne of David, and over his kingdom,
>   to establish it, and to uphold it
> with justice and with righteousness
>   from this time forth and for evermore.
>   (Isa. 9:6-7)

It is only too easy to take this passage out of its context and apply it at random to whatever one likes, but that would result in totally misunderstanding its import. The context is international Middle Eastern politics of the eighth century BC. Israel, the northern Jewish kingdom, had allied itself with Syria against Judah, the southern Jewish kingdom. Playing the usual game of international checkerboard politics, Ahaz, king of Judah, decided to ally himself with the great power of the day, Assyria, in order to avert the threat. This international backdrop is depicted for us by Isaiah at the beginning of his seventh chapter. But the prophet does not endorse Ahaz's policy. To name the rulers of Israel and Syria is evidently proof enough for Isaiah of their weakness (7:8-9). The obvious conclusion is therefore that an Assyrian alliance was as unnecessary as it was dangerous.

It is in order to persuade Ahaz to follow his advice that the birth of the child Emmanuel is to take place (Isa. 7:14). This is described as a divine "sign"—*not*, of course, because it was to be a virgin birth, for, as we have already seen it was to be no such thing. In what sense then *was* it to be a divine sign? The unborn infant is not described in supernatural terms. Indeed, all that is said of him is that "he shall eat curds and honey when he knows how to refuse the evil and choose the good" (Isa. 7:15), or better, "he *will be eating* curds and honey" at the time when he learns to understand the difference between good and evil. The mention of the curds and honey is evidently just an indication of the extreme youth of the child (and *not* of economic hardship, as some commentators have suggested) and serves to date the really crucial statement which comes next: "For before the child knows how to refuse the evil and choose the good, the land before whose two kings you are in dread will be deserted" (Isa. 7:16).

So far, it is clear, the message is one of hope for Judah: her enemies are about to be destroyed and there is no need for her to enter into a dangerous "alliance" with (that is, subjection to) her real natural enemy, Assyria. But then comes a verse which has often been interpreted in an opposite sense, as prophesying the destruction of Judah irself:

> The Lord will bring upon you and upon your people and upon your father's house such days as have not come since the day that Ephraim departed from Judah—the king of Assyria. (Isa. 7:17)

The phrase "the king of Assyria" must be disposed of at once. As most commentators agree, it is probably an interpolation inserted by an early annotator and it certainly seems quite out of place here. It is evidently meant to "explain" the first part of the verse, but it would appear to result from a fundamental misunderstanding of the prophet's message.

The prophecy is addressed to King Ahaz of Judah, but what does it mean? Does it mean that days are about to come which are so bad that, in the words of a commentator, "the loss of the ten tribes was as nothing to the loss of population that now awaits Judah" (*International Critical Commentary,* Isaiah I, G. B. Gray, p. 137)? Or does it mean that days are about to come which are so good that their like has not been seen since the loss of the ten tribes? The Hebrew is equally amenable to both interpretations, but the second seems to me to be more in keeping with what Isaiah has been saying up to this point. In other words, therefore, this is no prognostication of doom for Judah but exactly the opposite, a message of hope and good cheer.

But, if so, what are we to make of the following verses?

> In that day the Lord will whistle for the fly which is at the sources of the streams of Egypt, and for the bee which is in the land of Assyria. And they will all come and settle in the steep ravines, and in the clefts of the rocks, and on all the thornbushes, and on all the pastures.
>
> In that day the Lord will shave with a razor which is hired beyond the River—with the king of Assyria—the head and the hair of the feet, and it will sweep away the beard also.
>
> In that day a man will keep alive a young cow and two sheep; and because of the abundance of milk which they give, he will eat curds; for every one that is left in the land will eat curds and honey.
>
> In that day every place where there used to be a thousand vines, worth a thousand shekels of silver, will become briers and thorns. With bow and arrows men will come there, for all the land will be briers and thorns; and as for all the hills which used to be hoed with a hoe, you will not come there for fear of briers and thorns; but they will become a place where cattle are let loose and where sheep tread. (Isa. 7:18-25)

This extremely difficult passage has been variously interpreted. Though the last part of it is clearly a picture of utter desolation, that description hardly applies to verses 21 and 22, which speak of an "abundance of milk." The way out of this is probably to take G. B. Gray's reading based on the Septuagint: "And it shall come to pass in that day, (if) a man shall preserve alive a young cow and two (milch) sheep, then it shall come to pass that owing to the abundance of the yield of milk, every one that is left in the midst of the land shall eat curds and honey" (*Commentary,* p. 140). The eating of curds and honey is not to be seen here as a sign of privation any more than it is to be thus regarded in the Emmanuel prophecy. But the point seems to be that the milk from a single young cow and two sheep will be enough to feed the whole surviving population of the land, an image of depopulation that is corroborated in the next few verses describing the infestation of once fertile land with briars and thorns.

This brings us to the main problem posed by this passage: what land is it describing? Is this a picture of a desolate Judah or of the ravaged lands of Israel and Syria? Both views have their champions, but the internal evidence seems quite unequivocal: there is a clear reference to Assyria in the phrase "the Lord will shave with a razor which is hired beyond the River" (Isa. 7:20). This can only be a reference to Assyria, even if the explicit naming of it which we have in verse 20 is an interpolation as in verse 17. In what sense could Assyria be said to be the hired razor of God? Presumably in the sense that Assyria was being used as the divine agent in punishing Judah's enemies.

If we do not understand the passage in this sense but rather as pointing to the future destruction of Judah itself, then it would have to mean that Isaiah was predicting that Judah's destruction would be inflicted upon her by Assyria, whereas in fact it was at the hands of the neo-Babylonian empire that Judah was to fall. Our optimistic (for Judah, that is) interpretation is further confirmed by what we read in the next few verses. Here God gives Isaiah a sign in the shape of a son born to his own wife ("the prophetess," 8:3) and he is told specifically that "before the child knows how to cry 'My father' or 'My mother,' the wealth of Damascus and the spoil of Samaria will be carried away before the king of Assyria" (8:4).

In the year 701 BC the Assyrians *did* move against the kingdom of Judah, but they were bought off by tribute, as we learn in 2 Kings 18:13-16). It is this attack that is referred to in the next few verses of Isaiah's eighth chapter (8:5-8), but this must not be confused with the *destruction* of Judah, which took place one hundred and fifty years later. The destruction of the kingdom of Israel and Syria, on the other hand, did indeed take place in Isaiah's own lifetime, in the eighth century BC.

A week, in Sir Harold Wilson's memorable phrase, is a long time in politics. Isaiah's prophecies have often been seen as referring to a period centuries after his own time, but a close reading, of the sort to which we have just subjected chapters seven and eight, reveals just how illusory such a view is. Isaiah is commenting on the situation—political, religious, and moral—of his own day and his prophecies look only a few years into the future. This, in fact, is something he lays great stress upon: the very imminence of the cataclysms he predicts. Hence the imagery of a child learning how to address his parents and knowing the difference between good and evil. Both are simply graphic ways of representing short periods of time (the one, of course, longer than the other), just a matter of a few years. The prophecy that in sixty-five years time Ephraim (Israel) would be "broken to pieces so that it will no longer be a people" (Isa. 7:8) is not really at variance with the prediction of the destruction of the *kingdom* of Israel as such within a few years, as the deportation and scattering of the ten tribes may not have been completed until well after the conquest. Nevertheless, this sixty-five-year prophecy is probably an interpolation.

In fact, Syria was destroyed in 732 BC and the end of the kingdom of Israel came a decade later, probably no more than twenty years after Isaiah had predicted it.

It is worth noting that in the Emmanuel prophecy the child, though as yet unborn, was evidently already conceived. That, at least, is the understanding of the prophecy that we must adopt if we follow the grammar of the Hebrew, the literal meaning of which is: "Behold, the young woman *is* pregnant and will bear a son" (Isa. 7:14; italics added). How old would the child be by the time he knew right from wrong? The conventional answer would probably be something like five. But, says Isaiah, it was to be *before* this that Syria and Israel would be deserted.

But, if the Emmanuel prophecy is short-term in its range, so to speak, what are we to make of the even more famous prophecy in chapter nine quoted at the beginning of this section? And, above all, to whom does this prophecy refer? Does it refer to the same person as the Emmanuel prophecy (whoever that may be) or not?

The point about the Emmanuel prophecy is that the identity of the child "Emmanuel" is totally unimportant; he is not invested with any special qualities at all and there is no indication that he is to be a Messianic figure of any kind—or, indeed, any form of ruler. Whether or not Isaiah has a particular child in mind for "Emmanuel" is therefore irrelevant. The definite article in the Hebrew, "Behold, *the* young woman," may not be as significant as it seems in translation, as Hebrew usage would allow this to mean "*a* young woman" or even "young women" in the plural as well as "the young woman." It cannot be sufficiently stressed that it is *not* the conception or birth of "Emmanuel" that is to constitute the divine sign. The sign is to consist in the fact that within five or so years of this birth the two kingdoms threatening Judah are to perish. In other words, the "Emmanuel" prophecy is just a poetic way of predicting the imminent destruction of two enemy states.

The prophecy in chapter nine is of course quite different. Here the identity of the child is crucial, as he *is* invested with exceptional qualities. But before trying to identify him, let us turn our attention to the time-scale involved. If "Emmanuel" was already conceived though not yet born at the time of the prophecy in Isaiah's seventh chapter, the child in chapter nine clearly *is already born* at the time of the prophecy: "For to us a child *has been born,* a son *has been given"* (9:6) would be the literal translation of the Hebrew text. Unless this is waved aside as poetic license, Isaiah could hardly be referring to someone who was to be born seven centuries later.

And what of the attributes of the child? Here clarity reigns supreme: "And the government will be upon his shoulder" (9:6), the word rendered as *government* being the Hebrew *misrah,* which comes from a root meaning "power," "rule" or "dominion" and is related to the word *sar,* meaning a "prince" or "chief." There can be no doubt about it: what we are dealing with here is an earthly ruler governing an earthly kingdom, which, as we have already seen, is quite normal in Jewish Messianic prophecy. The next verse amplifies this initial description:

> Of the increase of his government and of peace
>   there will be no end,
> upon the throne of David, and over his kingdom,
>   to establish it, and to uphold it
> with justice and with righteousness
>   from this time forth and for evermore.
>   (Isa. 9:7)

Here is no airy-fairy spiritual "kingdom" but a real territorial monarchy, identified in so many words as David's kingdom, namely the original united Jewish kingdom of the twelve tribes. The phrase "to establish it" (line 4) does not imply that a kingdom is to be set up from scratch but rather that an already existing kingdom is to be set on a firm foundation.

The reign of the new king is to be marked by peace coupled with expansion (in practice a rather rare combination!), presumably so as to reestablish David's kingdom in its entirety, that is, with the addition of the northern kingdom. And when was this dynamic new dispensation to begin? So imminent is it that the prophet can say, "from this time forth and for evermore" (line 6).

To sum up our findings so far, what we have here is the delineation of the reign of a just and righteous king who will bring peace and who will reunite the Jewish people in a single kingdom that will last forever—a king, moreover, who was already born at the time of the prophecy. There could be no doubt about the identity of this new king: it could only be Hezekiah, who is described in the second Book of Kings as follows:

> He trusted in the Lord the God of Israel; so that there was none like him among all the kings of Judah after him, nor among those who were before him. For he held fast to the Lord; he did not depart from following him, but kept the commandments which the Lord commanded Moses. And the Lord was with him; wherever he went forth, he prospered. He rebelled against the king of Assyria, and would not serve him. He smote the Philistines as far as Gaza and its territory, from watchtower to fortified city. (2 Kings 18:5-8)

There is a definite concern here to portray Hezekiah as flatteringly as possible, glossing over the fact that he became a tributary to Assyria but stressing instead his resistance to that power. But, though he did not succeed in reuniting the Jewish state, he did at least make some inroads on Philistine power. Above all, he removed all traces of idolatry from public worship and proved a just and humane king. Here indeed was a king after a prophet's heart.

As we know not only from Isaiah's own writings but also from the second Book of Kings, the prophet was a contemporary of Hezekiah (see 2 Kings 19:2). Isaiah himself in the prologue to his prophecy tells us that he prophesied "in the days of Uzziah, Jotham, Ahaz, and Hezekiah, kings of Judah" (1:1). The famous vision of his sixth chapter is dated "in the year that King Uzziah died" (6:1), which presumably represents an early stage of the prophet's career. There is absolutely no reason to disbelieve this date, as the prophecy in question is not historical in any sense but is the timeless vision of seraphim proclaiming the holiness of God. The traditional date for Uzziah's death is 756 or 757 BC. Hezekiah's dates are unfortunately a bit more problematical, some saying he began his reign in 729 BC (on the basis of 2 Kings 18:1) and others dating his accession to 716/15 BC (according to 18:14). As he became king at the age of twenty-five (2 Kings 18:2), he would have been born either in 754 or 741/40, both dates falling well within the period of Isaiah's prophetic career. In other words, whichever date is the right one for Hezekiah's birth and wherever in the course of his career we place the prophecy, Hezekiah will indeed already have been born when the prophecy was first uttered, which is exactly what the prophecy requires.

So far so good. But surely, you may object, is this not a prophecy of a divine being, thus ruling out its application to a mere mortal king like Hezekiah, who, however saintly, cannot possibly measure up to the description embodied in the composite name that Isaiah says the child is to bear? The name is indeed unique even in the company of the most extravagant biblical names: "Wonderful Counselor, Mighty God, Everlasting Father, Prince of Peace." (9:6)

The first and most obvious problem here is that, if these names *are* indeed the attributes of a divinity, how could they also apply to a human Messiah? *This would be a breach of the first of the Ten Commandments, the most fundamental of all Jewish beliefs, the principle of monotheism. Moreover, at no time have Jews anywhere believed in a* divine *Messiah.* In this categorical sweeping statement I include Jesus' own *Jewish* followers, who give no indication in their writings or in the reports of their actions that they believed that Jesus (or any other human being) was a god. In short, there is no possibility whatsoever that Isaiah could have intended his readers to expect a divine Messiah, a human being who was also a god.

This has been recognized even by some Christian scholars, and the New English Bible renders the relevant verse thus: "And he shall be called in purpose wonderful, in battle Godlike, Father for all time, Prince of peace." (9:6). But this is not really a satisfactory translation of the Hebrew text, as it departs too far in the direction of an interpretation.

In Hebrew, there is no word for *is, am* or *are.* To put it in conventional grammatical terms, there is no present tense of the verb *to be.* This means that in order to express the sentence, "I am a lion," you must say simply "I lion." Similarly, "he is hungry" becomes "he hungry" and "we are young" must be expressed as "we young." To those who have been brought up on Tarzan comics ("Me Tarzan, you Jane") this form of expression will not appear unduly strange, and on the whole it works well enough in Hebrew. But ambiguities will inevitably arise, especially where, as in a name, we are not sure whether we are dealing with a complete grammatical sentence (that is, containing a finite verb) or just a phrase.

In English and most (if not all) modern cultures, a name is *not* normally in the form of a complete sentence and we therefore do not expect to find a verb in ancient names either. Yet, many a biblical name is a complete sentence in itself and does contain a verb. The name of Isaiah's son, Shear-jashub (Isa. 7:3), is a case in point; the name means "a remnant shall return." Here the verb *is* expressed in the Hebrew, since it is not the verb *is*. But Isaiah's own name, literally "the Lord salvation," makes sense only if we insert the verb *is* into the translation: "the Lord is salvation." And the same applies to many other Hebrew names, among them the name Emmanuel, which literally translated means "God with us," but which must be rephrased as "God *is* with us."

If we adopt the same approach to the series of Messianic names in Isaiah's ninth chapter, what we get is something like this: "A wonderful counsellor *is* mighty God, an eternal father *is* the prince of peace." Translated in this way, which does no violence to the Hebrew, the whole import of the name is completely altered. Instead of representing attributes of the Messiah, the name is seen to characterize attributes of God. Which means that, instead of blasphemy, what we have here is a perfectly acceptable name (by Jewish standards, that is) on a similar pattern to many other biblical names, which, like *Isaiah* and *Emmanuel,* proclaim the greatness not of man but of God.

If anyone objects that King Hezekiah was not given this name, however it is translated, the retort must be that neither was Jesus! Moreover, we are told simply of the new ruler that "his name will be called" the eight Hebrew words we have just discussed. The point is that it is *passive,* not active as in the case of *Emmanuel,* which was discussed in chapter one. His name will *be* called etc. etc.—but by whom? There is no indication that this long sequence of epithets describing God is to be the Messiah's actual given name, but merely that this is what he "will be called," quite possibly in some informal sense. Indeed, as he was already born at the time of the prophecy, as Isaiah himself indicates, his formal naming could not possibly still be in the future. So this long series of names is to be seen rather as a sobriquet given to a good king by his appreciative subjects.

The key to it all appears to lie in the last line of the same verse, a rather neglected line: "The zeal of the Lord of hosts will do this." (Isa. 9:7). The reference is to the coming reign of peace, justice, and righteousness. *This,* says the prophet, will be achieved by God's zeal (9:7). How fitting, therefore, that the attributes of the new king, Hezekiah, are credited to God, which is exactly what the "name" does: "A wonderful counsellor is mighty God, an eternal father is the prince of peace."

Though no Jew would ever have taken this "name" as conferring divine attributes on the Messiah, that understanding of the "name" is also quite in conformity with the Hebrew words as they stand. It is unlikely that the Christian promotion of Jesus from "the Son of God" to "God the Son" owes its origin to this verse of Isaiah's but rather to long-standing pagan concepts, in which the dividing line between the idea of "god" and that of "man" was much less clear-cut than in Judaism. But, once Jesus *was* thought of as a god, it is hardly surprising to find that view read back into Isaiah.

Fitting the Text to the Story

In the examples discussed so far, the life of Jesus was made to conform in every detail to the Jewish Messianic prophecies. It is almost as if the Christian scripture writers regarded the prophecies as a sort of advertisement for a vacant post in the "Situations Vacant" column of a newspaper:

> WANTED: *Messiah for Israel.* Must be of Davidic stock and born in Bethlehem. Virgin birth a recommendation—must have been anointed with oil. Must ride into Jerusalem on an ass (two asses optional). Priestly status will be an advantage. Preference will be given to candidates capable of miracles. Dead heroes need not apply.

Most of these requirements could be met by adding details to Jesus' actual curriculum vitae, which is what the Gospel writers fall over one another in doing. But, what they found far more difficult was to square certain details of Jesus' life—and death—with the requirements of the job. There was at least one such tricky detail which was bound to count against him: his crucifixion.

The Messiah had always been thought of as a scion of the house of David who would come to free the Jewish people from the oppression of a foreign yoke and reestablish Jewish independence in a lasting and indeed eternal kingdom under his own sovereignty. In short, the Messiah had to be successful in ordinary down-to-earth political terms. Defeat and death at the hands of the enemy could only be seen as a sign that the defeated hero was *not* the Messiah.

When, for example, about a century after Jesus' death, Simon Bar Kochbah raised the standard of revolt against Rome, the famous Rabbi Akivah pronounced the nationalist leader to be the Messiah. The failure of the revolt, however, put an end to this, and there was never any attempt afterwards to resurrect Bar Kochbah's Messianic claims.

Jesus himself clearly saw his own execution in much the same light. His cry of anguished despair from the cross, calling out to God, "My

God, my God, why hast thou forsaken me?" (Mark 15:34; Matt. 27:46), is an admission of defeat and, however one may try to explain it away, characterizes the crucifixion as a sign of divine disfavor—anything but the glorious culmination of a predetermined divine plan for the salvation of believing Christians. The fact that this cry is quoted in (transliterated) Aramaic, the language actually spoken by Jesus (albeit with one significant difference between the two versions), together with the fact that it goes against all later Christologies, points strongly to its genuineness. Here is a failed Jesus torn between self-pity and anger directed toward the God who had turned against him. Unlike the case of many another about-to-be executed leader, there is no rousing speech to reassure his followers of the justice of their cause and to hold out hope of its ultimate triumph; there is no mention of resurrection; no attempt to justify the apparent setback as part of a divine plan for salvation. In short, there is here, unlike elsewhere in the Gospels, no attempt to whitewash the patent failure of Jesus and his movement.

If the Roman historian Tacitus is to be believed, Jesus' death was indeed followed by a decline in the Christian movement (*Annals* 15:44). This is exactly what might have been expected, as the ignominious death of a Messianic claimant could only be taken by most Jews as a sign that the claim had not been genuine. For this reason among others, as Paul especially came to realize, the only hope for the survival and growth of the movement lay in attracting into it non-Jewish adherents, and it was on this point that the first major split in the Christian movement took place.

But, even though any attempt to explain Jesus' death away would be unlikely to persuade Jews of the authenticity of Jesus' Messianic claims, the whitewash employed in the process was nevertheless compounded of a biblical base, carefully diluted and with an admixture of pigments drawn from elsewhere.

The Jewish Bible was ransacked in the hope that it would yield prophecies that could be interpreted as pointing to a suffering and despised Messiah instead of the more usual exultant and triumphant one. To this end a perusal of the book of Psalms proved particularly rewarding.

As it happens, Jesus' cry of anguish from the cross was itself a quotation from Psalm 22, which, for this among other reasons, quickly established itself as a Christian favorite and is sometimes referred to as the "Passion Psalm." It contains such verses as these: "A company of evildoers encircle me; they have pierced my hands and feet" (Ps. 22:16); "They divide my garments among them, and for my rainment they cast lots" (Ps. 22:18). Such detailed and indeed minute correspondence between what was taken to be "prophecy" and the Gospel accounts of the crucifixion appeared so uncanny as to point to only one conclusion: the truth of such "prophecies." Or so, at least, did Christian commentators use to argue.

Upon closer inspection, however, these correspondences begin to melt away. For one thing, though the Revised Standard Version has followed the King James Version in describing hands and feet in Psalm 22 as being "pierced"—thus providing a convenient preview of the crucifixion—the Hebrew word in question means nothing of the kind. The verse may well be corrupt, as the literal translation of the Hebrew Masoretic text is: "A company of evildoers encircle me, my hands and feet like a lion" (Ps. 22:16). This does not make a great deal of sense. The Septuagint offers a more promising reading: "A company of evildoers encircle me; they dig into my hands and feet." This makes good sense and the whole verse will now read: "Yea, dogs are round about me; a company of evildoers encircle me; they dig into my hands and feet." The verse is no longer very reminiscent of a crucifixion scene. What we have depicted before our eyes instead is the quite different scene of someone attacked by a pack of fierce dogs, who knock him down and savage his limbs. As for the sharing out of the garments, something which is mentioned in all four Gospels (Mark 15:24; Matt. 27:35; Luke 23:34; John 19:23), it is by no means impossible that the Roman soldiers *did* indeed behave in this fashion. But, can we really view this as a "fulfillment" of Psalm 22, as John makes a point of telling us (19:24)?

What, after all, is Psalm 22 about? It is certainly of the type traditionally referred to as a lamentation. But who is doing the lamenting? The psalm is written in the form of a lamentation by a single individual, who finds himself deserted by God in his hour of need, at a time when he is confronted by deadly enemies. If saved, he vows to praise God in the congregation (of the Temple). So far, there is no Messianic element in the psalm at all and it is only in the last five verses that anything approaching prophecy can be said to occur:

> All the ends of the earth shall remember and turn to the Lord; and all the families of the nations shall worship before him. For dominion belongs to the Lord, and he rules over the nations.
> Yea, to him shall all the proud of the earth bow down; before him shall bow all who go down to the dust, and he who cannot keep himself alive. Posterity shall serve him; men shall tell of the

Lord to the coming generation, and proclaim his deliverance to a people yet unborn, that he has wrought it.

(Ps. 22:27-31)

The great glory promised here to God is essentially conditional upon his saving the supposed speaker from his present dangers. But the speaker himself is quite helpless to save himself or anybody else—and is therefore hardly a Messianic figure.

Who then is this mysterious speaker? It can be none other than a personification of the Jewish people, as becomes clear if tested on the last few verses. If God answers the call of the people of Israel and frees them from the clutches of their enemies, His glory will be such as to attract all nations to His worship.

To return to the garments, the reference in the psalm can be seen for what it really is: a graphic description of the dismemberment of the Jewish state at the hands of its enemies, an event which has been repeated more than once in history. It gives no support to *any* Messianic ideal, let alone to Christianity, and the same applies to Psalm 22 as a whole, which when examined in context turns out not to be a Messianic psalm at all!

The chief technique at work here is that of interpreting the psalm—seen of course in terms of prophecy—so as to square with the most undeniable and awkward fact of Jesus' life, his crucifixion. But there is also an element of the other technique, the one already dealt with, namely that of fitting the facts to the biblical text. The story of the Roman soldiers dividing Jesus' garments among themselves is an example of this technique, as is Jesus' expression of thirst, which, as John candidly remarks, was made "to fulfill the scripture" (19:28), the relevant passage being verses 14 and 15 of our psalm.

One verse of Psalm 22 repeats a vivid image used by Isaiah (or vice versa): "But I am a worm, and no man; scorned by men, and despised by the people" (Ps. 22:6). The relevant verse of Isaiah corroborates our identification of the speaker of Psalm 22 as the Jewish people: "Fear not, you worm Jacob, you men of Israel! I will help you, says the LORD; your Redeemer is the Holy One of Israel." (Isa. 41:14) This introduces us to one of the major themes of the Book of Isaiah, namely that of the "suffering servant":

> Behold my servant, whom I uphold,
>   my chosen, in whom my soul delights;
> I have put my Spirit upon him,

> he will bring forth justice to the nations.
>
> (Isa. 42:1)

This is a characteristic verse. But what is the identity of this servant of God's? Isaiah leaves us in no doubt whatsoever on this score:

> But now hear, O Jacob my servant,
> Israel whom I have chosen!
> Thus says the LORD who made you,
> who formed you from the womb
> and will help you:
> Fear not, O Jacob, my servant,
> Jeshurun whom I have chosen.
>
> (Isa. 44:1-2)

God's servant, therefore, is not an individual at all, but the Jewish people as a whole, and, as if to hammer this point home, Isaiah uses no fewer than three names for God's servant—Jacob, Israel, and Jeshurun—all of which refer to the Jewish people.

Once it is accepted that God's servant in Isaiah is to be identified as the Jewish people, this leaves us very little option but to accept the same identity for the suffering servant of Chapters 52 and 53, a notoriously vexing passage of scripture.

> He was despised and rejected by men; a man of sorrows,
>   and acquainted with grief;
> and as one from whom men hide their faces
>   he was despised and we esteemed him not.
>
> Surely he has borne our griefs
>   and carried our sorrows;
> yet we esteemed him stricken,
>   smitten by God, and afflicted.
> But he was wounded for our transgressions,
>   but he was bruised for our iniquities.
>
> . . . .
>
> He was oppressed, and he was afflicted,
>   yet he opened not his mouth;
> like a lamb that is led to the slaughter,
>   and like a sheep that before its shearers is dumb,
>   so he opened not his mouth.
>
> (Isa. 53:3-5, 7)

If any passage in the Jewish Bible prophesies a suffering Messiah, this surely is it. Or so, at any rate, have Christians argued over the centuries. Indeed, it has seemed so obvious in many cases as to require no argument at all. Yet, once it is realized that the whole catalogue of woes depends on this initial identification of the sufferer, any Christological application begins to jar:

> Behold, my servant shall prosper,
>> he shall be exalted and lifted up,
>> and shall be very high.
> As many were astonished at him—
>> his appearance was so marred,
>> beyond human semblance,
>> and his form beyond that of the sons of men—
> so shall he startle many nations;
>> kings shall shut their mouths because of him;
> for that which has not been told them they shall see,
> and that which they have not heard they shall understand.
> (Isa. 52:13-15)

The sufferer, it is clear, is still God's servant, the people of Israel. And who can say that the prophecy was not fulfilled? The sufferings of the Jewish people are only too clearly marked in blood across the pages of history.

Alternatives to Messiahdom

It should be abundantly clear by now that, despite the strenuous efforts of the Gospels, Jesus cannot possibly be identified as the Messiah prophesied in the Jewish Bible. He was neither of the house of David nor a priest of the stock of Aaron; he was not a patriotic Jewish leader against the Romans; and, above all, from the Jews' point of view he was a failure. But, if Jesus was not the Messiah, as the Gospels are intent on proving, what then was he?

There are essentially two alternatives: (1) He may either be reduced to something less illustrious than a Messianic figure, or (2) he can be elevated to something higher. Both these positions have been claimed for him at one time or another by different writers on the subject. It has become painfully obvious to an increasing number of modern scholars that the traditional unquestioning acceptance of Jesus as the Messiah is no longer tenable, and so the two alternatives just mentioned have become more and more popular. But neither is without serious difficulties.

It may perhaps seem strange that even theologians who recognize the difficulties in the way of accepting Jesus' Messianic claims often find no barrier to believing in him as a divinity. But this may be less of a paradox than it seems. After all, to the pagan mind there was no reason why a human being should *not* be or become a god. Kings in the pagan Middle East were regularly worshiped as gods in their own lifetime and foreign generals such as Flamininus, the Roman conqueror of Greece, likewise found themselves deified on the spot by their new subjects.

But, if it was easy in pagan thinking for a human being to be elevated to divine status, it was partly at any rate because gods were not seen as being *so* very much above human status to begin with. The Greek gods, for example, were always portrayed in very down-to-earth terms. There was a great deal of fighting and bickering amongst themselves; marital fidelity meant very little to them; and they were as greedy, as vain, and as egocentric as any human being. Most ancient pagan societies were sharply divided between nobles and commoners, with the gods seen as simply the next step up beyond the aristocracy, the gap between god and noble being no greater than that between noble and commoner. In the Homeric epics, for example, gods are forever coming down to earth in human (invariably aristocratic) guise, and many illustrious nobles are themselves partly of divine or semi-divine descent. Examples include Achilles, Odysseus, and Helen of Troy, to name but three.

There was no shortage of divinities in most pagan religions, and Greco-Roman paganism was especially inclined to add alien gods to its pantheon. People collected gods and cults in much the same way as children now collect bottletops or matchbox labels. Any new god discovered in any part of the Roman Empire was eligible for inclusion in the assemblage of divinities. Many of these exotic deities offered a much more exciting form of worship and belief than the rather drab Roman state religion and attracted to themselves huge crowds of frenzied followers.

One particularly popular cult was that of the goddess Isis, imported from Egypt, a cult that combined mysticism with deep emotion and gave its devotees a sense of belonging to a select group without requiring them to give up the worship of the ordinary state gods of Rome. The Iranian cult of Mithras appealed particularly to Roman soldiers. Mithras was pictured as doing battle with the forces of evil, in the shape of a bull, which he is usually portrayed as stabbing to death with no great sense of enjoyment. Then there was the widespread, originally Anatolian, cult of Cybele, "mother of the gods," whose priests castrated themselves in frenzied passion for the "Great Mother," as Cybele was often called.

It would have been easy enough to see the name "Jesus Christ" as referring to yet another of these oriental deities, and there are some points of similarity between Christianity and the pagan mystery cults. For one thing, all of them had some form of initiation ceremony. In the case of Mithraism, this was exactly the same as in Christianity, namely baptism. The cult of Cybele had a slight variation on this theme, the so-called *taurobolium*, a ceremonial bathing in the blood of a slaughtered bull. The central concepts of the cult relate to procreation and immortality. In castrating themselves, Cybele's priests were supposedly following the example of the goddess' young lover, Attis, whose death (on March 22) and resurrection three days later form the pivot of the cult calendar and bear more than a passing resemblance to the most central celebration of Christian worship.

But, if Easter owes much to Cybele, Christmas is largely derived from Mithras (plus the old Roman festival of the Saturnalia, a jolly occasion on which gifts were exchanged). Mithras, associated as he was with the sun, gave Christianity December 25 as the date for Christmas, a date with no Jewish associations (except the festival of Chanukah, which normally happens to fall in December but is not associated with any particular date in the solar calendar). What is more, Mithras, like Jesus, was believed to have had a miraculous birth and to have attracted, as an infant, the attention of neighboring shepherds. In addition, Mithraism, like Christianity, had a sacramental meal as part of its ceremonial.

But perhaps the most important element common to Christianity and the pagan mystery cults was the concept of salvation. In one sense or another, Isis, Cybele, and Mithras were all seen as saviors, and it is this which, in no small part, accounts for the historical popularity of their cults.

Christianity *could* easily have taken its place as yet another mystery cult, with the only real difference between it and the other cults being its exclusivity. Isis, Cybele, and Mithras could all coexist (sometimes a trifle uneasily) with one another and with the state religion of Rome, even within the breast of a single worshipper, but acceptance of Christianity entailed the rejection of all other forms of religion, not that that would have stopped Christianity from competing on equal terms with the pagan mystery cults.

I use the word *could* advisedly. Christianity *could* have taken its place alongside the pagan mystery cults. Why, then, didn't it? In short, because of its Jewish origin and its dependence on historical events.

Mithras, as we have seen, was supposed to have had a miraculous birth, but no prospective initiate to the Mithraic cult would have asked for proof of that. Mithras was accepted as being a mythical figure and was in any case by definition divine, as were Isis and Cybele. Only by severing all ties with Judaism, by renouncing all Messianic claims and, for that matter, by departing from the Christian scriptures, could Jesus be thought of as a divinity plain and simple. But, if this were done, Jesus would be just another "pagan" divinity and Christianity just another mystery cult.

With this we touch upon one of the great dilemmas of Christianity, which though present under the surface all of the time comes into view only periodically: the stronger the belief in Jesus' divinity the greater the tension between Christianity and monotheism, and even between Christianity and the Christian scriptures themselves, which can only, with a great deal of difficulty, be made to yield an image of a divine Jesus.

In the whole corpus of Christian scripture there are only *eight passages* which can be said to refer to Jesus as divine, and all of these without exception are highly dubious; so much so, indeed, that modern Christian theologians are themselves now increasingly prepared to accept the fact that the concept of Jesus' divinity is *not* to be found in the Christian scriptures.

But, it is of course precisely *because* a belief in Jesus' divinity flies in the face of monotheism that it is a convenient escape-hatch for those wishing to get away from the difficulties surrounding Jesus' Messianic claims. The problem, though, is that this solution frees Jesus from the toils of Messianic prophecy only to eject him, as we have seen, into the void of pagan mysticism.

Several titles are applied to Jesus that manage to steer clear of the Messianic trap while at the same time avoiding the quicksands of divinity. Such titles are "Savior," "Son of God," and "Son of Man."

Son of Man

"Son of Man" has a sort of mystical ring to it, and it has attracted a great deal of scholarly attention. The fact that the same term occurs in a prophetic passage of the Book of Daniel was seized upon as a sign of the prophetic import of the title, but it is perhaps worth looking more closely at the relevant extract:

> I saw in the night visions,
> and behold, with the clouds of heaven
>   there came one like a son of man,
> and he came to the Ancient of Days
>   and was presented before him.
> And to him was given dominion
>   and glory and kingdom,
> that all peoples, nations, and languages
>   should serve him;
> his dominion is an everlasting dominion,
>   which shall not pass away,
> and his kingdom one
>   that shall not be destroyed.
>   (Dan. 7:13-14)

That this is a Messianic prophecy there can be little doubt. The "Ancient of Days" is probably to be taken as a personification of God and the other figure, who "came like a son of man," is evidently the Messiah.

But that certainly does *not* mean that "son of man" is some sort of special title for the Messiah. This is well demonstrated in the very next chapter, where Daniel himself is addressed as "son of man" (Dan. 8:17). As has now been amply demonstrated, notably by Geza Vermes, the phrase "son of man" was commonly used in Aramaic (the language of this part of the book of Daniel and also the language spoken by Jews in the time of Jesus) to mean simply "man" or the indefinite "one" or "someone." The Messianic figure is described as "like a son of man" to indicate that it appeared in Daniel's dream as a human figure by contrast with the "four great beasts" described just prior to this (Dan. 7:3-8).

The oft-repeated suggestion that "son of man" as a description of Jesus in the Gospels has some special Messianic connotation derives from a belief that the phrase bears such a connotation in Daniel. As it clearly does not, its use in referring to Jesus also cannot have any Messianic significance.

Why then is "son of man" so frequently found as a reference to Jesus in the Gospels—sixty-six times, to be precise! One very significant fact about its use in the Gospels is that it is not only used exclusively *of* Jesus but also only *by* him. In other words, it is used by Jesus as a sort of impersonal alternative to *I*. This is exactly what we find in its use in Jesus' supposed reply to the high priest's question, "Are you the Christ, the Son of the Blessed?": "I am; and you will see the Son of man seated at the right hand of Power, and coming with the clouds of heaven" (Mark 14:61-62). This statement is of course very self-consciously modeled on the prophecy in Daniel, yet even so "son of man" is clearly nothing other than a modest synonym for *me*. To say "you will see *me* seated at God's right hand" might have sounded even more daring and arrogant than the already extremely daring and arrogant statement which Mark puts into Jesus' mouth. (The other synoptics tone it down still further, as we have had occasion to see in another connection.) Elsewhere it is even more obvious that "son of man" has no Messianic connotations. Take, for example, the well-known remark attributed to Jesus after his disciples have been reprimanded for picking ears of corn on the Sabbath: "The sabbath was made for man, not man for the sabbath; so the son of man is lord even of the sabbath" (Mark 2:27-28; Matt. 12:8; Luke 6:5). Here "son of man" may not even refer to Jesus himself but to "man" generally, the implication being that, as the Sabbath had been made for man and not vice versa, therefore man was master of the Sabbath.

But, you may well ask, if it *is* so obvious that the term "son of man" has no Messianic connotations, why have so many Christian commentators seen such connotations in it? The short answer must be that "son of man" offers an irresistible escape route from the Messianic dilemma. For here is a term which, without in so many words investing Jesus with the Messianic title (a difficult mantle for him to carry off, as we have seen) enables him to claim it on the sly, as it were!

Son of God

"Son of God" has almost exactly opposite characteristics to "son of man." If "son of man" has no Messianic connotations, "son of God" most certainly *does*. And, whereas "son of man" is used *only* by Jesus, "son of God" is *never used by him either in reference to himself or to anyone else*. One thing the two titles have in common is their use by modern scholars to enable Jesus to have all the aura of the Messianic title without actually laying claim to it directly. In the case of "son of man" this approach founders on the slightly inconvenient fact that it is not a title at all but merely an Aramaic substitute for an indefinite pronoun! What about "son of God"? The attempt to use this title— and this time there can be no doubt that it *is* a title—as a foil to *Messiah* is equally unsuccessful, precisely because "son of God" was so *closely* identified with Messianism that investing someone with the title of "son of God" is tantamount to hailing him as the Messiah.

The idea that the Messiah was in some special sense the son of God is an extension of the idea among the Jews that their king was the son of God. "I will be his father and he shall be my son" (2 Sam. 7:14) is a noteworthy formulation of the relation between God and king, with particular reference to Solomon and the house of David, which is promised eternal rule (7:16). The second psalm, evidently a hymn recited at royal coronations, puts it more poetically:

> I will tell of the decree of the LORD:
> He said to me "You are my son,
>   today I have begotten you.
> Ask of me, and I will make the nations your heritage
> and the ends of the earth your possession.
> You shall break them with a rod of iron,
> and dash them in pieces like a potter's vessel."
>   (Ps. 2:7-9)

Though the whole Jewish people, or indeed the whole of mankind, may be seen as the children of God, his fatherly relationship to the king is clearly something different, something much closer. Hence the stress in the psalm on the idea that only now, at the moment of coronation, does the king become the son of God. And so close is the relationship seen to be that God undertakes in advance to refuse his son, the king, nothing, but promises him universal power.

This close connection between the Messianic (or kingly) title and that of "son of God" is recognized in the Gospel story of Jesus' examination by the high priest, who asks him: "Are you the Christ, the Son of the Blessed?" (Mark 14:61). In Matthew this is phrased slightly differently: "I adjure you by the living God, tell us if you are the Christ, the Son of God." (Matt. 26:63). How many questions does the high priest put to Jesus, one or two? Just one. This is equally clear in both versions. He does not ask Jesus (1) whether he is the Christ (that is the Messiah) and (2) whether he is the son of God. The two titles are so identified in his mind that "son of God' is seen as merely an extra attribute of the Messiah. There is no possibility of answering *yes* to being the son of God and *no* to being the Messiah, or vice versa, because the two titles are merely two facets of the same thing.

Of course, there is in addition the quite different usage of terms referring to divine parentage in pagan religions, something to which I have already alluded in a previous chapter. Thus, to take but one example, the Emperor Augustus called himself *divi filius*, or "son of a god," the god in question being the deified Julius Caesar, whose adoptive son the emperor was. The idea of gods coupling with human beings to produce semidivine offspring is a commonplace of Greco-Roman mythology, and the story of Jesus' virgin birth clearly owes something to that tradition.

If we discard the Jewish tradition of regarding the king as in some special sense the son of God, then the use of the title in reference to Jesus is consigned wholly to the pagan conception of divine parentage, an association which most Christian theologians would probably prefer to avoid. But, by the same token, taking "son of God" as some sort of Messianic title that somehow bypasses and transcends the difficulties associated with claiming for Jesus the Messianic title itself is just not possible.

Savior

A comparatively early Christian symbol was the fish. This had a double meaning, as it referred on the one hand, to the milieu from which at least some of Jesus' disciples were drawn while at the same time being a pictorial representation of an acrostic: the Greek word for *fish* is *ichthus,* the letters of which were deemed to stand for the Greek equivalent of "Jesus Christ, son of God, Savior." But, though the concept of Jesus as the savior of those who believe in him is central to Christian belief, the word *savior* itself occurs surprisingly rarely in the Christian scriptures themselves, and particularly so in the Gospels, and, moreover, where it does occur it is as likely to be used in reference to God as to Jesus. In fact, the name *Jesus* itself, as was mentioned earlier in another connection, or its Hebrew form, *Joshua,* refers specifically to this divine quality of salvation—the bearer of the name, it must be stressed, being not the savior but rather *the object of God's salvation,* someone saved by God. Nevertheless, there was also a Jewish tradition of regarding certain human beings as saviors—notably, once again, kings. Indeed, one of the very first attributes of monarchy which we hear about in the Bible is this quality of salvation:

> Now the day before Saul came, the LORD had revealed to Samuel: "Tomorrow about this time I will send to you a man from the land of Benjamin, and you shall anoint him to be prince over my people Israel. He shall save my people from the hand of the Philistines; for I have seen the affliction of my people, because their cry has come to me" (1 Sam. 9:15-16).

As always, the salvation referred to here is of a down-to-earth, military and political nature. Nevertheless, it is clearly to this, another attribute of the Jewish kings, that the concept of Jesus as a savior owes its origin. Once more, without this Messianic association, Jesus' depiction as a savior can only be pagan—in the mold of the salvationist mystery deities, Isis, Cybele, and Mithras.

Christ/Messiah?

Such is the anxiety on the part of Christian theologians to extricate Jesus from the tricky problems associated with the Messianic title that there has even been a theory recently propounded that contrives to sever the title *Christ* from any Messianic connotations, the argument being that *Christ* was not a title at all but a sort of surname given to Jesus *not* because anyone thought he was the Messiah but rather in reference to a particular verse of Isaiah:

> The Spirit of the Lord GOD is upon me,
> because the LORD has anointed me
> to bring good tidings to the afflicted;
> he has sent me to bind up the brokenhearted,
> to proclaim liberty to the captives,
> and the opening of the prison to those who are bound;
> to proclaim the year of the LORD's favor,
> and the day of vengeance of our God;
> to comfort all who mourn. (Isa. 61:1-2)

It is hard to understand why the application to Jesus of the title *Christ* should refer specifically and solely to this passage—except of course that it enables one to invest Jesus with all the attributes of the Messiah without any of the concomitant problems! The plain fact is that *Christ* or *Christos* is simply the Greek equivalent of the Hebrew *Mashiach,* or *Messiah,* both of which literally mean "anointed," and, though the king was not the only person to be anointed in ancient Jewish society (priests, for example, also were), the term had by Jesus' time come to refer specifically to the king, and, more precisely, to a king, whether past or future, of the house of David. The coronation psalm which we have just cited is a case in point:

> Why do the nations conspire, and the peoples plot in vain?
> The kings of the earth set themselves,
>   and the rulers take counsel together,
> against the LORD and his anointed, saying,

"Let us burst their bonds asunder, and
cast their cords from us." (Ps. 2:1-3)

That is how the psalm begins. There is no explanation of the term
anointed, but we may quite safely conclude that it refers to the king of
Israel. In other words, the term *anointed*—that is, Messiah or Christ—
was already used without any qualification to refer to the king. It
would therefore have been most surprising if Jesus could have been
called by this title by his supporters unless they wished to signify a
Messianic claim on his behalf.

But, as a matter of interest, who *is* God's "anointed" in Isaiah's
sixty-first chapter? Is this not a portrayal of the Messiah too? If not, it
is a picture of a messenger-type character similar to that expected to be
played by the prophet Elijah, a role reserved in the Christian Gospels
not for Jesus but for John the Baptist!

This clarifies the dilemma in the minds of many modern Christian
theologians, who recognize how difficult it is to claim that Jesus was
the Messiah. But what alternative is there? *Unless* Jesus can by hook or
by crook be invested with the Messianic title, he must either become
just another pagan deity—or a mere human being.

Jesus: Teacher, Prophet and Ideal Human Being?

On the face of it, this alternative would seem to be the most common-
sensical solution. Of course, to have any significance Jesus would
have to be portrayed as an *extraordinary* human being, not just a
teacher but a great teacher, a prophet, and an ideal of humanity. This
should surely pose no problem. This is a description to which one can
easily subscribe without even being a Christian in any sense. Or is it?

If there is one word that tends to be associated with Jesus the
man, it is the word *love,* and his teachings certainly contain many
injunctions to "love." But what about his own life? He tells his followers not only to love their neighbors, a Jewish injunction, but also
their enemies. But what about himself? Does he ever love *his* enemies
and bless them? Not at all. On the contrary, he roundly condemns the
Pharisees, repeating at least four times the well-known phrase. "Woe to
you, scribes and Pharisees, hypocrites!" (Matt. 23:13, 15, 16, 23; Luke
11:42, 43, 44). There would not appear to be much love lost on the
Pharisees here, but, in view of the injunction to "love your enemies"
(Matt. 5:44; Luke 6:27), we may well ask: Who is the real hypocrite?

Jesus' lack of affection for his family has already been discussed.

But there are of course one or two incidents in the Gospels that stand out as exemplars of love and humility, the best known probably being the story of Jesus washing the feet of his disciples at the Last Supper (John 13:4-17). This scene, described only by John, is invariably taken as an example of Jesus' humility. But is it?

The purpose of the whole elaborate and laborious process is not left to commentators to work out. John puts a very explicit explanation into Jesus' own mouth:

> When he had washed their feet, and taken his garments, and resumed his place, he said to them, "Do you know what I have done to you? You call me Teacher and Lord; and you are right, for so I am. If I then, your Lord and Teacher, have washed your feet, you also ought to wash one another's feet. For I have given you an example, that you also should do as I have done to you. Truly, truly, I say to you, a servant is not greater than his master; nor is he who is sent greater than he who sent him. If you know these things, blessed are you if you do them." (John 13:12-17)

A careful reading will reveal that, far from being an example of humility, this episode represents an assertion of authority on Jesus' part over his disciples. He is most anxious for his gesture *not* to be interpreted as a sign of his reducing himself to the level of his disciples. That is why he specifically informs them that it is *right* for them to address him by titles of honor (whereas they themselves, as he says elsewhere, are *not* to claim any titles of distinction for themselves). Just in case they have not got the message, he then repeats his own two titles, Teacher and Lord, in reverse order. Then comes the hammering home of the message: "a servant is not greater than his master." Once again, as if addressing a group of dim-witted ten-year-olds, he feels it necessary to ram the point home, just in case the disciples did not understand that *they* were the "servants" (the Greek word is better translated as *slave,* which makes it even more pointed) and *he* the master. Hence the reference to "sender" and "sent." The whole thing can be summarized as a sharp warning to the disciples to obey Jesus' injunctions, and the quoted extract is followed by a clear admission by Jesus that he did not trust all his disciples.

The story of the woman taken in adultery is another example of an incident generally interpreted as a reflection of Jesus' great humanity. But, once again, all is not as it seems.

The story occurs only in John (7:53—8:11), though it is sometimes tacked onto the end of Luke's twenty-first chapter. The woman in question, as the text makes quite plain, has been caught in the act when she is brought to Jesus by the scribes and Pharisees (8:3-4). It is often assumed by commentators that Jesus was to pronounce judgment on the adulteress, but this seems unlikely (assuming, that is, that the story is true to begin with, which it may very well not be). We are, after all, told explicitly that the woman was brought to Jesus by the Pharisees "to test him, that they might have some charge to bring against him" (8:6). This hardly gives us the impression of their coming to Jesus as a judge. Jesus certainly never held any official office, and in this instance he is clearly in the dark about the legal position and has to ask the woman herself, "Has no one condemned you?" (8:10). In other words, Jesus does not even *know* whether the woman has already stood trial or not. His own "examination" of her can therefore have been only of the most informal nature, a fact which is further corroborated by Jesus' failure to call witnesses or to treat the matter in any proper judicial manner.

The story is generally regarded as an example of Jesus' great sympathy and humanity, for two reasons. One is his remark to the woman's accusers: "Let him who is without sin among you be the first to throw a stone at her" (8:7); and the other is his parting words to the adulteress herself, once it is clear that she has not in fact been formally tried or even indicted: "Neither do I condemn you; go, and do not sin again" (8:11). These two pithy remarks are among the best known of the sayings attributed to Jesus, especially in the beautiful rolling prose of the King James version: "He that is without sin among you, let him first cast a stone at her" (8:7); "Go, and sin no more" (8:11).

But both of them have serious problems. Since, as it turns out, the woman has not yet been found guilty by a court of law, the whole question of stoning is premature, and it would certainly have been wrong for anyone to start stoning her—not, of course, that the Pharisees were doing so or had any inclination to do so, for if they *had,* would they simply have gone away and left the woman alone with Jesus? So, what then *does* Jesus' reference to stoning mean? If, as seems likely, it is meant to be taken in a metaphorical sense, as referring not so much to executing the woman as to pronouncing her guilty, then it is utter nonsense. If no one with the slightest blemish has the right to sit in judgment on anyone else, then no system of justice can ever operate.

This rather leaves the alluring fabric of Jesus' first saying in tatters.

What about the second saying? It is noteworthy that, despite the absence of a trial, Jesus himself readily assumes the woman's guilt, as we see from the fact that he tells her not to sin *again*. In Jewish law, two independent eyewitnesses are required to establish guilt, but at no time does Jesus try to ascertain whether there had been such. Moreover, having paid the woman the dubious compliment of taking her guilt for granted, Jesus then takes it upon himself to forgive her for what was, after all, a mortal sin (or capital crime) and an offence against the Ten Commandments. This was not only arrogant on his part but also grossly hypocritical, if any store is to be laid by the tradition of Jesus' pronouncements on sexual matters:

> Every one who divorces his wife and marries another commits adultery, and he who marries a woman divorced from her husband commits adultery. (Luke 16:18)

> It was also said, "Whoever divorces his wife, let him give her a certificate of divorce." But I say to you that every one who divorces his wife, except on the ground of unchastity, makes her an adulteress; and whoever marries a divorced woman commits adultery. (Matt. 5:31-32)

> You have heard that it was said, "You shall not commit adultery." But I say to you that every one who looks at a woman lustfully has already committed adultery with her in his heart." (Matt. 5:27-28)

Here Jesus is advocating the expansion of the definition of adultery to include not only all the categories already found in Jewish law—including whatever category it was that the "woman taken in adultery" fell into—but in addition the second marriage of any divorced man or woman—and, most remarkable of all, even looking "lustfully" at a woman! So far, therefore, from being the "liberated" moralist that he may appear to be from the story of the woman taken in adultery, Jesus was evidently much more straitlaced even than the Pharisees.

How is his hypocrisy to be explained? One possibility is of course that Jesus' sentiments have not been accurately reported. Another is that he held one view at one time and the other at another. But that too would require explanation, if it were true, and would not in itself rule out hypocrisy in any case. There is however one important common element to be found in the hyper-Puritanical attitude to sexual morality given him in the Gospels and his forgiveness of the adulteress. In both cases Jesus is taking a deliberate stand against the

Pharisees. Here, I believe, we have the crux of the matter.

In the case of the adulteress, she is brought to Jesus by the Pharisees in order to challenge him, as we are specifically told. He certainly rises to the bait. In his preachments on sexual morality, he clearly differentiates his views from conventional Jewish teaching, by mentioning the certificate of divorce (then as now a perfectly acceptable legal document in Jewish law) and the seventh commandment—in order to disagree with the one and greatly to expand the operation of the other. In other words, there is a common polemical basis to the two contradictory positions he adopts: an antiestablishment, and more particularly, anti-Pharisee-establishment position, setting *himself* up as the voice of authority. Of course, this in itself entails a further example of Jesus' hypocrisy, for are not the Pharisees the very people of whom Jesus said: "The scribes and the Pharisees sit on Moses' seat; so practice and observe whatever they tell you, but not what they do; for they preach, but do not practice" (Matt. 23:2-3). Yet here we find him rejecting not the Pharisees' deeds but their teachings—the very thing that Jesus enjoined his followers to "practice and observe." And Jesus calls *them* hypocrites!

Jesus a Prophet?

Was Jesus a prophet? Of course, the word *prophet* is not confined to someone who predicts the future but may have a much broader meaning. Moses has always been considered the greatest of the Jewish prophets, yet he is not noted for any "prophecies" in the modern sense. Rather, in his case the word *prophet* (Hebrew: *navi*) refers rather to his speaking out a divinely inspired message. But, to return to our question, was Jesus a prophet? We shall first consider his "prophecies" in the usual sense and then go on to discuss his abilities, if any, as a speaker-out of ethical teachings under the head of "teacher" rather than "prophet." (See page 141.)

All Jesus' prophetic utterances as reported in the Gospels essentially boil down to a single one that the end of the world is at hand, to be replaced by the "kingdom of heaven," symbolized by the coming of the Messiah, identified as Jesus himself.

This sort of prophecy is probably most closely associated not with Jesus but rather with John the Baptist, whose cry is reported to have been: "Repent, for the kingdom of heaven is at hand" (Matt. 3:2), adding: "I baptize you with water for repentance, but he who is coming after me is mightier than I, whose sandals I am not worthy to carry; he will baptize you with the Holy Spirit and with fire" (Matt. 3:11).

What exactly is the meaning of the term "the kingdom of heaven"? And does it *necessarily* imply what we today would colloquially call "the end of the world"? The phrase "kingdom of heaven" is not unknown in Jewish writings, where it generally does *not* imply the end of the world. Thus, as Rabbi Eleazar ben Azariah, a leading Talmudic authority, put it, obeying certain commandments was equivalent to accepting "the kingdom of heaven" (Sifra Kedoshim 9:10). A better translation would be "the king*ship* of heaven," meaning divine sovereignty, something that can, of course, quite easily coexist with the ordinary physical and material world. In Greek as in Hebrew, the word translated as *kingdom* is the same as that translated as *kingship*, (Hebrew: *malchut;* Greek: *basileia),* despite the very different connotations that the two words have in English.

Even when the term used in the Hebrew is "the world to come," the implication in Jewish writings is usually *not* of an extraterrestrial or purely spiritual world but rather of the world as we know it transformed by the coming of the Messiah, marking not the end of the world as such but the beginning of a new age of peace, harmony, and prosperity. Such a view is quite in keeping with the prophetic visions of Isaiah and the other biblical prophets, which we have already had occasion to consider. So great is the correspondence between the visions of the prophets on the one hand and the Talmud on the other that despite the lapse of time between them there is no reason to see anything other than a direct continuity.

Of course, within this generalized picture of peace and happiness there is room for a variety of interpretations, ranging from the view that in the new age there would be no death (Exod. R. 15:21) to the more cynical view that not even poverty would disappear but that the only change would be the triumph of the Jewish people over the heathen kingdoms, which would become subservient to Israel (Ber. 34b). Certainly, whatever other features were expected in the Messianic age, it is always seen in the Talmud—once more, totally in keeping with the biblical view of the Messiah and his mission—as essentially the salvation of the Jewish people:

> The Holy One, blessed be he, said to Israel, "In this world I set before you blessings and curses, good fortune and disasters, but in the world to come I will remove from you the curses and disasters and bless you, so that all who behold you will declare you to be a people of the blessed." (Tanchuma Re'eh 4)

Some Talmudic writings, however, *do* see the coming of the Messiah as marking the end of the world:

> After 4,291 years from the creation of the world, the world will be destroyed, partly by the wars of the sea monsters, partly by the wars of Gog and Magog, and then will the days of the Messiah occur; and the Holy One, blessed be he, will not renew the world until after seven thousand years." (Sanhedrin 97b)

This would place the end of the world AD 531. In another Talmudic anecdote we read that the school of Elijah had predicted the coming of the Messiah after a period of eighty-five Jubilees from the time of creation (a Jubilee being a period of fifty years), the eighty-fifth being also the last Jubilee (Sanhedrin 97b).

To which of the two traditions did Jesus belong? It is quite clear, as is now accepted by most recent scholarship, that he belonged to the latter tradition, seeing the advent of the Messianic age in terms of the end of the world. Such verses as the following immediately spring to mind: "When they persecute you in one town, flee to the next; for truly, I say to you, you will not have gone through all the towns of Israel, before the Son of man comes" (Matt. 10:23). And: "Truly, I say to you, there are some standing here who will not taste death before they see that the kingdom of God has come with power" (Mark 9:1). These verses both look forward to the early coming of the Messiah, but neither specifically mentions the end of the world or even implies that the coming of the Messiah will be accompanied by such an event.

In a later chapter, however, there *is* a clear statement of a belief on Jesus' part of the imminent end of the world, a statement which, with slight variations, is found in all three of the synoptics (Mark 13; Matt. 24; Luke 21:5-33; 17:31-37, 26-30). As usual, we cannot be sure that these predictions, all placed in Jesus' mouth in the Gospels, really did emanate from him. The opening prophecy of the physical destruction of the Temple is more than a little suspect, for a start, and probably owes its presence in the Gospels to the actual event itself, which of course did not occur until the year 70, a generation and more after Jesus' death. But that does not mean that we can discount Jesus' authorship of the prophecy as a whole—except that it is not particularly original, deriving as it does to a considerable extent from the Book of Daniel, which is actually mentioned by Matthew (24:15). The author of the latter part of Daniel evidently identifies the Messianic age with the Maccabean victory over the Seleucid empire of

Antiochus IV Epiphanes, which had probably already occurred by the time that part of the book was written. But the language of Daniel is so obscure as to lend itself to circumstances never envisaged at the time of writing. What is more, the scenes of destruction described in Daniel may easily be used to support the view that the coming of the Messiah was to be attended by the end of the world, which appears to be a mistaken interpretation of Daniel (see especially Dan. 12:1-3), but which obviously suited other purposes, including the Christian one.

The timetable according to the Gospels (supposedly quoting Jesus) is as follows: (1) the rise of many false Messiahs coupled with wars, famine, and eathquakes, all this being termed the "birth-pangs"; (2) Jesus' followers will be harassed and put to death, and many will be attracted away by "many false prophets," "but he who endures to the end will be saved" (Matt. 24:13); (3) "and then the end will come" (Matt. 24:14), entailing "great tribulation, such as has not been from the beginning of the world until now, no, and never will be" (Matt. 24:21); (4) an eclipse of the sun and the apprarance of "the Son of man" in heaven sending out his angels to "gather his elect from the four winds" (Matt. 24:31). Finally, we learn, "this generation will not pass away till all these things take place" (Matt. 24:34).

This last statement which occurs in all three of the synoptics, predicts the end of the world within a matter of decades. This may well be an updated version of what Jesus himself had actually predicted, because it is sufficiently vague not to have been proved wrong by the time the Gospels were written (depending of course on their dates, a highly vexing question).

Was Jesus a prophet? If he did indeed prophesy the imminent end of the world (or at least within a matter of decades)—the only real prophecy which stands in his name—then he clearly was not much of a hand at prophecy!

Jesus the Teacher

But, if Jesus was no prophet (in the modern sense of the word) he clearly *was* a teacher. Even if we cannot always be sure what his exact teachings were, we can hardly doubt that he *did* teach and preach. The question, though, is: What is his stature as a teacher? How great a teacher was he?

Most people, Christian and non-Christian alike, would hardly see this as a problem at all. Jesus is, almost by definition, *the* teacher par excellence, the greatest teacher the world has ever seen. So at least most people would say.

His ability to put a point graphically—always assuming, of course, that at least some of the parables and sayings attributed to him really are his—is undoubted. But what we are more concerned with is the originality of his teachings and the quality of mind that they reveal. Most of the teachings that have come down to us under Jesus' name are decidedly not original, even where they depart from the mainstream of Jewish teaching. We are told, for example, that in order deliberately "to test him" the Pharisees asked Jesus: "Teacher, which is the great commandment in the law?" (Matt. 22:36). Why is this question made out to be such a challenge? Because the really cautious and conservative Pharisees would not wish to single out one or two laws above the rest, and this indeed is why the great Pharisaic teacher Shammai chased away the prospective proselyte who had asked him very much the same question, as we observed in another connection.

But Rabbi Hillel, the other leading Pharisee of the day, had not been so dismissive. On the contrary, his reply was to encapsulate the whole of Jewish law in the dictum, "Do not do to your neighbor that which is hateful to yourself," adding: "That is the whole law; the rest is just commentary." (Shab. 31a). In the light of this extremely radical reply of Hillel's, Jesus' answer to the Pharisees is almost tame by comparison, for, while Hillel deliberately turned the biblical injunction to love one's neighbor as oneself (Lev. 19:18) into a negative formulation, thus making it more easily attainable, Jesus merely repeated the biblical text as it stood, and added to it an injuncion which had long formed part of the traditional Jewish profession of faith, the so-called *Shema* prayer (beginning "Hear, O Israel," Deut. 6:4-5):

> And he said to him, "You shall love the Lord your God with all your heart, and with all your soul, and with all your mind. This is the great and first commandment. And a second is like it, you shall love your neighbor as yourself. On these two commandments depend all the law and the prophets. (Matt. 22:37-40).

Christians generally assume that these sentiments—and especially the injunction to *love* God and your neighbor—are especially Christian and not Jewish at all. Nothing could be further from the truth. Another basic point must be stressed: Jesus is here formulating his summary *not* of some new religion called "Christianity" but of the religion to which he belonged, Judaism. And, as I have just said, his formulation is a less radical departure from the conservative Pharisee position (as epitomized by Shammai) than Hillel's was. This is not just because Jesus encapsulated the Torah in two commandments whereas Hillel summarized it all in one. What is really significant is that Jesus' two commandments cover the two aspects of Jewish law (as represented, for example, by the two halves of the Ten Commandments), relations between man and God on the one hand and, on the other, relations between man and man.

Hillel's single commandment, however, deals only with man's relations with his fellow man, the implication being that if one got this relationship right, all else, including one's relationship with God, would flow from it. In this vital respect Hillel was more radical and original than Jesus, with Shammai of course occupying the extreme conservative position.

But that is not to say that *none* of Jesus' views were original. In going beyond one's love for one's "neighbor" and enjoining love for one's "enemy," Jesus was indeed striking out on his own (if indeed this injunction can be attributed to him rather than to a later Christian source)—in a direction, however, as we shall see in Chapter 8, which could lead nowhere but to total hypocrisy. And the same applies to the well-known injunctions to "turn the other cheek" and the like, none of which, it must be added, did Jesus himself—according to the Gospel record itself—ever show the least sign of putting into practice in his own life.

As for the teachings attributed to Jesus that have at their heart the moral that in Paul's words, "the letter killeth, but the spirit giveth life" (2 Cor. 3:6), this once again was hardly a new idea. One has only to go back to the Jewish prophets to find condemnation after condemnation of empty ceremonial and insincere ritual. Here is one typical example, the words quoted being attributed to God himself:

> I hate, I despise your feasts,
>   and I take no delight in your solemn assemblies.
> Even though you offer me your burnt offerings
>   and cereal offerings,
> I will not accept them,
> and the peace offerings of your fatted beasts
>   I will not look upon.
> Take away from me the noise of your songs;
>   to the melody of your harps I will not listen.

But let justice roll down like waters,
and righteousness like an ever-flowing stream.
(Amos 5:21-24)

These words were penned seven and a half centuries before Jesus'
birth. So much for his originality in this regard!

VII

Christianity Without Christ

Unlike Judaism, which as we have seen is a communal religion, Christianity is a creed religion. The difference comes out particularly clearly in regard to conversion. It was not only because Shammai believed that it was impossible to teach the whole of Jewish law while standing on one leg that he chased away the prospective convert; it was also because he was not particularly keen on the whole idea of conversion.

Shammai's negativism is perhaps extreme, but it is really only an exaggerated form of an attitude that has always been typical of the more conservative Jewish viewpoint. Starting from the communal basis of the religion, this conservative attitude has always required conclusive evidence that the prospective convert was prepared to commit himself not only to the Jewish form of worship and to the Jewish monotheistic belief but also to membership in a group, entailing therefore the assumption of a whole new identity. It is the difficulty involved in achieving this that has led to the negative attitude toward conversion to Judaism that has prevailed throughout most of Jewish history.

Christianity of course takes exactly the opposite view of conversion, which has always been encouraged and often enforced, not infrequently with the aid of violence and bloodshed. Pronouncing the approved formula of belief of the particular church or sect of Christianity that one wishes to join is generally all that is required on the part of the convert, who is then duly baptized as a Christian.

The Creed

It is important to test the Christian creed against the conclusions we have reached on the basis of the evidence adduced so far. We shall use the form of the so-called Apostles' Creed as it stood in the year 600, a composite and brief resume of the essentials of Christian belief. It is probably worth our while to quote it in full.

I believe in God the Father Almighty:
And in Jesus Christ, his only begotten Son, our Lord;
Who was born of the Holy Ghost and Virgin Mary,
And was crucified under Pontius Pilate, and was buried;
And the third day rose again from the dead.
Ascended into heaven, sitteth on the right hand of the Father;
Whence he shall come to judge the quick and the dead;
And in the Holy Ghost;
The Holy Church;
The remission of sins;
And the resurrection of the flesh, Amen.

It should be noted that no fewer than six of the eleven articles are concerned with Jesus. Let us take them one by one:

1. That Jesus was the Christ or Messiah. As we have seen, and despite some doughty efforts to deny it, there is no way of escaping the equation Christ = Messiah, the only snag being that Jesus cannot possibly lay legitimate claim to either the former or the latter. QED.

2. That Jesus was the son of God. This idea too, as we have noted, originated from the special father-son relationship that was always believed to exist between God and the Jewish kings, and therefore between God and the Messiah. This father-son relationship, however, carried no implication whatsoever of God's physically "begetting" a son, a pagan concept that, from the Jewish point of view, lowers the stature of God and is therefore totally unacceptable. Nevertheless, despite this pagan development of the idea, the basic original concept of the Messiah as God's "son" in some special sense is decidedly an ancient Jewish one.

3. That Jesus had a virgin birth. This is another untenable myth (see Chapter 1), but it is linked to a Messianic claim.

4. That Jesus was crucified under Pontius Pilate and buried. It is true, but why was he crucified? Yet again, as we saw in Chapter 5, the answer is: because of his Messianic claims.

5. That Jesus was resurrected. Yet another myth, as was shown in Chapter 4, but, as usual, a myth required in order to make it possible to believe that Jesus was the Messiah, because a failed and executed Messiah was seen as a contradiction in terms.

6. That Jesus ascended into heaven and sits at God's right hand. This belief obviously owes something to the biblical story of Elijah's ascent, but it is also necessitated by the belief in the Resurrection. After all, the Resurrection, according to the Gospels, was not a coming back to life for any length of time but only long enough to demonstrate Jesus' triumph over death. But, if belief in the ascension is necessitated

by acceptance of the Resurrection, then, as we have seen, the idea of Resurrection itself is a prerequisite of the validity of his Messianic claims. The only other problem with the ascension is a total lack of evidence to support it.

7. That Jesus will come down to earth "to judge the quick and the dead," a reference to the belief in a Day of Judgment, or in a so-called Last Judgment, a Jewish idea found already in the prophecies of Isaiah (3:13; 5:16), where it is associated with the Messianic age. It is hardly surprising, therefore, that Jesus should be envisaged by Christians as presiding over the Last Judgment. It is also worth nothing that in the ancient world generally—including the Roman Empire—monarchs were invested not only with executive powers and functions but also with legislative and judicial ones. The same mix of functions is also found at a lower level. Thus, the so-called "judges" of the biblical book of that name, including such famous names as Deborah, Gideon, and Samson, were most certainly not purely judicial officials but were a form of local ruler with executive and military duties as well. This is well demonstrated by the Hebrew title used to describe them: *shofet,* which is the same word as the Punic (a Semitic language) *sufet,* used of the members of the ruling oligarchy of Carthage. Similarly, the king in the ancient world was always supreme judge of his people as well as chief executive, which brings us back to the central element of the Messianic concept: its monarchical character. Accepting Jesus' role in the Last Judgment therefore depends not only on belief in such an event but also on accepting Jesus as the Messiah.

In short, all the claims made for Jesus in the Christian creed are untenable. What is more, all of them hinge on accepting him as the Messiah, which in itself is untenable, as we have seen. What effect does this have on our view of Jesus and on Christianity?

If Jesus was not the Messiah, what was he? Even his claims to being a great teacher, prophet, and ideal human being will not stand up to scrutiny as we discovered in the previous chapter. What then is left?

Jesus clearly was the leader of some sort of religious group within Judaism, though how big it was is hard to say. It certainly was by no means the only group of its kind, that of John the Baptist being another. That Jesus himself claimed to be the Messiah is more than likely, as was argued in an earlier chapter. But in this regard too he was not exceptional: there was no shortage of Messianic claimants at the time, and the Baptist may possibly have been one too. What is certain is that even if John the Baptist did not himself make that claim for himself, some of his followers clearly did.

But, you may object, that cannot possibly be all there was to Jesus. Christianity is, after all, one of the biggest success stories in history. Surely, therefore, there must be some truth to its claims! Such objections are found even in the writings of Christian theologians, including liberal theologians.

> Jesus died on the cross, and for a period beginning two days later his disciples had experiences of seeing him, which convinced them that he was alive, raised from death and exalted to God's presence in power. Without such conviction it is impossible to explain the survival of the church. (M. Goulder, "Jesus, the Man of Universal Destiny in *The Myth of God Incarnate*, 54-55)

This is an important question: How are we to explain the survival and success of Christianity if all its claims are demonstrably false?

The first fact that needs emphasizing is a paradox: that, though Christianity was esentially based on the belief that Jesus was the Jewish Messiah, this claim was never accepted by the majority of Jews, especially after Jesus' death. If Christianity had depended for its continued existence on *Jewish* acceptance of Jesus as the Messiah, which was initially the whole basis of the apostles' mission, as we have seen, then it is most unlikely that it would have lasted.

Not only the survival of Christianity but its very existence as a separate religion resulted from the fact that an active campaign to recruit non-Jews was embarked upon—pagans who were not only not much interested in the idea of a Messiah but who were also quite ready to accept a human being as a god. So, though the Christian creed is based essentially on the claim that Jesus was the Jewish Messiah, in practice Christianity did not depend upon this claim. It is for this reason, among others, that the success of Christianity in no way "proves" the truth of the claims it makes for itself.

It can, however, never be sufficiently stressed that neither Jesus nor those who after his death became the leaders of the so-called "Jerusalem church" had any intention of breaking away from Judaism. *Jesus died a Jew and his movement was a Jewish movement.* This is something that was established in Chapter 2. How, then, and why did the movement change to the extent of forming a new and quite separate religion?

The Birth of a New Religion

Even Paul, "apostle to the Gentiles," the man responsible for the existence of Christianity as a separate religion with its converts drawn from
pagan non-Jews, clearly saw the movement as part of Judaism:

> Then what advantage has the Jew? Or what is the value of circum-
> cision? Much in every way. To begin with, the Jews are entrusted
> with the oracles of God. (Rom. 3:1)

The argument Paul uses here is that the specially favored position
enjoyed by the Jewish people in the eyes of God was the result of their
faith and not of their deeds. Jews may have sinned, but that did not
abrogate God's favor, which was based on Jewish belief in Him as the
only true God. Even the patriarch Abraham, says Paul, the first Jew to
be circumcised, was justified in the eyes of God not by his deeds, including the act of circumcision, but by his faith, which in any case pre-
dated his circumcision (Rom. 4:1-12). In proof of this fundamental
assertion Paul quotes a verse from the Book of Genesis (15:6):
"Abraham believed God, and it was reckoned to him as righteousness"
(Rom. 4:3). This is an accurate enough version of the biblical verse in
question, but does it really prove what Paul wants it to prove, namely
a Jewish belief in justification by faith alone?

According to the Book of Genesis, Noah and his family were the
only human survivors of the flood. Noah had three sons, Shem, Ham,
and Japheth, who were the ancestors of all the peoples on earth,
Shem's descendants being the "Shemites" or Semites, Ham's being the
dark races of Asia and Africa (hence the term "Hamite" formerly used
in linguistic studies) and Japheth's being essentially the "Aryan"
peoples of the north and west of Europe and of European Russia. In
Chapter 10 we are given a list of the "generations" of these three father
figures, each of whom had a goodly number of children, more grand-
children, and more descendants in later generations, Abraham being of
the ninth generation of the descendants of Shem.

Abraham himself was one of three brothers, the other two being
totally unknown: Nahor and Haran. Why was Abraham singled out by
God for special treatment rather than either of his brothers, cousins, or
more distant relations? *Was* it, as Paul asserts, because of Abraham's
faith in God? No. Decidedly not. *When,* after all, does God signify the
special favor with which he views Abraham? Paul is quite right in
dating it before Abraham's circumcision but wrong in attributing it to
his faith—because it occurs before anything at all is said of Abraham's
faith. Here is the relevant passage:

> Now the LORD said to Abraham, "Go from your country and
> your kindred and your father's house to the land that I will show
> you. And I will make of you a great nation, and I will bless you,
> and make your name great, so that you will be a blessing. I will bless
> you, and him who curses you I will curse; and by you all the
> families of the earth shall bless themselves. (Gen. 12:1-3)

Abraham's first act of worship occurred only after this, when he
built an altar to God at Shechem (Nablus) (Gen. 12:7). What then of
the passage quoted by Paul to prove that Abraham's faith was the
cause of the divine favor he enjoyed? Like the clever debater that he
was, Paul has taken the passage out of context. It occurs after God has
promised Abraham a "great reward" and Abraham has objected that
such a promise was meaningless as long as he remained childless (Gen.
15:1- 3). God then reassures Abraham that "your own son shall be
your heir" (15:4) and takes him outside, where he points to the heavens
and makes the well-known promise to give Abraham descendants as
numerous as stars. It is this promise that is being referred to in the
verse cited by Paul: "And he believed the LORD; and he reckoned it
to him as righteousness" (15:6). The faith referred to here is therefore
not Abraham's belief in God as such but something much more specific:
his belief in a particular divine promise. And, moreover, the "righteousness" which is credited to Abraham for believing in this (improbable) promise is *not* the cause of the divine favor bestowed on him:
for he has already enjoyed such favor for three whole chapters.

Paul is therefore clearly wrong in his interpretation of the biblical
text dealing with Abraham's divine favor. This may well be deliberate
on Paul's part, because it enables him to establish the chief principle
differentiating Christianity from Judaism: the concept of justification
by faith alone. Just as Abraham had been singled out for special divine
favor because of his belief in the only true God, says Paul, what now
qualifies a person for divine favor is acceptance of Jesus as the
Messiah, again a matter of faith. In this way Paul is able to relegate the
question of circumcision to total insignificance and elevate the question
of faith in Jesus as the Christ to take its place as the hallmark of
membership in a divinely favored community.

> Circumcision indeed is of value if you obey the law; but if you
> break the law, your circumcision becomes uncircumcision. So, if a
> man who is uncircumcised keeps the precepts of the law, will not
> his uncircumcision be regarded as circumcision? Then those who
> are physically uncircumcised but keep the law will condemn you

who have the written code and circumcision but break the law.
For he is not a real Jew who is one outwardly, nor is true circumcision something external and physical. He is a Jew who is one
inwardly, and real circumcision is a matter of the heart, spiritual
and not literal. (Rom. 2:25-29)

In this remarkable passage Paul is at pains to reinterpret the whole
nature of circumcision. But why does he bother? Why could he not
have said simply: "Circumcision is necessary to become a Jew, but in
order to become a Christian it is not required"? *The answer is that
even he does not think of Christianity as being something separate
from Judaism.*

The problem was that in order to become a Jew a male convert
had to undergo the painful operation of circumcision, which was also
considered by the Greeks and Romans to be disfiguring. This demand
could only make Judaism very much less attractive to non-Jews than it
would otherwise have been. Hence Paul's solution. Without severing
his ties with Judaism, he reinterprets circumcision in such a way as to
make it meaningless. What he says boils down to a rejection of circumcision as the mark of a true Jew and its replacement by keeping the
law, that is, the Jewish Torah.

His argument so far is: the true Jew is not the person who is
circumcised but the one who, whether circumcised or not, keeps the
law. Keeping, that is, obeying, the precepts of the Torah was indeed a
central tenet of Judaism, so this part of what Paul had to say was not
so radical. In the Book of Leviticus Jews are enjoined: "You shall
therefore keep my statutes and my ordinances, by doing which a man
shall live" (Lev. 18:5). This was interpreted by rabbinical commentators as meaning that even a non-Jew who obeyed the Torah was
the equal of the High Priest (Sifra to Lev. 18:5; Sifra Acharei pereq
13:13; Sanders, *Paul and Palestinian Judaism,* p. 207). But, even
though the equal of the High Priest, such a non-Jew would not be
deemed to be a Jew, any more than the repentant Ninevites in the
Book of Jonah were thought to have become Jews through their acceptance of the divine warning communicated to them by that most
reluctant of all reluctant prophets, Jonah (see Chapter 2).

Herein lies the crucial difference between the Jewish view of
conversion and Paul's view of it. As Judaism is and has always been a
communal religion, no one can become a Jew without becoming a
member of that community in a very real sense. Circumcision is only
one aspect of that identity, but a necessary one nevertheless, together

with obedience to the Torah in all its rigor. For Paul, though, his abandonment of circumcision as a requirement for conversion *to Judaism* and his replacement of it with obedience to the Torah is only the first step to the conclusion we have already glimpsed.

His argument now takes a more circuitous route. The Torah, he says, is a manifestation of God's righteousness, but it is not the *only* manifestation of God's righteousness" another being "faith in Jesus Christ" (Rom. 3:21). Therefore, what is required in order to become a true Jew is belief in Jesus as Christ. This now becomes the chief criterion of conversion to Judaism *according to Paul.* Since acceptance of Jesus as the Christ had eclipsed obedience to the Torah in Paul's scheme of things, it may well have seemed to his hearers that he was now relegating the Torah to the same oblivion to which he had sought to consign circumcision. On this point, however, he demurs: "Do we then overthrow the law by this faith? By no means! On the contrary, we uphold the law" (Rom. 3:31).

This may seem a strange thing for Paul to say, especially in view of his radical departure from so many basic Jewish tenets. But the fact that he says it is itself significant. It indicates a strong desire on his part *not* to be thought to be breaking away from Judaism. However radical his departures from Jewish practice and belief may have been, *it seems clear that he did not see himself as starting a new and separate religion* but merely as redefining the question of membership in the Jewish community.

But, in replacing a communal identity with a belief—belief in Jesus as the Christ, or Messiah—Paul *had* in fact started a new religion, a creedal religion as against the *communal* religion into which he had been born.

The seriousness of the changes Paul was advocating did not go entirely unnoticed. The hostility with which the Jews greeted Paul after he preached in the synagogue at Antioch in Pisidia is recorded for us in Acts (13:45, 50); it was evidently this which had made him turn to the Gentiles (that is, non-Jews) in the first place (13:46-47). But within the Christian movement itself there was evidently some concern about this. That is why Paul is addressed by Jesus' brother James and the elders of the Jerusalem church in the way described in Acts:

> You see, brother, how many thousands there are among the Jews of those who have believed; they are all zealous for the law, and they have been told about you that you teach all the Jews who are among the Gentiles to forsake Moses, telling them not to circum-

cise their children or observe the customs. What then is to be done? They will certainly hear that you have come. Do therefore what we tell you. We have four men who are under a vow; take these men and purify yourself along with them and pay their expenses, so that they may shave their heads. Thus all will know that there is nothing in what they have been told about you but that you yourself live in observance of the law. But as for the Gentiles who have believed, we have sent a letter with our judgment that they should abstain from what has been sacrificed to idols and from blood and from what is strangled and from unchastity. (Acts 21:20-25)

James and the elders are anything but delighted to see Paul, who is evidently an embarrassment to them. They are particularly unhappy about Paul's activities amongst the Gentiles. Their phraseology is diplomatic, but what they are esentially telling Paul is that there is no shortage of good, observant Jews who accept Jesus as the Messiah and it is not therefore necessary to convert Gentiles. Such is the concern of these elders for their movement to continue to be accepted as Jewish that they instruct Paul to undergo a purificatory ceremony. The fact that there are already four men, presumably members of the Jerusalem church, who have already taken such a vow (presumably a Nazarite vow), is itself indicative of their Jewish identity.

They realize full well the threat to this identity posed by Paul's conversion of Gentiles, and their remarks on these Gentiles is most instructive of all. They do *not* demand of the Gentiles what Paul demands of them in his Letter to the Romans, namely full obedience to the Jewish Torah. Paradoxically, Gentile converts are required by James and the leaders to observe only a few much more basic and therefore easy-to-obey precepts, all negative. This is not the only time that these prohibitions are mentioned. The whole letter referred to here had already been quoted in full in Acts 15, which clarifies the matter by adding before the prohibitions the words: "For it has seemed good to the Holy Spirit and to us to lay upon you no greater burden than these necessary things" (Acts 15:28). But, why should these four prohibitions be singled out as the *only* injunctions that the Gentile brethren had to obey?

The particular prohibitions appear to derive from the so-called "Commandments of the Sons of Noah," a traditional Jewish compilation of laws (not found in the Bible as such), which non-Jews were expected to obey. These included prohibitions against immorality, idolatry, bloodshed, and the eating of flesh cut from a living animal

(Sanhedrin, 56ab); based on Genesis 9:4 ff. The point about these basic laws is that they were regarded as constituting the barest of bare necessities for a civilized society but certainly *not* as qualifying those who observed them to become converts to Judaism. It would appear, therefore, that it was not because they approved of what Paul was doing that they agreed with him that the Gentile brethren should not be required to be circumcised, but precisely because they strongly disapproved. In placing the very light burden of the "Commandments of the Sons of Noah"—and nothing else—on the Gentile "brethren," what the Jerusalem elders were tactfully signifying was that these Gentiles were *not* to be regarded as converts at all!

Though Paul himself would obviously not have agreed with that, he still continued to regard himself not only as a Jew in some nominal sense but indeed as an *observant* Jew, and those Gentiles whom he had converted he regarded as converts *not* to some new religion but to Judaism. Hence the accusation leveled against him by "Jews from Asia" that he had "brought Greeks into the temple," which was not permitted (Acts 21:28). The charge is denied by Luke, who explains it as referring to the fact that "they had previously seen Trophimus the Ephesian with him in the city, and they supposed that Paul had brought him into the temple" (21:29).

But, whether true or not, the very fact of his being accused of such a thing only underlines Paul's Jewishness. Someone who had deliberately broken with Judaism and established a new religion would surely never want to set foot in the temple! We know that Paul did not adopt this view, but unquestioningly obeyed James' order to undergo the Jewish purificatory ritual. Moreover, when on trial Paul several times reiterated his Jewishness, on one occasion actually claiming to be still a Pharisee: "Brethren, I am a Pharisee, a son of Pharisees" (Acts 23:6).

Later on, when haled before the Roman governor, Felix, he defined his movement as a branch of Judaism in the following terms: "But this I admit to you, that according to the Way, which they call a sect, I worship the God of our fathers, believing *everything* laid down by the law or written in the prophets, having a hope in God which these themselves accept, that there will be a resurrection of both the just and the unjust" (Acts 24:14-15; italics added). This is really a plea in favor of being considered an observant and orthodox Jew.

What Paul is saying here is that though his Jewish accusers ("they") would regard the Christian movement as a "sect," this "sect" actually accepted the whole of Jewish law; therefore its members were no sectaries but true orthodox Jews. Finally, when he appears before the next governor of Judea, Festus, he puts his position in these words: "Neither against the law of the Jews, nor against the temple, nor against Caesar have I offended at all" (Acts 25:8).

We may of course dismiss these repeated pleas as merely examples of expediency. But, in that case, why should he place such emphasis on his Jewish orthodoxy and comparatively so little on his loyalty to Rome? The procurator Felix certainly was no friend to the Jews, and was actually accused of gross atrocities after his period of office by the Jews of Caesarea. He is most unlikely therefore to have been much impressed by Paul's protestations of loyalty to Jewish law. In this connection the contrast between Paul and Jesus is stark; at *his* trial Jesus does *not* go out of his way to depict himself as an ultraorthodox Jew. Paul appears to have a different motive: a genuine intention of convincing not so much the Roman governor as his Jewish accusers— *and himself*—of his Jewish orthodoxy.

Hence, too, his fastening onto his belief in resurrection as the real reason for his being accused: "With respect to the resurrection of the dead I am on trial this day" (Acts 24:21). This does *not* refer to the resurrection of Jesus but to resurrection in general, as is clear from the passage quoted above in which Paul specifically speaks of his belief "that there will be a resurrection of both the just and the unjust" (Acts 24:15), a belief which in the same speech he correctly labels as an orthodox Jewish belief, more particularly a Pharisaic one, as he is well aware when confronted by both Sadducees and Pharisees in the San-hedrin, where he causes dissension between the two groups by mentioning his belief in resurrection, "for the Sadducees say that there is no resurrection, nor angel, nor spirit; but the Pharisees acknowledge them all" (Acts 23:8).

In this respect Paul is being less than completely honest. He must have known that his belief in resurrection was *not* the real reason for the Jewish hostility towards him. The real reasons clearly were his belief that Jesus was the Messiah (see Acts 28:23-24) and his conversion of Gentiles. Why then does he keep harping on this question of resurrection? Clearly in order to close the gap between himself and his Jewish foes and paint himself in the most orthodox Jewish colors possible.

Which brings us back to the question of Paul's motivation for turning to the Gentiles for converts. It is worth noting that, despite his many rebuffs at the hands of Jews in a number of different cities, even finally in Rome he still tries to convert them to his way of thinking, and it is only when they to fail to be convinced that Paul angrily rounds on them and concludes: "Let it be known to you then that this salvation of God has been sent to the Gentiles; they will listen" (Acts 28:29), a sentiment echoed in the famous verse in Romans: "For I am not ashamed of the gospel: it is the power of God for salvation to every one who has faith, *to the Jew first* and also to the Greek" (Rom. 1:16; italics added).

It is worth nothing in this connection that the term *Christian* was not initially applied by Christians to themselves. It was in fact a term of abuse applied to them by pagans, while the Jews referred to them as *Nazarenes* (from Nazareth). It took a long time for Christians to regard themselves as anything but Jews, and the Jerusalem church only ceased to be regarded as Jewish about half a century after Jesus' death, while members of this conservative branch of Christianity continued to regard themselves as Jews down to the fourth century, continuing the practice of circumcision and the observance of Jewish law as a whole.

Earlier in this chapter we asked the question: How can we explain the survival and success of Christianity if its claims are untrue? We are now in a position to supply an answer, and it is a paradox. Had Jesus and his disciples managed to persuade their Jewish compatriots of the truth of their claims—notably that Jesus was the Messiah—it is most unlikely that Christianity would ever have come into existence as a separate religion at all. Nor is this purely hypothetical, for, as we have just seen, there *were* groups of Jewish-Christians who *did* accept Jesus as the Messiah but continued to practice their ancestral Jewish faith. Had Jews as a whole accepted Jesus as the Messiah, this belief could quite easily have been incorporated into Judaism without starting a new religion.

Why then *did* Christianity become a new and separate religion? Precisely because the bulk of the Jews were *not* persuaded of the truth of the claims made for Jesus. And *why* were they not persuaded? For the reasons given in detail in the previous chapters of this book: in short, because these claims clearly were *not true*. Why then were these claims so much more attractive and acceptable to pagan non-Jews? Because pagan religions were not concerned with historical truth, and it was in any case a matter of indifference to non-Jews whether Jesus (or anyone else, for that matter) was or was not the Jewish Messiah. What is more, the polytheistic pagan mind did not see the concepts of "man" and "god" as separated by the same great and unbridgeable chasm as appeared from the strictly Jewish vantage point.

The way was now open for the development of a number of totally un-Jewish and frankly pagan features in Christianity: (1) the Trinity, a concept as alien to Judaism as it was repugnant to it, and in effect a negation of true monotheism; (2) the cult of the Virgin Mary, combining two frequent pagan motifs: virgin birth and female mother-deities (for example, the Egyptian goddess Isis); (3) the sprouting of images, icons, and relics in Christian churches, many of which came to be invested with supernatural powers of their own—a return to idolatry, if viewed from the Jewish point of view; (4) the growth of an army of saints to whom Christians could appeal to intercede on their behalf, another polytheistic feature; (5) monasticism, a development of a type of extreme asceticism that has never had any place in maintream Judaism but which is to be associated with the East and with an ascetic streak in Greek thinking that went back to ancient times.

Creed Community

One distinguishing feature of the new religion, which may seem difficult to trace back to polytheistic paganism, is Christianity's extreme intolerance. After all, as we have seen, a polytheistic pagan religion such as that of Rome could always make room for a new god here and a new cult there—always provided that these new fads did not demand exclusive loyalty at the expense of the total eclipse of the "official" state religion and its gods. But this, of course, is precisely what Christianity *did* demand—total and exclusive loyalty, with the pagan gods (who, interestingly enough, were *not* said to be nonexistent) demoted to the rank of "demons" (not originally a term of opprobrium).

Judaism also demands total and exclusive loyalty—and has indeed been much less accommodating of pagan ideas and practices. Why then is it that Judaism has never been as intolerant of other religions—nor indeed of divisions within itself—as Christianity has been? The answer brings us back to the central difference between the two religions, the difference between a communal and a creedal religion. Being a communal religion, Judaism demands the exclusive loyalty of members of the Jewish community and of anyone who wishes to join the Jewish fold, but, by the same token, it has no claim—and wants no claim—on anyone outside the Jewish community. The only time in history when any degree of compulsion was employed on non-Jews to become Jews was in the time of the second temple, when, especially under King John Hyrcanus, a great expansion took place in the extent of the Jewish state. Among the conquered territories was Galilee, and there as in the other conquered areas the Jewish faith was imposed on the local population.

Far from being a denial of Jewish principles, this only underlines them, being nothing other than a direct application of the communal religious mentality. According to this communal outlook, religion and group identity are identical. In order to join the Jewish *religion* one has to join the Jewish *people*—and vice versa, which was the case in the reign of John Hyrcanus: the Galileans and others were now part of the Jewish *people;* therefore they had also to become Jews in *religion*.

We saw a different aspect of this same phenomenon in Chapter 2 in connection with the Book of Jonah, in which, though the people of Nineveh accept God and repent of their evil doing, and are in turn forgiven, there is never any question that they should become Jews. Jonah's is not a proselytizing mission in the Christian sense of the word. Another very well-known biblical text which brings out this basic dichotomy between the two religions is worth quoting:

It shall come to pass in the latter days
that the mountain of the house of the LORD
shall be established as the highest of the mountains,
and shall be raised up above the hills;
and peoples shall flow to it,
    and many nations shall come and say:
"Come, let us go up to the mountain of the LORD,
to the house of the God of Jacob;
that he may teach us his ways
    and we may walk in his paths."
For out of Zion shall go forth the law,
    and the word of the LORD from Jerusalem.
He shall judge between many peoples,
    and shall decide for strong nations afar off;
and they shall beat their swords into ploughshares,
    and their spears into pruning hooks;
nation shall not lift up sword against nation,
    neither shall they learn war any more;
but they shall sit every man under
his vine and under his fig tree,
    and none shall make them afraid;
    for the mouth of the LORD of hosts has spoken.
For all the peoples walk
    each in the name of its god,
but we will walk in the name of the
    LORD our God
    for ever and ever. (Micah 4:1-5)

The phrase translated here as "in the latter days" (line 1) may well have contributed to the belief that Jesus evidently shared with certain other Jews of his day that the coming of the Messiah would mark the end of the world, something which is clearly *not* intended if we continue reading, because the prophecy as a whole is one which, while depicting a very changed world indeed, clearly envisages the changes taking place in our same physical and material world. For example, though there is to be universal peace, there will still be separate nations—each still worshiping its own god, as we learn in the last verse. This, many commentators believe, is at variance with the initial picture of many different peoples going up to the mountain of the Lord, an interpretation which is aided by the fact that this same passage occurs in the Book of Isaiah, minus the last two verses, from "but they shall sit . . . " (Isa. 2:2-4).

From the Christian point of view, there certainly does seem to be a serious contradiction here. What, after all, this view maintains, could the first few verses mean if not that many nations from all over the world will accept the truth of Christianity *by converting to it?* If this Christian interpretation is adopted, then the last part of the quotation must certainly appear to contradict it.

But this, I believe, is a totally false reading of the passage as a whole and imposes Christian-type notions, based on creed, upon a text written in quite a different spirit. The acceptance of the teachings of God by many nations is surely to be understood in much the same way as the acceptance of divine guidance by the people of Nineveh in the Book of Jonah (see Chapter 2): recognition of God's wisdom and power by non-Jews who remain non-Jews. Once the first few verses quoted are seen in this light, it will immediately be observed that there is no conflict whatsoever between them and the last two verses, which indeed are simply a continuation of the ideas already implicit in the earlier verses. The last verse but one ("but they shall sit every man under his vine and under his fig tree") is one of the most beautiful and evocative of all biblical pictures. If taken literally, it surely reflects the independence that will come to even the humblest farmer secure in the possession of his own little patrimony. But, may it not perhaps be taken in a slightly different sense, in which each "man" stands for a nation? If so, this verse makes the perfect transition between the preceding picture of peace and the last verse, which explains the basis of that peace: mutual tolerance, something which a communal system of religion *can* achieve but a creed religion like Christianity never can.

That Judaism is an exclusive religion is undeniable. Conversion to Judaism has not normally been encouraged and when permitted at all has not been made easy. Jews are expected to obey elaborate rules and regulations (613 in the written Torah alone, not counting the myriad additional ones in the "oral law"), while non-Jews are expected to do no more than observe the extremely basic "Seven Commandments of the Sons of Noah," a sign that non-Jews are regarded as morally inferior to Jews. Exclusive? Undoubtedly. But it is this very exclusivism that has made for tolerance, just the sort of tolerance that is reflected in the last verse of the quoted passage of Micah. Precisely *because* non-Jews are expected to remain non-Jews, their religious differences from Judaism are accepted as part of the normal state of affairs, so much so, indeed, that it is not expected to change even with the coming of the Messiah!

But if, paradoxically, *exclusivism* breeds *tolerance,* then we should not be surprised to find that *intolerance* is the product of *inclusivism.* If you expect everyone else to give up his religion and accept yours, then anyone who refuses to do so must surely be in the wrong and should be punished. This is exactly the Christian position. Christianity is not exclusive. Quite the reverse. Millions are spent every year in order to persuade non-Christians that Christianity—and Christianity alone—has, or indeed *is* "the truth" and that they should therefore convert to it and be "saved." *But the very propaganda employed to attract converts has to condemn all non-Christian religions as false,* since Christianity alone is supposedly "true." *Intolerance springs quite naturally from the inclusivist nature of the Christian religion,* and it did not take long before this intolerance spread within Christianity itself. Based as it is on belief, or creed, the slightest deviation in belief is quickly labeled "heresy" and treated accordingly, with the usual inclusivist intolerance.

So, that is one paradox that has been established in this chapter: that Judaism is exclusive but tolerant, whereas Christianity is inclusive but intolerant. The second paradox, which was established first, is that the survival and success of Christianity is explained *not* by the truth of the Christian claims but by their falsity.

This leads to yet a third paradox. We have seen that Christianity is not at all based on the true story of Jesus of Nazareth (and even the one we have is not particularly edifying). But what we have also discovered is that the view that Jesus was the Messiah, or Christ, is quite-untenable. In a very real sense, therefore, not only is Jesus the man-irreleant to Christianity, but so is "Jesus the Christ." The "Christ" of-Christianity is esentially a pagan god in an inclusivist, intolerant creed-religion.

VIII

A New Ethic?

"Thou shalt love thy neighbor as thyself," to quote the beautiful AV translation, is perhaps *the* best-known of all biblical injunctions. Christians quite often take it to be a peculiarly Christian teaching, and of course it *is* one of the two commandments singled out by Jesus as constituting the essence of the Jewish religion (Mark 12:31-33; Matt. 22:39-40). But the injunction itself in fact comes from that most temple-oriented of all the books of the Bible, Leviticus (19:18).

On another occasion, however, according to Matthew (but not Mark), Jesus quotes the "love your neighbor" injunction—with a choice addition—only to dismiss it out of hand:

> You have heard that it was said, "You shall love your neighbor and hate your enemy." But I say to you, Love your enemies and pray for those who persecute you, so that you may be sons of your Father who is in heaven; for he makes his sun rise on the evil and on the good, and sends rain on the just and on the unjust. For if you love those who love you, what reward have you? Do not even the tax collectors do the same? And if you salute only your brethren, what more are you doing than others? Do not even the Gentiles do the same? You, therefore, must be perfect, as your heavenly Father is perfect. (Matt. 5:43-48)

If this is really what Jesus said, it does not reflect at all well on his capacity for biblical exegesis but reveals weaknesses similar to his interpretation of Psalm 110, which we have already had occasion to discuss. For one thing, he adds to the "love your neighbor" commandment a negative injunction, entirely of his own invention: "and hate your enemy." Why does he make so crude an "addition" to the biblical commandment? The only possible explanation, in view of what he goes on to "deduce" from this, is that he has added the nonexistent negative commandment to the real positive one in order the better to be able to disparage the positive "love your neighbor" teaching and to replace it with his own "love your enemy." His argument, however, is dishonest throughout. After grossly distorting the commandment by means of his unwarranted addition to the text, he then proceeds to misinterpret it outrageously—and, without doubt, deliberately. It is hard to believe that this is the self-same law he is to single out only a few chapters later, in the same Gospel, as one of the two "great" commandments on which "depend all the law and the prophets" (Matt. 22:37-40).

He equates "love your neighbor" with "love those who love you," which is not the same thing at all, but this certainly makes it easy for him to characterize it as something that even tax a collector would do without any prompting and therefore is not a moral injunction at all. It may well be that "love your neighbor" originally referred only to one's fellow Jews. The context certainly would support this view:

> You shall not hate your brother in your heart, but you shall reason with your neighbor, lest you bear sin because of him. You shall not take vengeance or bear any grudge against the sons of your own people, but you shall love your neighbor as yourself. (Lev. 19:17-18).

But even loving your compatriot is by no means equivalent to loving only those who love you. Private enmities frequently arise between people living in close proximity to one another and sharing the same nationality, religion, and social background—probably more frequently than between people of totally different backgrounds who are less likely to come into sufficiently close contact for open hostility to arise. It is therefore far from meaningless to say "love your neighbor as yourself." On the contrary, it is so difficult for most people to love anyone else *nearly* as much as themselves that it may well turn out to be true that *no one* has *ever* put this basic precept into practice.

In the midst of advocating loving your enemy Jesus gives himself away by disparaging the Gentiles, that is, non-Jews. So much for Jesus' own observance of his new doctrine. Not of course that he was any more successful in practice in obeying the "easy" original "love thy neighbor" doctrine. Who, after all, were his neighbors if not the Sadduces, whom he excoriated, and the Pharisees, whom he reviled?

We are still left with a puzzle, though: Why did Jesus put forward the "love your enemy" doctrine at all—always supposing of course that he actually *did*—especially in view of his later endorsement of the very doctrine which he here contemptuously waves aside, "love your neighbor as yourself." I believe the reason is the same we have seen in connection with certain other of his pronouncements: no reason other than to differ from the conventional Jewish position. This may seem to beg more questions than it answers. Why, after all, *should* anyone disagree just for the sake of disagreeing? In order to set himself up as *the* great authority, an attitude that squares only too well with the mentality of a man who believes, in the face of all evidence, that he himself is the Messiah!

The story of the Good Samaritan is supposedly told by Jesus in answer to the question put to him by one of his interlocuters: "And who is my neighbor?" (Luke 10:29). In the story a man, presumably a Jew, "fell among thieves," who beat and stripped him, leaving him half dead by the roadside, and he is then ignored by a Jewish priest and a Levite, who both "passed by on the other side," and he is finally rescued by a Samaritan, who binds up his wounds, takes him to an inn, and pays for his upkeep out of his own pocket. "Which of these three, do you think," asks Jesus, "proved neighbor to the man who fell among the robbers?" (Luke 10:30-37). The point he is making is that one should treat everyone as one's neighbor. This is exemplified by his choice of a Samaritan as the hero of the story, a story which, it should be noted, does not claim to have any basis in fact. There was no love lost between Samaritans and Jews. The Jews looked down on the Samaritans, whose claim to Jewishness alternated with acts of treachery against the Jews, while the Samaritans hated the Jews for not recognizing them as true Jews. Therefore, for a Jew to love a Samaritan or vice versa was really so great an extension of the idea of loving your neighbor as to amount to loving your enemy.

But if this *is* the way one should interpret the word *neighbor*—so as to include anyone with whom one might happen to come into contact—then there is clearly no point in rejecting the injunction to "love your neighbor" and replace it with "love your enemy," for the term *neighbor* is here so broad as to be all-embracing and to include *enemy* within it.

This only confirms the explanation that I gave for Jesus' position: his willful arrogance. He first rejects "love your neighbor" as being meaningless and substitutes for it "love your enemy." But the next thing you know he labels "love your neighbor" one of the two greatest laws! Then finally he reinterprets it so that "love your neighbor" is *equivalent* to "love your enemy," thus making his initial repudiation of the first and its replacement by the second nonsensical.

On the whole, though, it may be said that Jesus adopts a more extreme position than the orthodox Jewish one, a position that takes the Jewish teaching not to its logical but to its illogical conclusion. "Love your enemy" is a prime example of this. It sounds good, but it is an unattainable goal, an unnatural ideal. But, you may object, what can possibly be wrong with aiming high? The trouble is that any man of even moderate honesty will not be able to help admitting to himself not only that he *cannot* reach this goal but also that more often than not he does exactly the opposite. At best one might ignore one's enemy, turn one's back on him, forget him and even possibly, in very rare cases, forgive him. But love him? And, in particular, love him as much as one loves oneself? Never. The insistence upon this impossible ideal can lead in only one direction: to hypocrisy.

Nor does this depend on the way one defines the term *enemy*. Christianity has had, in practice, a wonderful facility for *creating* enemies. By the time of Augustine, when Christianity had already become the official religion of the Roman Empire, there were no fewer than two hundred different "heresies," as that worthy himself informs us—and that does not of course include any non-Christian "unbelievers," but only Christian sects whose doctrines, often differing only in some minute particular from the orthodoxy of the day, earned their adherents persecution, torture, and death.

The "love your enemy" injunction appears in quite a different context in Luke from the one in which it is embedded in Matthew's Gospel:

> Woe to you, when all men speak weil of you, for so their fathers did to the false prophets.
>
> But I say to you that hear, Love your enemies, do good to those who hate you, bless those who curse you, pray for those who abuse you. To him who strikes you on the cheek, offer the other also; and from him who takes away your coat do not withhold even your shirt. Give to every one who begs from you; and of him who takes away your goods do not ask them again. And as you wish that men would do to you, do so to them. (Luke 6:26-31)

In Matthew the same concept that is expressed in the last verse quoted is found in slightly different surroundings:

> Ask, and it will be given you; seek, and you will find; knock, and it will be opened to you. For every one who asks receives, and he who seeks finds, and to him who knocks it will be opened. Or what man of you, if his sons ask him for bread, will give him a

stone? Or if he asks for a fish, will give him a serpent? If you then, who are evil, know how to give good gifts to your children, how much more will your Father who is in heaven give good things to those who ask him! So whatever you wish that men would do to you, do so to them; for this is the law and the prophets. (Matt. 7:7-12)

"Do unto others as you would have them do to you" is perhaps the most familiar form of the injunction found at the end of both these passages. In Luke, this idea is apparently tacked on to what goes before and adds to it. In Matthew it is merely a summing up of the foregoing verses and does not really add anything to them. But this enables us to understand the injunction better. As Matthew makes clear, this injunction essentially demands a standard of behavior equivalent to that of God. The argument is insidious and runs something like this: *Every man will give his children whatever they ask for. Yet all men are evil. God, who is good, will therefore do even more for His children than merely give them what they ask.* So far the argument is unobjectionable but what comes next does not follow logically from what has been said up to this point: *Therefore,* you (Jesus' followers) *must imitate God and give not only what is requested of you but much more.* And then comes the famous injunction: treat others *not* as they treat you but as you would *like* them to treat you. Presumably, therefore, if you would *like* everyone you meet to hand you a gold coin (and who would not like that?), then *you* must present a gold coin to each of them, even though they do *not* actually give you any!

Once again, the teaching is so idealistic as to be nonsensical, and once again can only lead to hypocrisy. Anybody who claims actually to have achieved these ideals in practice is an arch-hypocrite. Jesus himself could certainly not (honestly) have made such a claim, though he is commonly thought to have been a perfect human being. But, did he treat the Pharisees and, for that matter, the Gentiles (barring one or two individual cases which we have already discussed) as they *wished* to be treated? Certainly not.

The contrast between Jesus' "do unto others" doctrine and the version of it propounded by Rabbi Hillel is instructive. "Do not do to your fellow man that which is hateful to yourself" (Shabbat 31a) is his teaching. This does *not* require you to hand everyone gold coins just because that is the way you would like others to treat *you*. It *does* require you to abstain from beating people about the head, if that is something that you would *not* like done to yourself. In other words, it is a much more realistic and attainable—though still not *easy*—ideal.

There are several popular English expressions which reflect the psychological attitudes involved here. Once one has started doing something "bad," like eating a chocolate between meals (especially if one happens to be on a diet), it is sometimes thought that one might as well "go the whole hog." One could, in those circumstances, also have said that one "might as well be hanged for a sheep as for a lamb." What these expressions seek to convey is the idea that once you have crossed the supposed borderline between "good" and "bad," it does not really matter how far over the border you go. Once you have broken your strict diet by eating just one tiny little chocolate, that's it: your diet is broken, so it doesn't matter if you now have a second chocolate or even if you finish the whole box in one sitting! Of course, this is illogical. After all, one chocolate may add a few extra calories to your intake, but its effect can easily be counteracted by eating that much less later on. In practice, of course, things rarely work that way, and once one has "broken" one's diet without being struck down at once by a thunderbolt, the tendency is to continue to make further inroads into the sacred dictates of the diet.

Looked at from a slightly different point of view, this attitude can be expressed by the phrase "a miss is as good as a mile," which is usually used in relation to achieving a particular objective, such as passing an examination. If someone who has failed a particular examination is told by way of consolation that he has failed by only one mark, he may retort that a miss is as good as a mile. In that sort of context, we cannot but agree with him: in practice it makes no difference whether he missed obtaining a passing grade by one percentage point or fifty.

This miss-is-as-good-as-a-mile mentality is exactly what the Christian ethic encourages. Where Jesus is reported as advocating the "love your enemy" doctrine, he does not say: "Loving your enemy would be best, but if you can't manage it then loving your neighbor is still highly commendable." Not at all. On the contrary, he *rejects* "love your neighbor" as an ideal when enjoining "love your enemy." This does not of course mean that he is opposed to the idea of loving your neighbor; but he does not regard it as being an ideal worth striving for because he takes it for granted.

This means that "love your enemy," and not "love your neighbor," represents the Christian "pass mark" in ethics. The result is that (unless he rejects the criterion altogether and thus essentially ceases to be a Christian) *every single Christian must regard himself as a moral failure.* It is no good his saying, "I haven't managed to love my enemy, but I do sometimes love my neighbor as myself," because loving his neighbor cannot earn him a passing grade. Only loving his enemy can do that—and that is impossible!

In effect, therefore, the Christian is actually *discouraged* from loving his neighbor by an ethic which is supposedly "higher" than that. At the same time he is *encouraged* to boast of the superiority of his religion's ethical code—something Christians do all the time. The result is an unbridgeable chasm between theory and practice. In other words, hypocrisy.

The whole Christian ethic is well summed up in the last verse of the passage in Matthew quoted above advocating the doctrine of "love your enemy": "You, therefore, must be perfect, as your heavenly Father is perfect" (Matt. 5:48). Like so many Christian teachings, this is an extreme form of a Jewish one: "You shall be holy; for I the LORD your God am holy" (Lev. 19:2). This formula, uttered here by God himself, is repeated several times in slightly varying forms. The Hebrew word translated as *holy* is *qadosh,* which evidently derives from a root signifying separation, thus "set aside," "set apart," or "special." The *holiness* of God is therefore an expression of precisely that separation between God and man, that unbridgeable gulf between the human and the divine, that so distinguishes Judaism from the pagan religions.

This concept certainly places the Jews on a pedestal in relation to other peoples—a type of Jewish arrogance, if you like—but what it does not do is to claim that Jews are perfect. Yet, that is what Jesus instructs his followers to be. The "you shall be holy" of Leviticus becomes in Matthew, "You must be perfect"—a very different proposition altogether and once again an impossible one. The Greek word translated as *perfect, teleios,* comes from the word *telos,* meaning a "goal" or "limit." A *teleios* man is therefore one who has achieved his "goal," presumably the "goal" of the divine creation of man, which in a loose sense may be identified as "goodness."

In demanding that his followers be "perfect" Jesus was setting the pass mark at one hundred percent, thus making it impossible for anyone to reach it—and positively discouraging to anyone trying to reach a more reasonable and attainable level of goodness, which could by definition be awarded only a failing mark.

Turning the Other Cheek

In Luke, in the passage quoted above (6:27-31), the idea of doing to others as you would have them do to you is linked with the equally well-known injunction to turn the other cheek. Matthew puts this doctrine in a different, and once again, more easily intelligible, context:

> You have heard that it was said, "An eye for an eye and a tooth for a tooth." But I say to you, Do not resist one who is evil. But if any one strikes you on the right cheek, turn to him the other also; and if any one would sue you and take your coat, let him have your cloak as well; and if any one forces you to go one mile, go with him two miles. (Matt. 5:38-41)

Today the doctrine of "an eye for an eye" is commonly thought to be barbaric, a view which is not infrequently heard from Christian pulpits. By Talmudic times the doctrine was no longer applied literally but was taken to mean that suitable monetary compensation had to be paid by the guilty party. There is in fact an interesting discusion of "an eye for an eye" to be found in the Talmud, in which it is concluded that it would make no sense to take it literally, for what would happen if, for example, a blind man knocked out the eye of a sighted man? (B.K. 83b ff.). Nevertheless, it may well be that "an eye for an eye" *had* originally been taken literally. The wording of the doctrine in Leviticus seems to point in this direction: "When a man causes a disfigurement in his neighbor, as he has done it shall be done to him, fracture for fracture, eye for eye, tooth for tooth; as he has disfigured a man, he shall be disfigured" (Lev. 24:19-22).

But, whether taken literally or metaphorically, the basic principle is the same, namely that whoever is *responsible* for causing harm to another must be punished for what he has done, and his punishment must match the harm he has done.

Is that an unfamiliar doctrine? Not at all. Anybody in the modern world with the slightest familiarity with modern law and legal concepts will find it only too familiar. It is in fact the whole basis of all modern systems of criminal law and of tort (or delict). In both these huge areas of law, one of the fundamental questions must always be whether the defendant was responsible for the harm done. If, for example, a house collapses soon after it is built killing the householder, who is responsible? Is the builder responsible? Not unless the collapse was the result of his shoddy workmanship or negligence, and even then it would certainly not be considered right today to regard this as on a par with murder and to put the builder to death (or give him a sentence of life imprisonment), because one very important element is missing: intention. These two related concepts are paramount in any modern judicial system: responsibility and intention. What, after all, is the difference between accidentally killing someone in a motor accident and shooting him dead from the top of a high building? Intention. Hence only the latter can be regarded as a case of murder, the other only as manslaughter—even though the end-result is the same: a human being has lost his life.

In the Babylonian law code of Hammurabi, which predates the Mosaic code, we find a rather different attitude prevailing. If a builder puts up a house that collapses as a result of poor workmanship and kills the owner, the builder himself is to be put to death (section 229). Even this would today be considered unduly harsh, but Hammurabi goes on to say that if the person killed as a result of the collapse is the owner's *son,* then not the builder but the builder's *son* is to be put to death (section 230). To our way of thinking this is so preposterous as to be funny, but Hammurabi did not intend it as a joke. The point is that he was not working on the basis of the principle of responsibility. The fact that the builder's son had had nothing to do with the building of the house and cannot possibly therefore be held responsible for the collapse is irrelevant to his way of thinking. Nor is this an isolated example. If a man strikes another man's daughter and causes her death, who do you suppose is to be punished? Needless to say, *not* the murderer but his *daughter* is to be put to death (section 210).

Certain enactments of the Mosaic Code are clearly intended to correct and counteract such illogicalities and injustices. "Life for life, eye for eye, tooth for tooth, hand for hand, foot for foot" (Deut. 19:21) takes on a somewhat different coloring when seen against the background of the Babylonian Code. In Hammurabi the value placed on an eye, a tooth, or a life is by no means fixed: it depends entirely on the social status of its owner. So, in the case of the killing by a man of another man's daughter, that is not the whole story. The case mentioned above, in which the death of someone else's daughter is to be compensated for by having one's own daughter put to death, applies only if the families concerned are both noble. If, however, a nobleman causes the death of a commoner's daughter, then not only is the nobleman's daughter spared but the nobleman himself is only required to pay a (fairly stiff) fine (section 212). If it is a slave woman who has been killed the fine is rather less (section 214).

In the Mosaic Code, if free people are involved on both sides, their status is totally irrelevant, though slaves *are* treated as being of less value than free men. The general principle is the modern one of equality before the law: "You shall do no injustice in judgment; you shall not be partial to the poor or defer to the great, but in righteousness shall you judge your neighbor" (Lev. 19:15). This principle, together with those of responsibility and intention, are at the very heart of the Mosaic Code of laws as well as of modern Western judicial systems. But these principles are not to be found in the teachings of Jesus, who actually repudiates them. He rejects the principle of "eye for eye" in favor of the amoral principle, "Do not resist one who is evil," which if put into practice could only lead to a burgeoning of crime, violence, and dishonesty of every type (of which there is surely enough already, even without further encouragement). Jesus' forgiveness of the woman taken in adultery also ties in here as another example of an amoral attitude to justice.

Sexual Morality

But, while in conformity with Jesus' socially disruptive nonresistance to evil, his attitude to the adulteress is quite at loggerheads with his general attitude to sexual morality, which was anything but lax:

> You have heard that it was said, "You shall not commit adultery." But I say to you that every one who looks at a woman lustfully has already committed adultery with her in his heart. (Matt. 5:27-28)

Once again, as on so many other occasions, Jesus specifically differs from the normal Jewish law by taking up a much more extreme position. As usual, his position here is *so* extreme as to be meaningless. It equates the sin of "looking lustfully" at a woman with the much more serious sin of adultery as defined in Jewish law. If we take "looking lustfully" as being essentially synonymous with "coveting," then this was already a sin in Jewish law, and indeed in the Ten Commandments, but that still does not make it identical to adultery, which of course also earns special mention in the Ten Commandments. In certain circumstances (though not all) adultery carried the death penalty. But how was one to assess the punishment called for by "looking lustfully" at a woman? For that matter, how was one to prove whether a particular man was guilty of this offence or not?

Not that Jesus was unique in lumping lustful looks together with adultery proper. As we know from the Talmud, there were also some Jewish rabbis who took this view: "not merely one who sins with his body is called an adulterer, but he who sins with his eye is also so named" (Lev. R. 23:12).

Traditional Jewish practice has always tried to diminish the opportunities available for sexual arousal by segregating the sexes as much as possible. That is why, to this day, men and women sit separately in Orthodox synagogues. In some the women are obscured from view by a curtain, and in others they are confined to an upstairs gallery. Some very observant Jewish men will never shake hands with a woman, for the same reason, and traditional Jewish dancing is performed by separate groups of men and women. If a man and a woman *were* to dance together, they would take the floor with each holding opposite ends of a handkerchief.

Such practices may seem prudish in terms of the standards of the "permissive" age in which we live, but they are essentially an attempt to keep sexual feelings within bounds, not to suppress them altogether. They do *not,* for example, imply that lustful looks are equivalent to adultery.

If lustful looks *are* equated with adultery, then we must revise our opinion not only of lustful looks but also of adultery itself. Lustful looks may then appear to be no better than adultery, but adultery must by the same token be no worse than lustful looks. Moreover, once a man is guilty of lustful looks (and how many are not?), he must consider himself an adulterer. What then is to stop him from actually committing "real" adultery? Once again, the pass mark has been set at one hundred percent. A mark of ninety-nine percent is just as much a fail mark as twenty percent. So, once one little lustful glance has cost a man that one percentage point, why should he not go the whole hog?

But Jesus has not quite finished with the question of adultery:

> It was also said, "Whoever divorces his wife, let him give her a certificate of divorce." But I say to you that everyone who divorces his wife, except on the ground of unchastity, makes her an adulteress; and whoever marries a divorced woman commits adultery. (Matt. 5:31-32; see also Luke 16:18)

Divorce may certainly get out of hand, as has happened in the Western world in recent times, but it is essentially intended as a form of safety valve, to enable two "incompatible" people to stop torturing each other. To force every marriage, once contracted, to last until the death of one of the spouses can only result *in practice* in encouraging extramarital affairs, prostitution, and even "divorce Italian style" (that is, murder), all of which have flourished in Christian countries which have followed this supposedly "higher" morality.

Why, in any case, *should* divorce be regarded as inevitably leading to adultery? It is the result of an arbitrary definition on Jesus' part. Starting with the unwarranted definition of marriage as a lifelong bond which can never be dissolved, any married person who has sexual relations with anyone other than his or her initial spouse is by definition an adulterer, even though the original marriage has been legally ended and the person with whom the "adulterer" is supposedly committing adultery is his or her new—and perfectly legal—spouse. In short, it is a circular argument. If you do not recognize divorce, then any remarriage can only be classified as adultery. Why? Because you do not recognize the second marriage. Why not? Because you do not recognize divorce. QED.

Paul's "rather marry than burn" is really an extension of Jesus' ideas on sex:

> To the unmarried and the widows I say that it is well for them to remain single as I do. But if they cannot exercise self-control, they should marry. For it is better to marry than to be aflame with passion. (1 Cor. 7:8-9)

Once one has extended the bounds of adultery to include "lustful looking" and remarriage after divorce, it is not a tremendous leap to regard any form of sexual activity, including marriage itself, as essentially bad. With Paul celibacy became the Christian sexual ideal—one totally at variance with the Jewish outlook on life.

Judaism has always been concerned to recognize human nature for what it is—physical, material and selfish—and to keep it under control, within bounds. An attempt to curb selfishness is made by the requirement to "love your neighbor as yourself"—a difficult but not impossible ideal. The Jew is not enjoined to love his enemy, an unattainable and impractical ideal, as we have seen, and one which is more likely to do harm than good, but he is commanded to help his enemy in a practical way:

> If you meet your enemy's ox or his ass going astray, you should bring it back to him. If you see the ass of one who hates you lying under its burden, you shall refrain from leaving him with it, you shall help him to lift it up. (Exod. 23:4-5).

Here we have no fanciful ideal or high-sounding principle but a down-to-earth commandment which is well within the reach of anyone.

While helping your enemy, you are not required to "love" him, or even to like him, but such cooperation as is required of you here is undoubtedly more likely to reconcile you with your enemy than all the high-flown hypocrisy of those who proclaim "love" but do not even practise common courtesy.

Similarly, the Jewish attitude to sex is not to try to suppress it altogether but rather to channel the sexual desire along socially acceptable lines. Adultery is condemned, but it is carefully defined, and different types of adultery are distinguished from one another. If a married woman commits adultery, she is to be put to death together with her partner in crime (Deut. 22:22). If, however, the woman is betrothed but not yet married, both adulterers are to be stoned to death only if the adultery took place in an urban area, but if it happened out in the country then only the man is put to death, the woman going scot free (Deut. 22:23-27). But if the woman is a virgin who is not even betrothed, then all the man has to do is to pay the girl's father fifty silver shekels and marry her (Deut. 22:28-29).

Why these wide discrepancies in the treatment of the same crime? Surely adultery is adultery? Not at all. Here we have an excellent example of the practical approach of Jewish law. We may not agree with the premise—which runs right through the Bible—that a wife "belongs" to her husband, but once we have identified it we will find that the apparent inconsistencies between the different punishments meted out to the different kinds of adultery disappear. Thus, if we start from the assumption that a married woman "belongs" to her husband, then anyone committing adultery with her is clearly harming her husband, as she is herself by consenting. Hence the harsh penalty laid down for this type of adultery. By the same token, however, an un-married and unbetrothed virgin does not "belong" to any man (except, in a rather different sense, to her father), which is why adultery with her is punished so much less severely. The case of the betrothed but unmarried woman falls between these two extremes. As she "belongs" to her fiancé she is expected to resist the advances of any other man. That is why she goes unpunished if the act occurs in the countryside; she is presumed to have called out for help and her cries to have gone unheeded. But if it occurs in town, then it is known that she did *not* cry for help, which of course can only mean that she was a willing partner in the adulterous act and therefore she was party to the harm inflicted on her fiancé.

We find at work here once again the principles of responsibility and of making the punishment fit the harm done. Human nature is harnessed in the interests of the good of the community as a whole. Sex, it is assumed by Christianity as well as by Judaism, was intended by nature as a mechanism for the propagating of the species. On this basis it becomes quite understandable to condemn any form of sexual activity that cannot possibly lead to procreation—masturbation and homosexuality being just two examples. But it is not at all understandable to regard *all* sexual activity, *including sexual intercourse in marriage,* as being esentially bad. Yet that is exactly what Paul does, and in so doing flies in the face of nature and attempts to deny it. Therefore, as with the injunction to "love your enemy," so the elevation of celibacy as the sexual ideal is not only a forlorn attempt to replace a practical and attainable goal with an impossible ideal, but also an effort to substitute the unnatural for the natural.

But is Paul's really a more extreme position on sexual morality than that attributed to Jesus? Perhaps not. What, for example, are we to make of a very well-known but ill-understood passage, which, it is important to note, follows immediately after the passage in Matthew quoted above where Jesus equates lustful looking with adultery (Matt. 5:27-28) and comes immediately before his disquisition on divorce (Matt. 5:31-32)?

> If your right eye causes you to sin, pluck it out and throw it away; it is better that you lose one of your members than that your whole body be thrown into hell. And if your right hand causes you to sin, cut it off and throw it away; it is better that you lose one of your members than that your whole body go into hell. (Matt. 5:29-30)

This does not *appear* to have anything to do with the discussion of sexual morality, though it is found in Mark and also elsewhere in Matthew in a non-sexual context (Mark 9:43-47; Matt. 18:8-9). But what does it mean? In view of the extremism which is so characteristic of Jesus' teaching, it would be rash to jump to the conclusion that it cannot possibly be meant to be taken literally. And there most certainly were those who did behave in this fashion. There was the early Roman hero Mucius Scaevola, for instance, who is said to have plunged his right hand into a burning brazier in order to "punish" it for killing the wrong person (he had mistaken a court official for the Etruscan king Lars Porsenna, whom our hero had come to assassinate). Then, perhaps closer to home, there were the so-called *galli,* the priests of the cult of Cybele, who castrated themselves in their frenzy for the goddess.

Though neither Jesus nor Paul ever advocated castration and though Christianity continued the Jewish ban on full participation in religious life for those who were physically mutilated, nevertheless the basic underlying principle is essentially the same as that which made Paul praise celibacy as the ideal sexual state, a principle which is undoubtedly to be seen as at least one of the factors leading to the eventual rise of monasticism.

The fundamental point is a belief that sex in any form, including marriage, is essentially "dirty," a belief which has by no means died out even today. Once sex is seen as something "dirty," then it becomes something that one should try to avoid as much as possible. True celibacy, as many who have taken an oath of chastity have found, is by no means easy to sustain. Should one not then punish the offending organ which caused one to sin? This may possibly be the eye or the hand, which Jesus actually mentions, but could he not perhaps have been thinking of another organ altogether, one whose name he dare not utter, but one which is nevertheless more closely associated with sin—and especially of course with sin in this sexual context—than either the hand or the eye?

This interpretation also ties in with Jesus' view of temptation. "Lead us not into temptation" is his prayer, *not* "give us the strength to resist temptation."

But where did the idea come from in the first place that sex was dirty? It is certainly not a Jewish idea. For, though the Jewish religion has always had a somewhat prudish attitude and though it has always castigated any form of sex labeled as "unnatural," sex itself has never been so regarded, and the ideal in this area has always been sexual gratification in marriage.

For a long time before the birth of Jesus, however, there had been a strain of Greek philosophical and social thought that regarded sex in any form as, oddly enough, "contrary to nature," nature being defined in terms of the self-sufficiency of an individual living on his own. This school of thought, embracing the so-called Cynics and Stoics, rejected the whole of the physical and material side of life, believing that it was physical and material *pleasure* that was the worst enemy to human *happiness,* a purely spiritual virtue. "Pleasure" included not only sexual enjoyment but also the pleasurable sensations associated with wealth, good food, comfort, and any other physical or material delights.

The first thinker associated with these ideas was the famous philosopher Diogenes the Cynic, so-called from the Greek word for *dog* because he adopted so aggressively antisocial a stance that he was thought to "snarl" all the time. Diogenes lived in a barrel, deeming a house to be far too elaborate for his needs and therefore "contrary to nature." The barrel also served for clothing, as clothes too were "contrary to nature." Even the Roman emperor Marcus Aurelius, who lived over a century after Jesus' time and who was a noted Stoic philosopher, wrote in his memoirs: "A man may live well *even* in a palace." The point he was making was that living in the lap of luxury and ease, being waited on hand and foot, was "contrary to nature," since it induced pleasure, the very opposite of happiness. One could live much better, the assumption was, in a cave, a barrel, or a tomb. Another Stoic philosopher, Epictetus, was actually a slave, but far from advocating the abolition of slavery he saw it merely as an "external," part of the purely physical side of life and therefore of no consequence.

This sort of outlook on life could be summarized in the Greek slogan *sōma sēma*, meaning "the body is the tomb [of the soul]." The body—that is, the whole physical and material side of life, was seen as a shackle weighing down the spirit and preventing it from soaring aloft. Only by denying oneself all physical or material pleasure could one hope to preserve oneself as a truly human being, a spiritual being, and thereby attain true happiness.

Hard though it may be to believe, this type of outlook was influential for a very long time. Diogenes himself was an older contemporary of Alexander the Great, who paid the philosopher the ultimate compliment (not reciprocated) by saying, "If I were not Alexander, I should like to be Diogenes." But Stoicism was still flourishing five hundred years later, which is when Marcus Aurelius lived. The upper classes and the rich could protect their privileges behind a barricade of Stoic philosophy, declaring such things as wealth and social status to be matters of indifference or even positive disadvantages in the pursuit of happiness. To the lower orders, the poor, and even slaves Stoicism offered consolation for exactly the same reason: poverty, physical hardship, and privations were only "externals," which could safely be ignored or, better still, were actual advantages on the path to happiness, lightening the physical burden that the spirit had to carry. The only truly rich man, Stoicism taught, was the wise man, that is, the man learned in Stoic wisdom. This superior being was also the only true king and, for that matter, the only true free man (regardless of his social status), the rest of the population being slaves—slaves to their bodies, to money, or to pleasure.

In view of the widespread influence of the Stoic modes of

thought, it is hardly surprising that we should find strong reflections of it in Christianity. It need not have been a deliberate or even a conscious borrowing of Stoic ideas on the part of Christianity, merely the absorption of ideas that were very much in the air.

Rich and Poor

"The love of money is the root of all evil" (1 Tim. 6:10) is one of the best-known Christian texts, but it is a statement of pure Stoicism. When asked by a young man how to attain "eternal life" Jesus replies, "If you would enter life, keep the commandments." On being pressed, he singles out several commandments: "You shall not kill; you shall not commit adultery; you shall not steal; you shall not bear false witness; honor your father and mother; and, you shall love your neighbor as yourself" (Matt. 19:16-20). But Jesus' interlocutor is still not satisfied. Declaring that he has observed all the commandments listed, he demands, "What do I still lack?" (Matt. 19:20). Jesus' answer is surprising. Having replied purely in terms of Jewish law up to this point, he now diverges wildly:

> If you would be perfect, go, sell what you possess and give to the poor, and you will have treasure in heaven; and come, follow me. (Matt. 19:21).

Then, turning to his disciples, he adds:

> Truly, I say to you, it will be hard for a rich man to enter the kingdom of heaven. Again I tell you, it is easier for a camel to go through the eye of a needle than for a rich man to enter the kingdom of God. (Matt. 19:23-24, see also Mark 10:25; Luke 18:25).

Despite the gyrations of commentators, many of whom have found this doctrine as painful as the rich young man who had supposedly prompted it, the sense is quite plain. The rich man does not actually have to have *done* anything in order to be banned in this way; being rich is sin enough.

In the light of this, the parable of Lazarus and the rich man becomes less ambiguous than is commonly supposed. All we are told is that there was a rich man "who was clothed in purple and fine linen and who feasted sumptuously every day" (Luke 16:19). We are told no more about the rich man's way of life. We do not know whether he was generous or mean, honest or dishonest. We are not even given his name. We do learn, though, that there was a poor man "full of sores" named Lazarus who lay at the rich man's gate and "who desired to be fed with what fell from the rich man's table" (Luke 16:21). As there does not appear to have been any connection between Lazarus and the rich man, the fact that he remained at his gate evidently means that he *did* feed on the rich man's leavings. The rich man's punishment after death, torment in the fiery furnace of hell, was evidently meted out to him for no reason other than his wealth, as Abraham supposedly tells him when he complains of his unjust fate:

> Son, remember that you in your lifetime received your good things, and Lazarus in like manner evil things; but now he is comforted here, and you are in anguish. And besides all this, between us and you a great chasm has been fixed, in order that those who would pass from here to you may not be able, and none may cross from there to us. (Luke 16:25-26)

There is no mention here of any specific sin or catalogue of sins that the rich man has committed against Lazarus or anyone else. The doctrine expressed is simply one of automatic inversion: those who prosper in life will suffer in death, and vice versa.

A similar doctrine is found in Luke's version of the beatitudes:

> Blessed are you poor, for yours is the kingdom of God.
> Blessed are you that hunger now, for you shall be satisfied.
> Blessed are you that weep now, for you shall laugh.
>
> . . . .
>
> But woe to you that are rich, for you have received your consolation.
> Woe to you that are full now, for you shall hunger.
> Woe to you that laugh now, for you shall mourn and weep.
> (6:20-21, 24-25)

Once again, there is no implication whatsoever of any wrongdoing on the part of the rich and prosperous—other than their wealth and prosperity—and no implication of any merit in the poor and miserable— other than their poverty and misery. The better-known version of the beatitudes found in Matthew, is quite different in tone (Matt. 5:3-11). Here, it is not the poor who are blessed but the "poor in spirit," a different concept altogether. It is not the physically hungry, as in

Luke, who will be satisfied, but "those who hunger and thirst for righteousness." As for the rich, there is no mention of them at all. In short, the qualities singled out for reward in Matthew's list are spiritual qualities whereas those in Luke are material circumstances.

Which version is the more authentic? It hardly matters. Even if it turned out that Luke's version was a later reworked form of Matthew's version, there are enough other remarks of a similar type attributed to Jesus in the Gospels to make it hard to label the ideas of the "social Gospel" as deriving entirely from a time after Jesus' death. The same applies to attempts to reinterpret Luke's version in a metaphorical sense and thus essentially equate it with Matthew's version. Even if this were feasible —which I do not think it is—there would still be the unambiguous references to wealth and poverty in a material sense that we have already examined.

Both versions represent a departure from Jewish attitudes, but in different directions. The idea that those are blessed who "hunger and thirst after righteousness" is very close to the Jewish teaching, "Justice, and only justice, you shall follow" (Deut. 16:20), the Hebrew word translated here as *justice* being *tsedeq,* which is best represented in Greek by *dikaiosunē,* which indeed is the word we find in Matthew's beatitude translated as *righteousness,* which is also the usual translation for *tsedeq.*

So far so good. But "blessed are the meek" is decidedly not a Jewish belief. There is a great deal about hardship and suffering in the Jewish Bible, especially in the prophets—the sufferings of the Jewish people— but suffering is never held up as an ideal. The Jewish people are to be saved from their sufferings, but they are not to earn salvation *by* suffering. The suffering carries no merit itself. Not, of course, that meekness has ever been a Christian ideal either—*in practice.* It belongs to the type of concept to which "turn the other cheek" and "love your enemy" belong, ideals which are so impossible of attainment, as we have seen, as to lead only to hypocrisy.

Perhaps even more important than the unattainability of these ideals is their *unnaturalness.* Meekness is as much contrary to human nature as turning the other cheek and loving one's enemy, because it places the meek person at the mercy of his enemies. In other words, it is not much of a safeguard for *survival*—and survival is, without doubt, the prime natural instinct of any animal, including the human one. In the strict biological sense, therefore, as well as in the ordinary colloquial sense, such ideals are unnatural.

It is this unnaturalness that may be seen as the chief common factor between the two versions of the beatitudes. For, if it is unnatural to elevate meekness to a virtue, then so it is to declare poverty and misery as the social ideal. It is unnatural in the sense that man clearly has a natural instinct to enjoy himself and to live as comfortably as possible. To deny these instincts and to turn one's whole set of values about so that, as the Stoics insisted, *pleasure* becomes the opposite of *happiness* and happiness—the only worthy goal—becomes identified with a denial of any form of pleasure, is decidedly unnatural (though the Stoics of course redefined the term *nature* as well, as we have seen, making it mean the opposite of what it clearly should mean).

Judaism has always recognized human nature for what it is and, without attempting the impossible by remodeling it totally according to some abstract philosophical ideal, has tried to curb its worst excesses. Abraham, in whose mouth are placed those most improbable sentiments (quoted above), which he supposedly addressed to the rich man burning in hell, was himself a rich man according to the Book of Genesis, his wealth being one of the *blessings* given him by God. Similarly, in the Book of Job, wealth is a sign of divine favor. At the beginning of the book Job has seven thousand sheep, three thousand camels, five hundred oxen, and five hundred asses, together with a large slave establishment (Job 1:3). He is described as "the greatest of all the people of the east" (1:3). When he is put to the test, however, he loses everything, including even his children (1:13-19). Once he has "passed" his test his wealth returns: "and the LORD gave Job twice as much as he had before" (42:10).

But it is perhaps in the Book of Deuteronomy that this concept finds most direct expression:

> And if you will obey my commandments which I command you this day, to love the LORD your God, and to serve him with all your heart and with all your soul, he will give the rain for your land in its season, the early rain and the later rain, that you may gather in your grain and your wine and your oil. And he will give grass in your fields for your cattle, and you shall eat and be full. (Deut. 10:13-15)

Nothing could be clearer or more staightforward: obedience to God's commandments will earn tangible physical and material rewards. But, it cannot be sufficiently stressed, this does *not* imply approval of the indiscriminate amassing of wealth without concern for the plight of others.

On the contrary, every Jew is commanded as follows:

For the poor will never cease out of the land; therefore I command you, You shall open wide your hand to your brother, to the needy and to the poor, in the land. (Deut. 15:11)

This general injunction is backed up by more specific commandments, one of the most beautiful and at the same time one of the simplest being: "The wages of a hired sevant shall not remain with you all night until the morning" (Lev. 19:13). This touchingly simple law protects the interests of the day-laborer, who needs his wage paid promptly in order to sustain himself and his family. Another similar law, and one which, to my knowledge, has no parallel in any other legal code, is one which requires the Jewish farmer to leave a border of unharvested crops in his fields and vineyards and which forbids him to pick up ears of corn or fruit which may have fallen to the ground: "You shall leave them for the poor and for the sojourner" (Lev. 19:10). The practical application of this law of course forms the backdrop to the lovely romantic story of Ruth and Boaz, an indication that the law was no mere airy-fairy eloquent ideal but a practical program of poverty relief.

But, of all the books of the Bible none is so preoccupied with the fate of the poor than the Book of Psalms, where the attitude to poverty and wealth is perhaps closer than anywhere else to the Christian view. The poor are often identified as righteous and wickedness is associated with wealth:

For the wicked boasts of the desires of his heart,
and the man greedy for gain curses and renounces the LORD.
In the pride of his countenance the wicked does not seek him;
all his thoughts are, "There is no God." (Ps. 10:3-4)

The recognition here that wealth and worldly success tend to make man ignore God and to see himself as divine cannot be gainsaid. It is an undeniable psychological tendency, which however is not universal. This recognition may well have been one of the factors leading to the Christian vilification of wealth, but the Jewish conclusion to be drawn from the recognition of this psychological truth is very different from the Christian one. Christianity advocates a quite unreasonable—and unnatural—shunning of wealth and the cultivation of poverty. But the psalmist has a different message:

Arise, O LORD; O God, lift up thy hand;
forget not the afflicted.

. . . .

> Break thou the arm of the wicked and evildoer;
> seek out his wickedness till thou find none.
>
> . . . .
>
> O LORD, thou wilt hear the desire of the meek;
> thou wilt strengthen their heart,
> thou wilt incline thy ear
> to do justice to the fatherless and the oppressed,
> so that man who is of the earth may strike terror no more.
> (Ps. 10:12, 15, 17, 18)

In the Gospels, as we saw, being rich is itself a sin—sin enough to earn one exclusion from the "kingdom of heaven." In the Psalms, by contrast, wealth is seen not as *equivalent* to wickedness but as a possible psychological *cause* of it. The wicked are not condemned for being rich but for being wicked. Another vital difference is in the attitude to meekness. In Matthew's beatitudes meekness is itself commendable, so commendable indeed as to earn one "the earth." The psalmist, however, sees meekness as a form of weakness which he prays God will overcome. Far from being an advantage, therefore, meekness is seen as a serious disability. The prayer is therefore not for meekness—an unnatural desire—but for the healthy, normal and natural quality of *strength*.

IX

Christianity and Truth

"What is truth?" Pilate's taunt echoes down the centuries. This ringing challenge, unanswered and unanswerable, is placed in the Roman governor's mouth by John in response to Jesus' declaration, which can be interpreted as being arrogant, that his purpose in coming into the world was "to bear witness to the truth" (18:37-38).

How true is the biblical account of creation? The publication of Darwin's *Origin of Species* in 1859 sparked off one of the biggest religious disputes in history, which has still not died away. Even today there are "creationists" who reject the theory of evolution out of hand as being in conflict with the Book of Genesis, which is assumed to be literally true. If the biblical account is understood in this way, then clearly evolution and creation are irreconcilable and mutually exclusive explanations of the same set of phenomena.

Less fundamentalist religious thinkers, however, have come to see the problem in quite a different light. It is no longer a question of Genesis being right and Darwin wrong, or vice versa. Both explanations may be true in different ways, provided the biblical account is not understood in a narrowly literal sense. Both accounts, after all, offer us much the same progression of life forms, starting with plants and culminating in man. The chief obstacles to agreement have been, first, the Bible's time-scale and, secondly, its attribution of the whole process, and indeed of every stage within it, to a divine will. But, as is now commonly recognized, neither of these obstacles is insuperable. If the Bible's "day" is understood as a figurative representation of millions of years, the first obstacle is easily cleared. As for the active role of God in creation, it does not really contradict anything in the Darwinian theory but merely offers a theological explanation of the motivating force behind the remarkable process of evolution.

Interestingly enough, the theological objections to Darwin's theory have come much more from Christians than from Jews. Indeed, seven centuries before *Origin of Species* the Jewish philosopher Maimonides had already declared in so many words that the biblical account of the creation was not intended to be taken literally, a view in which he was not alone among Jewish thinkers. Why then should Darwin's revelations have hit Christianity with such shattering force? The reason, I believe, is the same one we have already encountered on a number of previous occasions—namely, that, unlike Judaism, Christianity depends for its very existence upon the acceptance of an improbable historical assertion as fact. For this reason, Christianity has always been more vulnerable to historical attack than Judaism. It is no accident that it is Christians, rather than Jews, who are concerned to find the remnants of Noah's ark on the summit of Mount Ararat; and it is no surprise that the genuineness of the Turin shroud should have become so central an issue to Christian clergy and laity alike, even in this supposedly enlightened twentieth century.

If it were to turn out that Abraham never existed, that Joseph was an Egyptian all the time or that the miracles attributed to Moses never happened, the validity of Judaism would not be in the least diminished. Judaism is indeed rooted in history, the long history of the Jewish people, but it does not depend upon the literal truth or accuracy of any *particular* event or biblical episode. The broad lines of Jewish history are deeply and indelibly etched on the map of time, and it is this ancient heritage of culture, law, and life that has given Jews throughout history the unique sense of identity which is Judaism.

Paradoxically, therefore, the fate of Noah's ark or Moses' miracles is less crucial to Judaism than to Christianity. For the slightest rent in the fabric of literal biblical truth may bring down the whole Christian edifice, resting as it does upon one very shaky historical premise, the story of Jesus as the Messiah (not to mention the added stress placed on the whole sturcture by the inconsistencies within that story). If the biography of Abraham, the founding father of the Jewish religion and also a prophet of Islam, is under attack, how can that of Christianity's founder remain unscathed? If Moses' miracles are rejected, how can Jesus' miracles be rescued? If Elijah's translation to heaven lacks credibility, why should Jesus' resurrection or ascension carry more conviction?

Is it any wonder that the church hierarchy should have reacted so violently against the Darwinian theory of evolution? But Bishop Wilberforce and Darwin's other clerical adversaries were not the only theologians— whether consciously or unconsciously—to identify the fate of

Genesis with that of the Christian Gospel. Strangely enough, a very similar attitude is descernible amongst radical Christian theologians of the twentieth century. Just as their nineteenth-century predecessors felt the need to rally to the literal truth of Genesis in order to save the Gospels from attack, so they reject the literal truth of the Gospels as part of their "demythologising" of the Bible as a whole. The quotation that follows is a good illustration of the fate of some basic Christological doctrines under the impact of this attitude:

> Jesus is "the man for others," the one in whom Love has completely taken over, the one who is utterly open to, and united with, the Ground of his being. And this "life for others, through participation in the Being of God," *is* transcendence. For at this point, of love "to the uttermost," we encounter *God,* the ultimate "depth" of our being, the unconditional in the conditioned. This is what the New Testament means by saying that "God was in Christ" and that "what God was the Word was." Because Christ was utterly and completely "the man for others," because he *was* love, he was "one with the Father," because "God is love." But for this very reason he was most entirely man, the son of man, the servant of the Lord. He was indeed "one of us" . . . The life of God, the ultimate Word of Love in which all things cohere, is bodied forth completely, unconditionally and without reserve in the life of a man—the man for others and the man for God. He is perfect man and perfect God—not as a mixture of oil and water, of natural and supernatural—but as the embodiment through obedience of "the beyond in our midst," of the transcendence of love. (J. A. T. Robinson, *Honest to God,* 1963, p. 76).

There are essentially two equations here. The first equates the concept of "God" with a force *within* the individual rather than a God "up there" or even "out there." Then comes the equation of Jesus with this redefined "God." The resulting portrait is of a being who is at once fully human and fully divine, as the divine element is in any case no longer seen as something separate from the human element but as an integral part of it.

But what does all this really mean? Stripped of the jargon, the Jesus who emerges from this process of redefinition is no more than the usual exemplary "good man," an identification which creates more problems than it solves. The Jesus of the Gospels certainly *preaches selflessness but he does not practice it.* He tells his followers to turn the other cheek and to love their enemies, but we never catch him doing either. And, it cannot be stressed enough, *what we are talking about is the Gospel accounts of Jesus' life*—not some hostile Jewish tract or some biting pagan satire. And what do we find? We find Jesus calling down curses upon the heads of his enemies (for example, Luke 11:42-52) or even employing physical violence against them (John 2:15). But, not only does Jesus fail to live up to his own injunctions in respect of enemies: his own family—and not least his mother, Mary—receives short shrift from him, as we have had occasion to observe in a previous chapter. As for his proverbial humility, there is little sign of it in the Gospels. On the contrary, as we have also seen previously, he is repeatedly portrayed as pompous and self-important.

The surprisingly frequent glimpses in the pages of the Gospels of a decidedly less than perfect Jesus are doubly significant. Not only are they in stark contrast to Jesus' *teachings,* but, for that reason among others, they also constitute good prima facie evidence of the historical Jesus.

And yet, by dismissing the "quest for the historical Jesus" as irrelevant, the radical Christian theology of the twentieth century has only succeeded in replacing an at least roughly accurate—and, upon examination, none too flattering—portrait of Jesus the Jew, which emerges from careful scrutiny of the Gospels themselves, with a vague and shadowy, highly idealized image of "Jesus, the man for others," the product not of any historical evidence but of abstract theologizing.

But why, you may well ask, is there any need to attempt to portray Jesus the man at all—especially if the whole exercise is as irrelevant as the radical theologians maintain? The answer is that the figure of Jesus is so pivotal to Christianity that Christians are unable to avoid thinking of him as a human being, no matter how much high-minded theologians may eschew any such exercise as futile, irrelevant or both.

Yet, as was pointed out in Chapters 6 and 7, keeping Jesus on an elevated theological level in the guise of "God the Son," avoids many of the difficulties associated with that much more problematical character, "Jesus the Messianic claimant." But to adopt this approach would be to return Jesus to being just another pagan god in yet another polytheistic mystery cult. In other words, the essential appeal of Christianity would be lost—the appeal of a savior figure who is believed to have lived in the real world as a real flesh-and-blood human being.

There is also another reason why Christianity can never escape from the "quest for the historical Jesus," and that is the most important reason of all—namely, that the Gospels are clearly written in terms of a living, breathing, historical Jesus, whom they are intent on proving to have been the Jewish Messiah.

Even when disguised or hidden from view, the messianic claim lies at the very heart of Christianity. Most of the titles accorded Jesus and most of the powers with which he is invested stem directly or indirectly from this claim—whether he is portrayed as savior, priest, or king, "prince of peace," "the good shepherd," "the light of the world," or simply as "Son of God" or "Christ." Salvation, priesthood, and kingship are three basic facets of the messianic role, and hardly less fundamental aspects of it are the Messiah's function as teacher, human example, and his special position as God's chosen agent on earth.

The messianic claim is undoubtedly Jesus' greatest asset. But there is one small snag. The title is exclusive. Like Cinderella's slipper, it will fit the true claimant and the true claimant alone. And the snag is that Jesus' claim is bogus. He was *not* born in Bethlehem; he was *not* a scion of the royal house of David; and none of the messianic prophecies fits him.

So why bother? Why go to all the trouble of fabricating evidence, falsifying records, and even on occasion concocting nonexistent biblical "proof-texts" just in order to claim a Jewish title for Jesus—especially as the whole advertising campaign was directed not so much at a Jewish market as at pagans, most of whom would probably never have heard of Moses, let alone of King David or Bethlehem?

That is precisely Christianity's dilemma. Claiming the messianic title for Jesus entails falsifying the evidence—but *not* claiming it leaves little option to billing him as yet another pagan deity, which could hardly have appealed to the new religion's early leaders and propagandists—Jews almost to a man.

There was, in any case, a glut of new-fangled cults and exotic gods already on the market, and it would profit Christianity little to be thought merely to have swelled their number. Antiquity in a religion was the best claim to respectability. This was recognized by the church fathers, and it was for this reason that Tertullian, writing in 197, made a point of Christianity's antiquity in his *Apologeticus.* Christianity, he stressed, was based upon the "very ancient books of the Jews," which were older by far than any product of the people of the pagan world.

Should it come as a shock to learn that part of this same work was given over to an attack on Judaism and that Tertullian later wrote a separate treatise entitled *Against the Jews*? It should not. For what we have here is simply another manifestation of that same Christian dilemma mentioned above. Christianity had to derive its authenticity and respectability from Judaism, notably by laying claim to the messianic title for its founder. But it was a claim that could only be substantiated by detailed historical evidence. As no such evidence existed, it had to be invented, but even then it was so crude as to convince only very few Jews. Hence arose the strange spectacle of a religion centered on a Jewish founding figure, laying claim to Jewish titles of honor and depending for its validity on Jewish history and prophecy, but drawing its membership less and less from the ranks of the Jews and becoming increasingly hostile to Jews and Judaism alike.

It was Paul who first recognized this dilemma, saw a way out and in so doing became the true founder of Christianity as a new and separate religion. If the Jews would not accept Jesus as the Messiah, Paul decided, then those who did accept him would be dubbed the *true* Israel, the new Chosen People. And if those who were recruited to the new faith were not prepared to become Jews in the usual way, by circumcision, then the old covenant symbolised by circumcision would simply be deemed to have been superseded by a new covenant which dispensed with circumcision. The Jews' election as the Chosen People had been embodied in the "Old Testament," which was now joined by a "New Testament," which both supplemented and in practice also supplanted it.

In order to establish its independence of Judaism and to assert its superiority over it while at the same time resting upon Jewish concepts and beliefs, Christianity needed to prove that it was the true form of the ancient religion. "I am the way, and the truth, and the life" (John 14:6), a formulaic utterance supposedly spoken by Jesus, is a good example of this type of assertion. It is not enough for Christianity to claim to be true; It must claim to be *the* truth—the *only* truth. The two flanking equations are even more terrifying in their arrogance and intolerance. "I am the way" is further amplified by the following phrase: "No one comes to the Father, but by me." By contrast with Judaism, in which every worshipper has the right and indeed the obligation to approach God on a one-to-one basis, Christianity keeps the worshipper at arm's length from God and forces him to go "through channels," except that there is only one channel and that a narrow one indeed. Finally we have, "I am the life," a rather unsubtly veiled threat: nonacceptance of Christianity is equated with death.

Christianity is what I have termed a *creed religion,* a religion based upon the acceptance of a particular set of beliefs and standing in sharp contrast to the normal type of religion encountered in the ancient world, *communal religion,* a category embracing religions as diverse as Judaism, Hinduism and the Roman state religion. Communal religions tend to be exclusive: they are hard to join as membership in the religion entails membership in the social community, and vice versa, so that conversion to a communal religion is not only difficult but often practically impossible. Yet, paradoxically, it is precisely this exclusiveness which gives communal religions their generally tolerant attitude to other religions. After all, if you are reluctant for your neighbors to embrace your religion, you can hardly blame them for persevering in their own separate faith. Indeed, the whole outlook on life of the adherents of a communal religion takes it for granted that each separate nation, state or tribe will have its own religion—a formula for tolerance.

A creed religion like Christianity, by contrast, is constantly competing against all other religions—and, what is more, doing so on their own home grounds. Its success is measured in terms of the number of converts it makes.

There can be no doubt of the success of Christianity by this criterion, but it is strange to find the same criterion used not only as a measure of success but also as proof of Christianity's truth.

The basis for this may be the assumption that "you can't fool all the people all the time" and therefore that the wider the acceptance that an idea or belief enjoys the truer it must be! But perhaps Adolf Hitler's remark about the effectiveness of the "big lie," a subject on which he must be acknowledged an expert, is nearer the mark.

Yet the equation between popularity and truth persists in the common mind. (It is hardly ever to be found as a serious argument advanced by scholars, though it does put in a rare appearance in that runaway best-seller among serious works of (radical) Christian theology, *The Myth of God Incarnate,* published in 1967.)

There is of course another very important reason for the hardy persistence of this equation in religious thinking, and that is the centrality (in western religion at any rate) of the question of reward and punishment. If Christianity were not true, runs a common line of argument, then why should it have prospered as it so obviously has?

This argument of course rests squarely upon the assumption that the success of a religion in attracting adherents and amassing wealth is a mark of divine favor and an endorsement of its truth.

But Christianity took a long time to become successful, and the argument of "truth from success" would therefore simply not have served the interests of the early church fathers. Despite the occasional bouts of persecution by means of which the Roman imperial government (inadvertently) boosted the number of converts to Christianity, after three hundred years the number of Christians in the Roman Empire, according to modern estimates, amounted to no more than about ten percent of the total population. It was only in the fourth century after the conversion of the Emperor Constantine that Christianity became a major religion in numerical terms. It is now quite clear that it was not the success of Christianity that attracted Constantine to it but Constantine's conversion that led to the religion's success. The emperor's conversion gave Christianity an aura of respectability it had previously lacked, but, perhaps even more important, the statute book was soon bristling with laws discriminating against non-Christians.[1]

One need only take a glimpse at a much more recent religious success story in order to consign the "success-truth" formula forever to the dust heap to which it belongs. The success story I have in mind is that of the Mormons, or, as they prefer to be known, the Church of Jesus Christ of Latter-day Saints.

Joseph Smith, the founder of the sect, claimed that he had been guided by divine revelation to a place not very far from his home in Palmyra, New York, where under a large stone he had found a number of ancient gold plates covered in a form of Egyptian hieroglyphics. Together with these mysterious documents he claimed to have found two miraculous stones, with the aid of which and "by the gift and power of God," he was able to translate the contents of the gold plates into English. The whole work, divided into fifteen books was published in 1830 and forms part of the scriptures of the sect and is invested with divine authorship.

The ancient plates themselves, according to Smith, were returned to heaven by an angel and are therefore unavailable for inspection. As for the contents of the Book of Mormon, it claims to tell the story of Jews who migrated to America in 589 BC (over two thousand years before Columbus and sixteen hundred before Leif Erickson) and eventually established Christianity there—aided by a personal visit to America by Jesus—and spread it amongst the indigenous population.

Even if we ignore the similarities between the Book of Mormon and a novel written by the Reverend Solomon Spaulding (who died in 1816), and the charge made by handwriting experts in 1977 that twelve pages of Smith's manuscript were in Spaulding's handwriting, there is nothing in the way of historical evidence to encourage acceptance of any of the claims made by Joseph Smith or the Book of Mormon. And yet the claims are accepted by large numbers of highly educated, sophisticated modern Americans and other Westerners. Moreover, it cannot be sufficiently stressed, what the Mormons believe is the *literal* truth of the claims put forward by their founder. It may well be that the "latter-day saints" of two thousand years hence will entertain doubts about these claims and try to explain them away as myths. But, if that happens it will reveal more about the Mormons of the future than about the meaning or purpose of the Book of Mormon. For, whatever we may think, it is quite clear that the Book of Mormon was intended to be understood as *literally* true.

Exactly the same, I believe, is the case with the Christian Gospels. They too were written with the intention of being accepted as literally true—for, as I have tried to show in the course of this book, *Christianity depends for its validity upon the literal truth of the claims made for its founder.* There are, of course, millions of Christians who willingly accept the Gospels in this sense and who deny the label of "Christian" to anyone who does not share their own fundamentalist faith. (One such—a student of mine at Cambridge University—once confided in me his serious doubts as to whether the Pope was a Christian!) But, their intolerance at least has the virtue of being frank, forthright, and unabashed. Though their own belief in the truth of the Gospels is often total and they sometimes have trouble understanding how anyone can fail to share their commitment, it is nevertheless their very self-assuredness that makes them recognize that the question of acceptance of the Gospel claims for Jesus is the crucial test by which Christianity stands or falls.

Those Christians who adopt a more liberal, or even a radical, stance on this question are more difficult to pin down. These are people who cannot accept the Gospel claims as literally true but who also cannot bring themselves to admit that a rejection of those claims is a rejection of Christianity. They want to regard themselves as Christians without accepting the basis of the Christian faith. Hence the resort to high-flown jargon and the many attempts to explain the Gospel accounts away as mythical or figurative representations of a transcendent and not easily intelligible set of truths.

"Truth, in matters of religion," said Oscar Wilde, "is simply the opinion that has survived." It is in this sense, and in this sense alone, that Christianity can be said to be true. The only problem is that this definition of truth brings it dangerously close to what can only be called "the big lie."

NOTE

1. On the number of Christians in the Roman Empire in Constantine's time and on the Emperor's reasons for converting, see N. H. Baynes, *Constantine the Great and the Christian Church,* 1929; A. H. M. Jones, *Constantine and the Conversion of Europe,* 1948; and M. T. W. Arnheim, *The Senatorial Aristocracy in the Later Roman Empire,* 1972.

Bibliography

Ancient Sources

Besides the scriptural texts themselves the extant sources may be divided into three broad categories: pagan, Jewish, and Christian. On the whole, the upper classes of the Roman Empire, from whom almost all the literature of that society emanated, were little interested in the goings-on of an obscure eastern province of the Empire. Hence the brevity of the references to Judaism and Christianity to be found in such authors as Juvenal, Suetonius, and Tacitus. Pliny the Younger's letter to the Emperor Trajan on Christianity, together with the Emperor's reply (X.96 and 97), is an important source of information on Roman attitudes to the new religion.

Nicolaus of Damascus, a non-Jewish friend and adviser of King Herod, wrote a *Universal History* in no fewer than 144 books, which survives only in fragments but was extensively used by the Jewish historian Josephus as a source for his *Antiquities of the Jews,* an account of Jewish history from the earliest times to the outbreak of the Jewish revolt in the year 66. The revolt itself formed the main subject of Josephus' *Jewish War,* the first work that he wrote. His defense of Judaism in *Against Apion* is another important source. Less directly relevant to the origins of Christianity but nevertheless of great interest are the voluminous writings of the Hellenized Alexandrian Jewish philosopher Philo, a contemporary of Jesus, especially the account of his appeal to the Emperor Gaius to obtain Jewish exemption from emperor-worship, and his *Against Flaccus.*

There are no fewer than 386 volumes in the standard edition (by J. P. Migne) of the Church Fathers, but most of these date from a period well after the time we are chiefly concerned with. Eusebius' *Ecclesiastical History,* the first of a long line, traces the history of the church down to the year 324. Of the early theological writings, Tertullian's *Apologeticus* and *Against Celsus* are among the most important for our purposes, the latter being a rebuttal of the philosophical attack upon Christianity made by an educated pagan, many of whose arguments are preserved in Origen's treatise.

Probably the most accessible English translations of selections from the Dead Sea scrolls are those edited by T. H. Gaster and Geza Vermes.

Rabbinic Sources

First and foremost, in any study of Jewish law and lore, comes the Talmud, made up of the Mishnah and the Gemarah. The term *Talmud* is often used to refer to the latter alone. But, even when used in this sense, there is not one Talmud but two: the *Jerusalem Talmud (Talmud Yerushalmi)* and the *Babylonian Talmud (Talmud Babli),* the latter being by far the more substantial and more authoritative work. It exists in a thirty-five-volume English translation published by the Soncino Press between 1935 and 1952. The Mishnah was translated into English by Herbert Danby and published, together with copious notes, by the Oxford University Press, London, 1933.

The commentaries by the medieval Jewish exegetes "Rashi" (Rabbi Solomon ben Isaac, of Troyes) and Abraham ibn Ezra are of great importance, as are the writings of Maimonides, notably his *Guide for the Perplexed* and his *Letter to Yemen,* a work that deals specifically with the question of the Messiah and Messianism.

Modern Biblical Commentaries (Series)

The International Critical Commentary
The Cambridge Bible Commentary
Soncino Books of the Bible
Pelican New Testament Commentaries
The Westminster Commentaries
The Century Bible
The Interpreter's Bible
The Expositor's Bible
Torch Bible Commentaries

(*Note:* Individual volumes in these series do not have separate entries below.)

Modern Books

Arnheim, M. T. W., *The Senatorial Aristocracy in the Later Roman Empire,* 1972
Banks, R., *Jesus and the Law in the Synoptic Tradition,* 1975
Barbour, R. S., *Traditio-Historical Criticism of the Gospels,* 1972
Barclay, W., *The First Three Gospels,* 1966
Barrett, C. K., *Jesus and the Gospel Tradition,* 1967
Barth, K., *The Epistle to the Romans,* 1933
Baynes, N. H., *Constantine the Great and the Christian Church,* 1929
Blinzler, J., *The Trial of Jesus,* 1959
Bornkamm, G., *Das Ende des Gesetzes,* 2nd ed., 1958
———, *Jesus of Nazareth,* 1960

Bornkamm, G., G. Barth and H. J. Held, *Tradition and Interpretation in Matthew*, 1963

Bovon, F., *Les derniers jours de Jésus*, 1974

Bowker, J., *The Sense of God*, 1973

———, *Jesus and the Pharisees*, 1973

Brandon, S. G. F., *Jesus and the Zealots*, 1967

———, *The Fall of Jerusalem and the Christian Church*, 2nd ed., 1957

Braun, H., *Qumran and the New Testament*, 1966

Brown, R. E., *The Gospel According to John*, 1966

———, *The Virgin Birth*, 1960

———, *The Birth of the Messiah*, 1975

Bultmann, R., *The History of the Synoptic Tradition*, 2nd ed., 1968

———, *Primitive Christianity in Its Contemporary Setting*, 1956

———, *Jesus Christus und die Mythologie*, 1958

———, *Theologie des Neuen Testaments*, 1953

———, *The New Testament and Mythology*, 1953

Bultmann, R., and K. Kundsin, *Form Criticism*, 2nd ed., 1962

Burrows, M., *The Dead Sea Scrolls*, 1955

Cadbury, H. J., *The Making of Luke-Acts*, 2nd ed., 1958

Caird, G. B., *The Language and Imagery of the Bible*, 1980

Carroll, J. P., *When Prophecy Failed*, 1979

Casey, M., *Son of Man*, 1979

Catchpole, D. R., *The Trial of Jesus*, 1976

Chadwick, H., *The Early Church*, 1970

Cohn, H., *The Trial and Death of Jesus*, 1972

Conzelmann, H., *An Outline of the Theology of the New Testament*, 1969

———, *The Theology of St. Luke*, 1961

Cullmann, O., *Christ and Time*, 1951

———, *Early Christian Worship*, 1953

———, *Christology of the New Testament*, 2nd ed., 1963

———, *Salvation in History*, 1967

Dahl, N., *The Crucified Messiah*, 1974

Daube, D., *The New Testament and Rabbinic Judiasm*, 1955

———, *Collaboration with Tyranny in Jewish Law*, 1971

Davies, W. D., *Paul and Rabbinic Judaism*, 1948

———, *Christian Origins and Judaism*, 1962

———, *The Setting of the Sermon on the Mount*, 1964

———, *Invitation to the New Testament*, 1966

Derrett, J. D. M., *Law in the New Testament*, 1970

———, *Jesus' Audience*, 1973

Dibelius, M., *From Tradition to Gospel*, 2nd ed., 1934

———, *Gospel Criticism and Christology*, 1935

Dodd, C. H., *The Fourth Gospel*, 1955

———, *Historical Tradition in the Fourth Gospel*, 1963

———, *New Testament Studies*, 1953

——, *More New Testament Studies,* 1968
——, *The Founder of Christianity,* 1971
Donahue, J. R., *Are You the Christ?* 1973
Dunn, J., *Jesus and the Spirit,* 1975
Eissfeldt, O., *The Old Testament,* 1965
Falk, Z. W., *Introduction to Jewish Law of the Second Commonwealth,* 1978
Farmer, W. R., C. F. D. Moule and R. R. Niebuhr, eds., *Christian History and Interpretation,* 1967
Finkelstein, L., *The Pharisees,* 1963
Flusser, D., *Jesus,* 1969
Franklin, E., *Christ the Lord,* 1975
Freed, E. D., *Old Testament Quotations in the Gospel of John,* 1965
Fuchs, E., *Studies of the Historical Jesus,* 1964
Fuller, D. P., *Easter Faith and History,* 1965
Gager, J., *Kingdom and Community,* 1975
Gardavsky, V., *God Is Not Yet Dead,* 1973
Gaster, T. H., *The Dead Sea Scriptures in English Translation,* 1956
——, *Myth, Legend and Custom in the Old Testament,* 1969
Genest, O., *Le Christ de la Passion,* 1978
Gerhardsson, B., *Memory and Manuscript,* 1961
——, *Tradition and Transmission in Early Christianity,* 1964
——, *The Mighty Acts of Jesus According to Matthew,* 1979
Graetz, H., *Geschichte der Juden von den ältesten Zeiten bis auf die Gegenwart,* 4th ed. (11 vols.), 1908
Grant, M., *Jesus,* 1977
Grant, R. M., *A Historical Introduction to the New Testament,* 1963
Gundry, R. H., *The Use of the Old Testament in Matthew's Gospel,* 1967
Guthrie, D., *The Pastoral Epistles and the Mind of Paul,* 1966
——, *New Testament Introduction,* 3rd ed., 1970
Haenchen, E., *Der Weg Jesus,* 1966
Hahn, F., *The Titles of Jesus in Christology,* 1969
Harnack, A., *The Origin of the New Testament,* 1925
——, *The Sayings of Jesus,* 1908
——, *What Is Christianity?* 1901
——, *History of Dogma,* 3rd ed. (7 vols.), 1893
Harrison, R. K., *Introduction to the Old Testament,* 1969
Harvey, A. E., *Jesus on Trial,* 1976
——, *Jesus and the Constraints of History,* 1982
Hengel, M., *Judaism and Hellenism,* 1974
——, *Die Zeloten,* 1976
——, *Son of God,* 1976
——, *Crucifixion,* 1977
Hick, J., ed., *The Myth of God Incarnate,* 1967
Holladay, C. H., *"Theios Aner" in Hellenistic Judaism,* 1977
Hooker, M. D., *Jesus and the Servant,* 1958
——, *The Son of Man in Mark,* 1967

Hoskyns, E. C. and F. N. Davey, *The Riddle of the New Testament*, 1947
———, *The Fourth Gospel*, 2nd ed., 1947
Hull, J. M., *Hellenistic Magic and the Synoptic Tradition*, 1974
Jeremias, J., *The Parables of Jesus*, 2nd ed., 1963
———, *The Prayers of Jesus*, 1967
———, *Jerusalem in the Time of Jesus*, 1969
———, *New Testament Theology*, 1971
———, *Jesus' Promise to the Nations*, 1958
———, *Unknown Sayings of Jesus*, 2nd ed., 1964
Johnson, M. D., *The Purpose of the Biblical Genealogies*, 1969
Jones, A. H. M., *Constantine and the Conversion of Europe*, 1948
Keller, W., *The Bible as History*, 1956
Kelly, J. N. D., *Early Christian Creeds*, 1950
Klausner, J., *The Messianic Idea in Israel*, 1956
Knox, J., *The Church and the Reality of Christ*, 1964
Knox, W. L., *Sources of the Synoptic Gospels* (2 vols.), 1953, 1957
Kümmel, W. G., *Promise and Fulfillment*, 1957
———, *The New Testament: The History of the Investigation of Its Problems*, 1973
Lauterbach, J. Z., *Rabbinical Essays*, 1951
Lindars, B., *New Testament Apologetic*, 1961
Lindbloom, J., *Prophecy in Ancient Israel*, 1963
Machoveč, M., *A Marxist Looks at Jesus*, 1976
Marshall, I. H., *The Gospel of Luke*, 1978
Meyer, B. F., *The Aims of Jesus*, 1979
Moore, G. F., *Judaism in the First Centuries of the Christian Era* (3 vols.), 1927-30
Moule, C. F. D., *The Birth of the New Testament*, 1962
———, *The Phenomenon of the New Testament*, 1967
———, *The Origin of Christology*, 1977
———, *Miracles*, 1965
Neusner, J., *The Idea of Purity*, 1973
———, *Rabbinic Traditions about the Pharisees Before 70*, 1971
Nickell, Joe, *Inquest on the Shroud of Turin*, 1983
Nickelsburg, G., *Resurrection, Immortality and Eternal Life in Inter-testamental Judaism*, 1972
Nineham, D. E., ed., *The Church's Use of the Bible*, 1963
———, ed., *Studies in the Gospels*, 1955
Nock, A. D., *St. Paul*, 1938
North, C. R., *The Suffering Servant in Deutero-Isaiah*, 1955
Pancaro, S., *The Law in the Fourth Gospel*, 1975
Perrin, N., *Jesus and the Language of the Kingdom*, 1975
Popkes, W., *Christus Traditus*, 1967
Pritchard, J. B., *Ancient Near Eastern Texts Relating to the Old Testament*, 1950
Robertson, A., *Jesus: Myth or History?* 1946
Robinson, J. A. T., *Honest to God*, 1963
Roloff, J., *Das Kerygma und der irdische Jesus*, 1970

Russell, D. S., *The Method and Message of Jewish Apocalyptic*, 1964
———, *Apocalyptic, Ancient and Modern*, 1978
Safrai, S. and M. Stern, *The Jewish People in the First Century*, 1976
Sanders, E. P., *The Tendencies of the Synoptic Tradition*, 1969
———, *Paul and Palestinian Judaism*, 1977
Schillebeeckx, E., *Jesus*, 1979
Scholem, G., *The Messianic Idea in Judaism*, 1971
Schürer, E., *The History of the Jewish People in the Age of Jesus Christ*, rev. and ed. by G. Vermes, F. Millar, and M. Black (2 vols.), 1973, 1979
Schweitzer, A., *The Quest of the Historical Jesus*, 1910
Sherwin-White, A. N., *Roman Society and Roman Law in the New Testament*, 1963
Silver, A. H., *A History of Messianic Speculation in Israel*, 1927
Smith, W. Robertson, *The Religion of the Semites*, 2nd ed., 1894
Sox, H. D., *The Image on the Shroud*, 1981
Stauffer, E., *Jesus and His Story*, 1960
Stendahl, K., ed., *The Scrolls and the New Testament*, 1958
Tasker, R. V. G., *The Nature and Purpose of the Gospels*, 1944
Taylor, L. R., *The Divinity of the Roman Emperor*, 1931
Theissen, G., *Urchristliche Wundergeschichten*, 1974
———, *The First Followers of Jesus*, 1978
———, *The Sociology of Early Palestinian Christianity*, 1977
Vaux, R. de, *Ancient Israel*, 1965
Vermes, G., *Scripture and Tradition in Judaism*, 1961
———, *Jesus the Jew*, 1973
———, *The Dead Sea Scrolls in English*, rev. ed., 1968
———, *Post-Biblical Jewish Studies*, 1975
Wellhausen, J., *Einleitung in die drei ersten Evangelien*, 2nd ed., 1911
Westerholm, C., *Jesus and Scribal Authority*, 1978
Wiles, M. F., *The Remaking of Christian Doctrine*, 1975
Wilson, B., *Magic and the Millennium*, 1973
Winter, P., *The Trial of Jesus*, 1961
Yoder, J. H., *The Politics of Jesus*, 1972
Zeitlin, S., *The Rise and Fall of the Judean State*, 1962-67